FUNNY DATING STORIES TO HELP YOU KEEP YOUR HEAD IN THE GAME

ERIKA R. MCCALL
&
NIESHA FORBES

Los Angeles, California

Published by Don't Wait Create LLC
Los Angeles, CA
www.allgoodjustaweekago.com

ISBN-9781735302409 (HARD COVER)
ISBN-9781735302423 (PAPERBACK)

Cover by COLONFILM
Formatted by hDigitals Design Studio

This is my prayer: that your love will flourish and that you will not only love much but well. Learn to love appropriately. You need to use your head and test your feelings so that your love is sincere and intelligent, not sentimental gush. Live a lover's life, circumspect and exemplary, a life Jesus will be proud of: bountiful in fruits from the soul, making Jesus Christ attractive to all, getting everyone involved in the glory and praise of God.

PHILIPPIANS 1:9-10

CONTENTS

INTRODUCTION

"Okay, hold up wait a minute, all good just a week ago."

—CHILDISH GAMBINO, *3005*

In the world of dating, you can be at Red Lobster on Valentine's Day, sharing your last Cheddar Bay biscuit only to be suddenly heartbroken over the same person who fed you popcorn shrimp across the table just a week ago. You're left wondering what could have happened in those seven days, that you cringe at the thought of ever seeing their face again? In today's dating culture, people can quickly cancel or ghost you at the drop of a dime. When it comes to matters of the heart, sometimes we have to laugh to keep from crying. Opening up and being vulnerable is difficult when past experiences have hurt you. Our dating journeys have led to one of us being happily married to her soulmate while the other keeps her head in the dating game with full confidence that her king will show up at God's appointed time. We have both enjoyed living our best lives while laughing and, most of all, learning from the ghosts of our dating pasts.

There was a time when the two of us made a list of guys we wanted to thank for not wasting any more of our time. We even made a rap song about it called, *I thank you ninja,* But since we are no Cardi B, we decided to write about it. This book is not just any old dating book telling you what you need to do to prepare for your soulmate. We are sharing funny stories highlighting the mistakes we've made, red flags we've ignored, the counterfeit people, the sleepless nights we endured, and our thoughts on the stories that reflect the women we are today.

Now we have a different reason for wanting to thank the ghosts from our dating past. We appreciate each person who taught us something about ourselves, which oddly helped us learn and grow into the people we need to be. These people were only in our lives for a season, and we enjoyed the good times shared with them until it was time to exit the stage to the left.

We have invited some friends who have chimed in and shared some of their dating experiences. Whether you are single, in a committed relationship, or even married, this book will make you laugh and inspire you to believe in love while knowing we are all in this journey together. Most importantly, we want to spark conversations between men and women that continuously get swept under the rug. We are excited to start the conversation and explore new ideas while having some fun in between. Our reflections throughout this book are our opinions, and we invite you to join in on the conversation. We can collectively explore common behaviors that keep so many people from giving and receiving the love they deserve. The names and some of the locations have changed, but the stories remain the same.

PART I
LADIES EDITION

Woman Dating Confession: *When it comes to dating, I feel like I've done all of the right things with the wrong men.*

This book has two sections. Part I contains stories told by the ladies. Fellas, before you decide to fast forward to Part II, we invite you to stay. Don't worry; you will have your time. We still believe in chivalry, so ladies first. We ask that you open your hearts and minds to what some women go through during our journey of meeting a man like you. Maybe you will identify some similar mistakes you've made while trying to become your best self.

For years, people have made millions of dollars writing books or hosting seminars and coaching sessions that provide advice on how women can find, please, and keep a man. Most dating books are marketed to women searching for love, providing them with tips on how to get and keep a man. Making us feel like we are solely responsible for entering in and maintaining a relationship. You may have found yourself going from relationship to relationship until you finally met the person you were ready to spend the rest of your life with. Some of you might still be searching for your life partner or soulmate and experiencing situationship after situationship. Regardless of how long you've been in the dating game, all of us have stories that make us laugh and learn.

As children, we believed in the fairytale of kissing a frog before meeting our Prince Charming. Those frogs have come as emotionally unavailable men, cheaters, manipulators, and narcissists. In a lot of these instances, we are the ones who made the mistakes, and as much as we would like to believe, we are not always innocent. A few of us have acted a complete fool and embarrassed ourselves all in the name of love. But it's okay; you are not the only one. We've all been there. We might as well start with one of our personal stories. Let us tell you about the Smooth Operator.

CHAPTER 1
RED FLAGS & SITUATIONSHIPS

TALE OF THE SMOOTH OPERATOR

"No need to ask; he's a smooth operator."

— SADE, *SMOOTH OPERATOR*

ERIKA

It was a sunny day in Los Angeles, and I finally had a Saturday to myself. Still new to the city, I decided to explore the neighborhood and check out a few stores in the area. I had never shopped at ROSS; I was more of a Marshalls and TJ Maxx girl. So, I decided to see what all the hype was. While in the fitting room trying on clothes, I noticed my phone vibrating in my purse. By the time I picked it up to answer, I had missed the call. I got worried when I saw I had missed three calls from Niesha. As I frantically entered in my password, so I could return her call, she called again. I answered, and she was sobbing on the other end.

"Did someone die?" I always ask this question when someone calls me in a frenzy.

Through her sobbing, she barely mustered up a "No."

After two minutes of uncontrollable crying, she said, "I caught Papi Chulo cheating." Papi Chulo was Niesha's latest flame. It was hard to believe what she was saying because it seemed like the two of them were in a stable place and making their long-distance relationship work. Niesha had just moved to New York. She had gone home to Chicago to attend her cousin's bridal shower and visit Papi Chulo for the weekend. During the bridal shower, she received a phone call from a childhood friend, letting her know that she had spotted Papi Chulo on a date with some woman. Niesha's immediate reaction was to catch him red-handed.

As I paid for my items, Niesha replayed the incident over the phone. Coincidentally, she was only ten minutes away from the restaurant where Papi Chulo was canoodling with this unknown woman. Niesha ended her relationship that day, marking the first and last time I shopped at ROSS. I don't know if trying to comfort my friend during the midst of a heartbreaking moment led me to purchase items that didn't look as good as I thought they did when trying them on in the store. Whatever the case, ROSS always reminds me of the moment that led to the next couple of weeks that consisted of 3:00 am phone calls with Niesha sobbing on the other end.

We replayed the scene from Chicago repeatedly, trying to figure out where it all went wrong. She returned to New York with a bruised ego but has never looked back.

One thing I admire most about Niesha is that she's a love bug. She's always been willing to take a chance, and when a relationship didn't work out, she was on to the next. With each new bae, she didn't hold on to the baggage from her last one. While most people would use heartbreak as an excuse to put a wall around their heart, she always could love like she's never been disappointed. Her confidence in love is why we can laugh at a moment that once kept us up at the wee hours of the morning going over every detail.

"Girl, can you believe I thought he was my husband?" She says when we recall a moment that was once hard for her to stomach.

Laughing, I tell her, "You couldn't tell us baby teeth was not the one." Yes, this handsome man had baby teeth. To us, the two were the picture-perfect couple. But Papi Chulo was just in her life for a season. We were surprised the relationship ended the way it did, but it was time for them to part ways.

NIESHA

A week before this episode, I was on a late-night call with Papi Chulo discussing our plans to smash Harold's Chicken and kick it at his granny's house as soon as I landed in Chicago. I couldn't wait to get cozy next to him and lick the mild sauce from my fingertips. You couldn't pay me to believe that Papi Chulo was not the one for me. In my mind, all signs led to him being my king.

"You will meet your soulmate when you least expect it." A cliché, we all get fooled into believing. Papi Chulo seemed to arrive out of thin air at a time when everything in my life was going swell. I was single with no plans to mingle. While out at a swanky lounge with my girls having a grand time and just enjoying life, I noticed this chap eyeing me throughout the night. He approached me by joining in on a conversation with a mutual friend. When it was time to leave, Papi Chulo asked to walk me to my car. *Great manners. Oh, he's a gentleman.* I thought to myself. I must admit I was very intrigued. We talked outside for another forty minutes before he opened the driver's seat of my car for me to get in.

Papi Chulo told me he wanted to see me soon. Three days later, we were on our first date at church. Yep, you heard me right. Church. Not just any church, but my church. *Okay, God, I see what you're doing.* I instantly thought to myself. I was so hyped about this date that I immediately called Erika, who had just returned from Mexico on a mission trip. I gave her all the details about my new fella and her potential brother.

I was so excited on the other end of the phone. "E, he got a little misty-eyed from the message at church. This dude might be legit." I was not one to fool around with a man who didn't rock hard with God. When I saw him get emotional at church, I was like, *Yasssssssssssss Lord!* Unbeknownst to me, I would later think, *Oh no, Father!*

Papi Chulo loved the Lord, and that's all I needed to ignore the red flags, and one of the first ones was that he never mentioned a job. I often shared my career goals with him, so for him not to share his aspirations, I gave him the side-eye. When he told me that he made money doing small construction jobs while looking for a new gig, I told myself, *Oh, he's a handyman who may in the future become the owner of his own construction business.* After all, he had a good woman with the capacity to push him into something great.

When it became hard for Papi Chulo to land a gig, he finally informed me that he was in a legal stew of messes involving being shady with the Benjamins. Finding out about his felony charges made me sympathize even more. Being a Black man in America can be so hard, so when someone tries to turn over a new leaf, why not extend some grace? Learning about this information helped me understand why he was still living with his mama. He explained that she needed help, and he had decided to step in. I was so smitten and thought, *he has a good relationship with his mama, so of course, he treats women well.* Foolish of me to believe, especially considering the ending. But I see now I was forcing myself not to pick up on those fire engine red signs.

As our relationship progressed, many life-altering moments occurred that he was present for, such as my grandpa's cancer diagnosis, which shook me very badly. After a drunken, puke-filled evening, he stepped in to make sure I made it home safely. He supported me through a bleak time in my life. Upon my grandpa's transition, I decided to relocate to NYC. Papi was not a fan of this idea because his previous babe had done the same thing, and their relationship did not survive the long-distance. Being an alpha woman and only child, I was a little self-centered and cared nothing about the sour taste this put in his mouth. I ALWAYS wanted to live in NYC, and this relationship was not going to sway me to stay home.

After a lit going-away party, I left for NYC in January of 2014 with the confidence that a long-distance relationship would work. We talked every day. Papi even came to visit me for my birthday in April. Things seemed cute, and the vibes in the air were that love would be good to me on this run. I was hopeful.

However, the Lord knew he had to nip this thing in the bud for me and did he ever. A week after, I arrived in Chicago on a sizzling hot June day. Papi Chulo and I had a fun night which unbeknownst to me, would be our last. The next day, I went to my dearest sister-cousin Izoha's bridal shower. The night before had left me looking and feeling spicy. I showed up at the bridal shower in a short but tasteful skirt, which slightly hugged my curves. While partying and celebrating Izoha's upcoming nuptials, I received a call from my friend Krissy. She told me that my man Papi Chulo was at a restaurant with another chick. My face immediately became warm, and I politely told my sweet cousin that I had to make a quick run. She didn't question a thing because I appeared unbothered.

But it was the complete opposite. I had the bubble guts, a dash of rage, and a load of "how dare this fool." I was ready to pop off. I told Krissy to keep an eye on his activity as I was literally down the street from this action. I drove my car about fifty miles per hour down residential streets and even ran through some red lights. Luckily, I didn't hit anyone. The thing with rage is that you kind of blackout to anything going on around you because you're focused on getting to the target. I busted a U-turn in a hospital parking lot and strutted my glistening legs down to the foolery scene.

I walked into the restaurant and spotted Krissy and her hubby dining outside. We quickly made eye contact, and without using any words, she signaled where Papi Chulo and his "date" were sitting. Boom! I was in psycho mode and ready to check his soul while trying not to look crazy. I walked over to the bar where he was sitting, his back was facing me, and he never saw it coming. I tapped Papi Chulo on the shoulder and told him to grab me a tequila with a splash of pineapple juice. Instantly his face became distorted from fear. He looked like his bowels were about to move. This man quickly spurted out, "She's just my friend."

I asked why I never knew of her existence. Papi Chulo said it was because I lived in New York, and he had a lot of friends I had never met. I'm sure you can imagine the look on my face as I listened to this sorry mess of an explanation from a man who didn't even own a cell phone. I thought of all the times we spoke on his dad's cell and realized he didn't deceive me, I had misled myself. I thought about how he also didn't have a car (he was using Granny's whip) or a job, and I had been dating my own "Tommy from Martin," and from the beginning, the red flags were always there. I decided to call his bluff and asked him to introduce me to the chick that was supposedly just his friend. Papi Chulo turned pale, and I instantly knew I was indeed about to go in. I grabbed my drink out of his hand and walked over to the girl with her faux Furla bag inside a plastic grocery bag.

"Hello. My name is *Over It,* and I see that you're enjoying a nice lunch date with my boyfriend."

She laughed and gave a calm "yes," and I realized she knew about me, and I didn't know about her. This was crushing, but I continued to engage in conversation while Krissy and her hubby watched from afar. They anticipated me moving furniture around and laying hands. When I informed her of Papi Chulo's whereabouts eight hours before, the laughter quickly left his date's lips. I watched the confidence escape her eyes, and she, too, was gravely hurt with just a few short words. I walked off, and as I realized that this was the end, I caught his eyes take notice of my silhouette that he would never lay eyes on again.

Many apologies later, I was back in my NYC element and blocking Papi Chulo on all levels. He didn't have to know that I stayed up on multiple nights, replaying the details repeatedly with E. It was none of his business.

REFLECTIONS—NIESHA

Sometimes when dating someone, you allow the fun times to overshadow the warning signs that give us clues that you should not be entertaining that "special someone." Given that we were in a long-distance scenario, it was so much easier for his dishonesty to stay under wraps. Even when I came home to visit Papi Chulo, I dismissed red flags because we had good times eating Harold's chicken with a lovely Chicago backdrop to distract me from his issues.

RED FLAG

1. A warning signal or sign.
2. To identify or draw attention to a problem or issue to be dealt with.

In relationships, many of us get caught up in our feelings and neglect to acknowledge the red flags. In Niesha's case, the good outweighed the warnings. For starters, she and Papi Chulo had their first date at church. Let's admit it, ladies, a lot of us would take this as a potential sign from God. While this is great, it takes more than listening to a Sunday sermon together to recognize if the person you are dating is truly a man of God. As Tyrese Gibson says in *Manology,* a book he co-wrote with Rev Run, some MANipulators will use the church to bait you. As horrible as it sounds, these men will use anything, including the church, to pull you in. Merely going to church isn't enough when deciding if a man is the one for you. It's more about how he applies what he is learning. Another consideration is that no matter how the other woman behaves in addressing your concerns with the man, your issue always stays with him even though she may have known about you.

RED FLAG #1

Papi Chulo was living with his mom without a job or plan or even cell phone. Ladies, we need a man with a plan! Papi Chulo had no plans, so how could he also plan to date someone seriously?

RED FLAG #2

There were no plans for the two of them to live in the same city. It's essential to pay attention to how a man responds to your plans—individually and as a couple.

***

ROOKIE BALL

My rookie year, I was very immature.

—DENNIS RODMAN, *5X NBA CHAMPION*

ERIKA

I met Robert at a mutual friend's birthday party in the middle of October. My friend introduced the two of us and said we should know each other. We talked almost the entire party. I told him my plans to become an author, and he shared his dream of playing Major League Baseball. I was impressed. I had told myself if I ever dated an athlete, I would want it to be a baseball player. Superficial but true. Robert was in the minor league and had plans to attend a training camp in the spring.

My first encounter with Robert was so delightful that we talked almost every day after that. He was a few years younger than me but seemed mature. Hanging out with him was always a fun experience. I would meet up with him at his apartment. He would order takeout and play DJ while we sang and danced to the latest songs.

Robert's roommate Tyler came home during one of our hangouts one day. "Rob tells me you're a writer." I was flattered to know that Robert was talking about me to his friends. I've had guys whose friends acted like they "heard so much about me." But I could tell they were lying. The two of us weren't an item. Robert told me he wasn't ready for anything serious. However, I must note that his actions showed otherwise. We continued to see each other despite what he said, and naturally, as we spent more time together, we grew closer. During some of the most vulnerable times in my life, he was there, including the passing of my grandmother.

Robert and his friends threw a lot of parties and social events. While attending one of his bouts with a couple of my friends, Niesha and I noticed this chick by him the entire night, and it prompted me to inquire about her the next day. I asked Robert, "Who was the girl in your face last night?"

"Oh, that's my friend Yaya." He replied.

"Yaya? Oh, okay." I said.

It seemed like more than that, but since he was not my man, I left it alone. I continued enjoying my time with Robert until things changed one rainy Sunday afternoon. We were having a small brunch that he had whipped up: French toast, eggs, bacon, and mimosas on the side. As we had a good time, his "friend" Yaya rang the doorbell and rushed through the door with her two children. I wondered what was so urgent that she had to bring her small children to his house in the cold rain. She grabbed him so they could talk in the kitchen. The proximity between the kitchen and the living room made it easy for me to ear hustle. Yaya was questioning him about our brunch, who made it and had the nerve to ask who foot the bill for the groceries. Yaya didn't stay long because she had to tend to the two cuties patiently waiting for her in the living room. When she left, I asked Robert what was so important that she had to come to his house in the rain with her children.

"Is she your girlfriend?" I asked him.

"No, she's not my girlfriend! That is just my friend." He answered with a disgusted expression on his face.

I mean, Yaya probably saw what I also did, a handsome young man who stood at about 6'2 with a potential career in the MLB. I left the topic alone, and we went on about our business. About an hour later, however, while we were relaxing on the couch, there was a knock on the door. I answered the door, and once again, it was Yaya. This time, she didn't have her children. When she and Robert went upstairs to talk, I instantly got pissed. I was ready to know what was going on here, and if Yaya was not his girl, I couldn't tell.

After they finished talking, she came downstairs and started washing the dishes.

Since I had already asked Robert, I decided to inquire from Yaya about their relationship. "I'm his girlfriend." She told me as she proudly poured Dawn over our dirty dishes. Robert came downstairs while we were talking.

"Yaya, is your girlfriend?" I asked.

This young man looked me dead in my eye and said, "Yes, and I told you I didn't want to be with you." I don't know if it was the embarrassment or the shock that led me to his refrigerator. In my anger, I commenced throwing out its contents on the floor, because yes, I paid for that damn food, and he wasn't going to eat any more of it. With my feelings deeply hurt, I wanted him to feel just as bad.

"And you wonder why you're still playing rookie ball," I said as I threw eggs on the floor. Just two weeks earlier, I had picked him up from the airport because he was sent home after major league tryouts. His childhood dream seemed to be coming to an end. Robert wasn't my man. He had told me that he cared about me but wasn't ready for anything serious. However, Robert did the complete opposite of what he claimed not to be ready for. He spent quality time with me. He helped pay some of my bills. He was also there for me when I needed him emotionally. Although he told me he wasn't ready, I believed his actions instead of his words. Because I made assumptions based only on his actions and did not consider his words, I found myself standing in Robert's kitchen, looking like a complete fool.

Looking back at this moment, all I can say is, I was the rookie. I was seeking to be in a relationship with someone who told me he wasn't ready for what I wanted. This rookie left me with hurt feelings that could have been prevented by both parties. Thankfully, I can call Robert and laugh about this entire incident. We've become platonic friends who catch up with each other from time to time and have been able to dissect the Rookie Ball story and our overall situationship.

Because we are still friends, I called Robert to let him know I was going to share this moment that now makes us laugh. As my friend, he said, "Erika, I cared about you. I just wasn't ready for a woman like you." Of course, I was confused because when we talked, I was still living in my grandmother's basement, writing my first book. But he explained that he felt inadequate because he saw me as ahead of the curve. I used this conversation to let Robert know I felt confused because, as he told me he wasn't ready, he treated me as if we were in a relationship. We spent a lot of quality time together during some of the most trying times in our lives.

A common mistake some women make when dating is not listening to what a man is saying. If his actions don't align with his words or vice versa, it's up to us to value ourselves enough to become available for someone whose actions and words align. It is also up to us to set boundaries, so we don't operate in a gray area known as the "situationship." Ladies, if you view yourself as an exceptional woman, consider that men will take exception to you too. If he treats you well, as he should, do not mistake his proper treatment towards you as an advance. He may only be giving you the excellent treatment that you deserve. If a man told you that he is not ready and treats you terribly, you would be complaining. If you have goals for your life and a relationship is one of them, it is best to say you want something intentional in the very beginning. It gives the man the opportunity to be held accountable later if he proves that it is not what he initially presented himself to be. If he does "relationship" things but says he is not ready, in the end, he may call "a no harm no foul" and if he is not and you don't mind the man's company then at that point tread at your discretion. The blame is not on him because he is not ready for a relationship, wanting to treat you well or even liking you in the end. But it is your responsibility to guard your heart by defining the lines that feelings tend to blur.

Fellas, if you are not ready to be in a committed relationship, it is crucial that you also take clear definitive actions that align with what you say. Even if you develop feelings for this woman, as men are natural leaders, we cannot help but think you are leading us somewhere. We will not hear your "I'm not ready" because we believe as the followers we are following you, and all we need is patience. You shouldn't lead anyone on when you are not ready, even if you see things in your advantage and feel that it is not your responsibility. She could be in love with you today, but if she finds that you have not considered her feelings and you change your mind later, you would have destroyed any potential of a future.

NIESHA

When I got the call from E in total distress one evening saying that she was over Robert for real this time, I thought things had to be bad for her to throw up her hands and toss this guy. I wanted nothing more than to turn her tears of rage and sadness to some hearty laughs, but I was on a super casual date with a fella named Amir. Amir was a mutual friend of mine and E and had dope vibes all the time. Amir and I had been friends for an extremely long time and had recently reconnected. Our earlier days of knowing each other were no fun because he was my boss at an apparel store downtown. During that time, I was no fan of him at all. Almost a decade later, both of our tunes had changed, and we had been jamming heavy.

Since I couldn't chat with my heartbroken sister-friend over the phone, I told her to come over to my place. I figured she needed some wine, a little hookah, and laughter to get over this hump. Her friend was in town, so I invited her too. When they arrived, we immediately debriefed the kitchen fiasco. We debated why men do the dummy with "good girls," and concluded that some men just aren't for you. Go figure! Between the sobs of despair and the "you can do better, girl" chants we gave E, Amir came with a word and broke it down for us.

He suggested that if E didn't set boundaries for how she should be treated, men would try to have their cake and eat it too if they could. Aha! So aside from his gender sometimes being "greedy," they sometimes will not adjust your crown if they see it slipping off. I watched my dearest friend become so depleted and feel so out of sorts because she was unable to dismiss the fresh images in her mind of Robert's betrayal. She sat on my chair and cried while we were all discussing the moving-forward process. Meanwhile, Amir massaged her shoulders to help her breathe through her tears.

Talk about being a compassionate friend and a human being? Y'all already know what I was thinking at this moment. *This guy is not only caring to me but also those closest to me.* To some women, his gesture might have been perceived as inappropriate, but I was secure with Amir, and my sister was sad. If this massage would help her push through to the other side of this anguish, I had no problem. That evening E transformed from sadness to jubilee just off the strength of good energy and sound advice. When everyone left my apartment that night, I was confident that my sister exited better than she arrived and was on her way to victory. Thankfully, E had learned a great lesson about situationships.

SITUATIONSHIP

A relationship that has no label on it.

—URBAN DICTIONARY

The Rookie Ball story is a perfect example of how easy it is to get caught up in a situationship. Guy says he's not ready, and the girl still hangs around. Situationships are like cartons of milk you will enjoy while it's fresh, but once it spoils, it will be sour to taste and make you sick to your stomach. They have all of the benefits of a relationship without the commitment. If you've ever been in one, you probably operated in the gray area, some of us for years. You have no idea where it is going, but your heart is in it. Women are the ones catching feelings, while men aren't catching anything but flights.

To be honest, this type of relationship though it seems to be to the benefit of the man, what men miss totally when they habitually form them is that they are losing time, not sharpening the skills that develop from commitment. The man thinks he has it going on, but up against a committed man, he's a lot more inadequate than he thinks.

The best way to prevent a situationship is to communicate your wants and set boundaries based upon the result of the conversation, no matter how much you like a person. Men have somehow misled women to believe that we are crazy or desperate if we ask probing questions. In actuality, it is really because the man is ill-prepared or has no intention to step up. According to author and pastor RC Blake, "queens ask questions that only kings can answer," If he can't, chances are he's a peasant. A man should be able to take some heat, and he should not be afraid of your "big bad" questions.

CHAPTER 2
GIGGLES

Woman Dating Confession: *This guy I liked was my personal trainer, and while I was warming up before a workout, he walked up and got close to me. I was like, okayyyy this is cute. I started to blush as he began to whisper in my ear. Only to tell me he could see my underwear through my workout tights!*

Now that we've shared some of our personal stories that led us to write this book, it's time for laughter. We know we told you this is a book of funny stories to help you keep your head in the game, but not all of them were funny. It wasn't until after the dating experience that we were able to find light in what we experienced.

We will have some deep conversations about some of those stories but not before setting the tone and brightening the mood. We have some good girlfriends who have helped us achieve this goal. Grab your glass of wine or favorite beverage, and enjoy these stories we are about to share with you. Speaking of wine, let's get into the first story.

RED WINE

I was in my early 30s, and my sister and I decided to go out during Thanksgiving weekend. I wasn't seeing anyone seriously and was excited to meet someone new. We were enjoying ourselves when this very handsome, tall, and dark-skinned brother approached me. He looked like a retired basketball player, and it made sense when I found out he was an NBA referee.

After our first encounter, he would hit me up at some of the weirdest times during the day. It would be 2:15 pm, and I'd get a random call from him asking to meet up with me immediately. It was strange, so after about the third time when he randomly hit me up for an impromptu date, I asked the million-dollar question.

"Are you married?" He got super defensive and couldn't believe I asked such a question. I let him know that if he wanted to hang out, I needed a heads-up at least 24 hours in advance. Finally, he nailed down a time and day for us to hang. Our date was horrible. The conversation was whack, and he kept checking his phone. I told him if he had to go, I understood. He said, "No, it's all good." This guy was cute but distracted. I didn't call him after the date. He reached out a few times, and if I were bored, I'd pick up. Finally, the calls stopped altogether.

Almost a year after our date, a friend of mine asked me to join her at a party. She let me know it's one of her homeboys who threw some of the best parties. It was March Madness, so I figured it should be fun. When I arrived, a beautiful Filipino lady answered the door. She let me know that she was the girlfriend of the host. I was introduced to a lot of people before my friend said, "Let me introduce you to the host."

I followed her to the kitchen to meet the man of the hour. When she tapped him on the shoulder, he turned around. Guess who it was? Yep, you guessed it. It was my horrible date from the year prior. He was the boyfriend of the lady who answered the door. He wasn't married like I thought, but she was his girlfriend of 14 years. While he was in shock, trying to catch his breath, I acted as I'd never seen him before and carried on about my business. After all, I didn't want him, so I might as well enjoy myself.

I grabbed some food and sat down with my friends. I told them that the host was my horrible date from a few months earlier. As I twirled my glass and drank my wine, I replayed the look on his face. We had a hearty laugh about it. The wine splashed out as I continued to twirl my glass and landed on the white upholstered dining room chair. When we noticed the accident, I immediately tried to clean it up. If the host knew that I had done it, he might have thought I did it on purpose, and this was furthest from the truth. When we realized that the stain might be permanent, I made a fast exit to the door and never looked back.

21 QUESTIONS

It was the early 2000s. I was fresh out of college and new to the Atlanta scene. My cousin was playing for the Falcons, and I was introduced to various circles of guys, including some street dudes. A group of us were leaving Club 112 when I met this cute, brown-skinned guy with pretty hair. I'm a sucker for delicate hair. Curls, not waves, but I digress. He was tall and skinny, something I usually don't like, but it wasn't like I was trying to marry him. We talked and exchanged information.

We lived about 40 minutes apart and would always meet in the middle. He was flaky and often late for our dates. He would brag about wanting to take me to Spondivits, a legendary seafood restaurant. Instead of going there, we ended up at the movies because he wanted to see *Final Destination 2.* He showed up late for our date, so we had to see the film later. When we got to the theater, he bypassed the concession stand. I tried to let him know I wanted some popcorn, but he didn't hear me or at least acted like he didn't. But that's not even the worst part of the date.

As soon as the movie started, he began to rap in my ear. Not any old freestyle, it was the lyrics to 50 Cent's *21 Questions.* So as the film is playing and people are dying at every angle, he whispers, "If I fell off tomorrow, would you still love me? If I didn't smell so good, would you still hug me?" As I tried to adjust my seat and get as far away from his big wet lips whispering in my ear, he continued, "If I wrote a love letter, would you write back?"

In between rapping in my ear, he was answering phone calls. He came back from yet another 10-minute phone call and sat next to me. He continued, "And we could do what you like, I know you like that."

That's when I had enough. I turned to him and said, "Ssshhhuuuushhh." I didn't hear a peep out of him after that.

We went out a couple of more times. After all, I was young, bored, and broke. If we were both free, I didn't mind linking up. That was until he stood me up when we were finally supposed to go to Spondivits. While out with some friends, I told them about my encounter with this dude I will refer to as 21 Questions. They all replied, "Oh, you mean liar, liar? He's always on some BS girl. He's tried to talk to all of us." The joke was on me.

NO-LYE RELAXER

I was living in Indiana and was in a long-distance relationship with a guy from Washington, DC. It was a time in my dating life where I would entertain long-distance relationships. I did this to avoid getting hurt because it seemed easier to control the situation through the distance. I would date guys from different states or cities but only one man at a time. I went through a phase where I would meet someone; we would start talking over the phone and end up liking each other. Every 4-6 weeks, someone would have to fly.

This particular time, my man was coming to see me. I was getting ready and had planned everything—another reason I liked to import because everything would be perfect. There was no fighting or drama because there wasn't enough time for any of that. You had the excitement of going to the airport to pick them up, and then go home and enjoy spending quality time together over the weekend.

During my routine, which involved making sure my house was clean, and everything was planned, I was almost ready to get some beauty sleep. It was late, but I wanted to take my nightly shower. I'm not sure why, but I had decided that I was going to touch up my edges with some relaxer to make sure I was flawless for my gentleman caller. I put the cream on the edges, jumped in the shower, and grabbed the neutralizer to wash my hair. Something was different about my head. The way it felt was different. I looked at my hands, and they were covered with hair. I panicked and started washing some more, and more hair was coming out.

At this point, I was in a complete panic. I opened the bathroom sliding glass door and looked on the countertop. Lo and behold, I was so sleepy that instead of grabbing the relaxer, I used hair remover. The relaxer was just sitting there with the top still on. I put the hair remover, which was for my legs and armpits, on my head. I was slick bald all around my edges. Good thing I had long enough hair to wear a scarf and make it look pretty. I could also wear a hat. In tears of laughter, I called one of my good friends at 2 am. We both got a great laugh about this.

When I went to pick my date up from the airport, I also told him about the incident. He found it hilarious. My edges eventually grew back, but that was such a horrific moment.

MR. UNIVERSITY

I met my first love in the freshman dorm lobby. We were both entering our first semester in college and had so much in common. The two of us became immediate friends, and just before Christmas break, he asked me to be his girlfriend. We had so many great moments together. The one that stands out the most is the first time we were intimate. He was such a gentleman and made sure my first time was exceptional.

My first love was very popular. He was in school on a football scholarship, and during our sophomore year, he became SGA president. When he won Mr. University, all the women began to flock to him. I wasn't intimidated. I liked that out of all the girls who loved him; he chose me. He was even kind to my friends. When he got his first apartment, he let us store some of our belongings there. My world went crashing down on a bus trip when my friend told me my man wasn't as good as he portrayed himself. He spilled all the tea about the chick my boyfriend had been cheating on me with. When I told my friends, they were shocked because my boyfriend seemed to be so smitten with me. But behind the scenes, he was a playboy and a bit of a narcissist. We didn't see this coming.

After sharing this information with my friends, we went to his house to get our stuff and for me to break up with him. It was about three or four of us. I told my boyfriend I knew he was cheating and had evidence. While we were collecting our things, he started crying and shouting, "Don't leave me. I love you!" Then he passed out and was lying on the floor.

One of my friends said, "Come on y'all. Let's go." We stepped over him and walked out with our tubs. His neighbor, who lived across the hall and happened to be Miss University, saw what was happening.

She started yelling, "Oh, Jesus! Oh Jesus! Oh, my Jesus!" Meanwhile, we stepped right over the young man and kept it moving.

PROJECTILE VOMIT

I had a date scheduled with this guy I met but decided to go to a cookout first. There was some questionable looking food there, and I didn't see any coolers. I ate the potato salad and baked beans. Later on, I noticed nets and flies around the food but didn't pay it any mind. When it was time to go on my date, we met up at a sushi restaurant. We ordered the same thing. The food was good, especially the scallops.

After dinner, my date asked if I wanted to watch a movie. We went to his place and watched my favorite film at the time, Benjamin Button. While we were watching the movie, my stomach started feeling funny. I thought it would pass. We weren't even 15 minutes into the movie when I felt something coming up my throat. I asked where the bathroom was, and before I could close the door, it was projectile vomit. I was facing the door and vomited on the handle. I sprayed the entire wall and threw up all over the bathroom. It was like one of those scary movies where the person vomits, and it was a demon. I threw up some more in the toilet and realized I also didn't feel good enough to clean it up.

I was on my hands and knees by the toilet, praying. My date heard me and came knocking on the door. "Are you okay?"

"Um, yea. I will be out in a minute." I started panicking. There was vomit all over the walls of his beautiful bathroom. What's worst, there were no supplies around to clean it up. All he had was some decorative towels. I found a black rag that might be able to disguise the vomit. But it didn't. I couldn't hide the vomit on the cloth, and there was lint all over it. It was just horrible. I eventually gave up because my method of cleaning wasn't working. I came out of the bathroom and told him, "I'm not feeling well. Unfortunately, I messed up your bathroom and want to clean it up. Just point me in the direction of your cleaning supplies."

He said, "Don't worry about it. My cleaning lady comes on Monday." I insisted that I help clean it up, but he told me it was okay. I said, "Okay. I will be right back." I did it again. This time, I started with the door and continued to vomit all over the bathroom for a second time. I came back out and said, "I think I need to go home." At that point, I figured I was either going to die at his house that night or die peacefully alone and not as embarrassed. He was very nice about it and said, "It's okay. Just let me know you made it home safely." His cleaning lady ended up coming on Monday. We went out on another date about a week later, and he never mentioned what happened.

HOOD SQUAD

I'm sure this story will reveal my age when I tell you it starts with a Fat Joe and Jadakiss concert. My friend and I won tickets on the radio after the DJ challenged us to sing an R&B song in gospel and country. We had horrible singing voices but were willing to do what we needed to go to the concert. I don't know if the DJ felt sorry for us because the two of us couldn't carry a tune even if our lives depended on it, that he gave us the tickets to see Fat Joe and Jadakiss.

As we were leaning back and doing the rockaway while Fat Joe hit the stage, we kept getting disrupted by a group of people yelling, "Coooood Squad! Hoooood Squad!"

"Who in the heck is the Hood Squad?" I asked my friend.

"I have no idea." She yelled over the loud music as we both attempted to ignore the noisy crowd. Before Jadakiss could make an appearance, the concert had ended due to people shooting outside. People scattered, and we began to make our way to the car. Instead of going home, we tried to figure out what our next move would be. As we walked to our car, a group of guys in a limo full of people started to flirt with us.

"Hello, ladies." A guy peeked his head out of the window and introduced himself. "I'm with the Hood Squad."

"Oh, so you're with the people who were interrupting the concert?" We all laughed as I told them how loud and crazy we thought they were.

"We are about to go to a club down the street. Y'all want to come?" He gave us the address, and we met up with the Hood Squad. We skipped the line, had reserved seats, and popped bottles! The Hood Squad knew how to party. My friend and I had the time of our lives. We were no longer upset about the canceled concert. They were complete gentlemen and treated all of the women, including my friend and I, with nothing but the utmost respect.

At about 11 pm, our group of new friends decided it was time to hit up another spot. This time, we got in the limo. Before reaching our next destination, one of their rapper friends came in the limo to join in on the fun.

"I heard Hood Squad shut the concert down!" Their new rapper friend started giving everyone high fives.

"Yea, one of those New York dudes was talking crazy, and we had to let them know what was up." Another one of the Hood Squad members said this as he poured a shot of Hennessy in his cup.

"Shut down the concert?" My friend looked at me as we realized that we were hanging out with the group of people who shut down the concert by shooting it up. That's when we noticed an AK-47 under one of the limo seats. We were scared, nervous, and wanted nothing more than to get back to our car safely. Thankfully, the Hood Squad noticed the fear on our faces and immediately took us back to our car. We never got in a random limo again!

We can now laugh about this scenario, but God had His hands on us. The following weekend, there was a shooting at the club the Hood Squad had taken us to. They were involved, and someone died. That's all we needed to learn our lesson.

HI, SWEETIE!

While leaving work for home one evening, I ran over a pothole. I pulled over into the parking lot of a shopping center to check my tires. Just my luck, the tire on the front passenger side of my car had become flat. I was outside of a barbershop. There were about ten men in there waiting to get their haircut. One of them walked out with a fresh low Caesar cut with deep waves. He noticed a damsel in distress and asked if I needed some help.

"No, thank you. I have roadside assistance," I told him.

"But that can take about an hour. If you have a spare, you can be well on your way in about 15 minutes." I looked up at this tall and handsome man and figured, why not? After he fixed my tire, he started to engage me in conversation. "I'm Wayne, by the way." He extended his hand for a handshake.

I grabbed his firm but soft hand and introduced myself. "Thank you so much for helping me. You saved me a lot of time."

Wayne complimented me on my professional attire and asked what I did for a living. I told him I was a foster care worker. He seemed quite intrigued and told me about all of the work he was doing with young people in the community. He shared some of the nonprofit organizations he was working at. Our small talk turned into an hour-long conversation outside of the barbershop. I learned that Wayne had just moved back to Houston a couple of months ago. Not because he had relocated. He had been released after serving five years in prison on a drug charge. Now, let me say this. He had served his time, and it seemed like he was getting back on track. He even had a job.

We continued to talk about the violence in Black communities, and Wayne shared how he wanted to play a role in mentoring young Black men. Before we knew it, the sun was setting, and it was time for me to head home. "Well, I guess I better get going," I told him.

"Hey, do you think you can give me a ride home?" Wayne explained that he was currently taking public transportation to get around. He had issues with getting his license and was unable to drive at the moment. Since I had a cousin experiencing something similar, I agreed to give him a ride. Call me crazy, but I didn't feel scared to drive this ex-felon home. He was only 20 minutes away, and I knew how to handle myself if anything popped off.

When we arrived in front of Wayne's house, he asked for my number. He got out of the car and told me he would love to hang out soon.

The next day, I noticed Wayne had called me while I was at work. He did what most folks don't do anymore: left a voicemail. I checked the voicemail before calling him back. He started off the message with, "Hiiiiiii sweeettttiiieee!" in a high-pitched voice that sounded quite alarming. Something in his voice made me think this man could potentially be crazy. I know, I know, I was not bothered by the fact that he was an ex-felon and even had the nerve to drive him home. But that voicemail took me out. I called my best girlfriend and let her listen to it. We laughed at the crazy-sounding high-pitched voice and thanked God I made it home safely after driving Wayne home.

I didn't return Wayne's call, and he continued to blow my phone up for about three days. I had over 20 missed calls from him and about ten messages. The last voice message he left on my voicemail was quite irate. He was yelling and told me he didn't understand why I would give him my number and not call him back. The anger in his voice let me know that something wasn't right mentally with Wayne. Thank God I didn't find out the night I dropped him off at home.

NETFLIX AND EWWWW

What's better than one cute guy? Two, one for my friend, and the other one for me. Monique and I were at a party when we met equally attractive fraternal twins Jermaine and Jaiquan. Monique and Jermaine hit it off instantly. They spent the next week, texting back and forth all day every day.

A week later, I was the wingman on a double date. I found out at the party that Jaiquan was cute but not in the "I want to get to know you" kind of way. Nothing was exciting that made me want to learn more about him.

For the lack of a better word, Jaiquan seemed basic. However, I agreed to be with the wing woman.

When I found out it was a Netflix and chill situation, I was ready to renege on my offer. On a two-degree winter night in Washington, DC, Monique and I headed into an unknown situation. We pulled up in front of their apartment building and hurried to the door to get buzzed in. While walking upstairs, Monique's love interest Jermaine answered the door, and they greeted each other.

Jaiquan came from the back of the apartment and tried to swoop in for a hug from me. I gave him a handshake. "Aw, what's up, girl? I've been thinking about you."

In my head, I thought, *Really?* I wanted to tell him I was only there because Mo didn't want to come by herself. Instead, I gave him a half-smile. When we sat down in the living room, Jermaine suggested watching a scary movie. Monique let him know that I wasn't down for scary movies. Jaiquan used this opportunity to indicate that the two of us watch Netflix in his room, and I quickly declined. Instead, I sat on the couch. I didn't take off my jacket or gloves because it was freezing.

"Why is it so cold in here?" I asked.

"Someone is coming to fix the heat tomorrow," Jermaine explained.

I looked at Monique and rolled my eyes. She already knew the look I gave her meant, "Heifer, you owe me." Jaiquan told me it was warmer in his room. The unbearable cold must've taken hold of my brain because I followed him to his room where there was a space heater. The only place to sit was on his bed, so I sat down with my down, still wearing my coat. After Jaiquan closed the door, he said he was beginning to feel sleepy and started taking off his clothes. Watching him strip down, I wondered how this fool was taking off all his clothes when it felt like an icebox inside.

He then told me he missed me and had been trying to see me. I didn't do anything. I just sat stiffly on the bed. "Don't you want to take your coat off and lie down?" I quickly sent Monique a text and asked what the next move was because Jaiquan has gotten completely undressed and was begging me to lie down. She texted me saying Jermaine was lying in her lap.

Once I realized she wasn't ready to go, I tried to figure out how much time I had left to stomach this situation. Again, Jaiquan asked me to lie down on his bed. This time, he was on bended knee. I noticed a tattoo written across the top of his hands that said, "Get Money." He placed his hands on mine and attempted to unfold my crossed arms.

"Please, would you at least lie back?" After what seemed like 45 minutes of begging, I laid back in a fetal position and didn't take my coat or Timberland boots off. I was uncomfortable and cold. After a while, I asked to use the bathroom. When I turned on the light in his bathroom, I noticed cockroaches EVERYWHERE. I turned the light off and slammed the door. I went downstairs and interrupted Monique and Jermaine's quality time.

"Let's go. I'm not trying to leave with anything I didn't come with."

Monique looked sad. "Okay," she said. Both Jermaine and Jaiquan were upset; we left early.

"Yea, we gotta go," I said as I took a flight down the stairs. That was the last time I ever saw Jermaine and Jaiquan. I didn't talk to Monique much longer. She broke the girl code.

THE TIP

It was already kind of awkward when I went on a double date with my mom. But what the heck, I figured it would also be fun. These are the types of moments that you just can't recreate. You will leave with a great story or fond memory. From what I remember, the date went well. My mom and I looked good. We were both dressed to impress our nice-looking dates. The ambiance was refreshing. The food was delicious, and we had great conversations with lots of laughter. We had such a lovely evening, and I looked forward to doing it again. My mom's date offered to pick up the tab, and my mom insisted on leaving a tip.

My date was very appreciative and offered to pay the next time we went out. As our time together came to an end and we were leaving the restaurant, my date said he needed to use the restroom. We told him that we would wait outside for him. As we were waiting outside, we could still see inside the restaurant. My date didn't stay behind to use the bathroom. We watched him go to the table we had been seated. He took the tip my mom left for our server. LIKE REALLY? I was so embarrassed, and he had the nerve to walk out as nothing happened. He never got to pay for the next date because THERE WAS NOT ONE.

CHAPTER 3
HEARTACHES & DISAPPOINTMENTS

Heartbreaker, you got the best of me, but I just keep on coming back incessantly.
Oh why, did you have to run your game on me,
I should have known right from the start you'd go and break my heart.

— MARIAH CAREY, *HEARTBREAKER*

Entering the dating game means you will have your share of disappointments and potential heartbreaks. You are not alone in this. The thing about disappointment as it relates to potential baes is that even when you have no assurance of things working out, you still have hope that things will go your way. When your idea of a relationship is more of a fantasy than reality, it often leaves you heartbroken. In hindsight, usually what ends up happening when our mind bae doesn't become our real-life one is that we see how God was not only blocking us from disaster but protecting us from falling from grace. Sometimes, you orchestrate your heartbreak.

NIESHA

One of the biggest takeaways in life is that "man's rejection is God's protection." I hold this close to my heart because I believe it to be 1000% true. No loving parent wants to see their child make a fool of themselves or get their heartbroken. However, as adults, we tend to put our hands-on hot stoves to see if we'll get burned. It's life. The silver lining in it all is "what's for you is yours and (for the most part) nothing interferes with you getting it."

ERIKA

I love to hear Niesha say what's for you is yours. I remember when she did not want to listen to the phrase, "What God has for you." She knew it to be accurate but couldn't receive it due to certain circumstances she encountered. In the dating game, there's no way around heartbreaks and disappointments. Some will be harder to get through than others. The key is to take what you have learned and keep living a life full of love and laughter, especially when it seems hard to do.

IT'S MY PARTY I CAN CRY IF I WANT TO

It was my 27th birthday, and I was at a club crying in the bathroom stall. I was sad and cute at the same time. My sew-in and lip-gloss were popping, and my strapless multicolored dress hugged all the right curves. Let's just say, before I locked myself in the bathroom stall, I was turning quite a few heads. Over ten people who could have been anywhere in the world decided to spend their Friday night celebrating with me. But none of this mattered because the one person I wanted to show up failed to make an appearance.

Just a week earlier, I had brought friends and family to support the launch of his clothing line. He even made me a pre-birthday dinner and told me he couldn't wait to attend my birthday party. So, as I sat on the toilet with my birthday dress on, I tried to figure out what was so urgent that this young man missed my special day. My friends tried to console me, but I told them I wanted to leave immediately. I left without even acknowledging my new guests because I was too distracted by the one who didn't show up.

During the next two days, I investigated this dude's sudden disappearance. Had he been kidnapped? Murdered? After all, he lived on the South Side of Chicago in what was known as the "wild hundreds." I called his friends and even went to his house. When I didn't find him at home, I turned into Inspector Gadget. I should have been enjoying the fact that I had celebrated another year of life. Instead, I was trying to solve this mystery.

By the time Monday rolled around, I was too sad to go to work. I took a sick day and drove back to his house to see if he was home. I wanted to know why this guy didn't come to my party. He opened the door and immediately started apologizing for not showing up. No explanation, nothing. The only thing he could say was, "You don't deserve me," he was correct! I did not deserve his neglect and lack of consideration. But what did I do? I tried to convince him that I did.

As cliché as it sounds, it wasn't me; it was him. The guy standing before me knew I did not deserve the treatment he was dishing to me. There was something in his eyes that made me feel bad for him. Although I tried to make him realize he deserved me, I knew this was the end. We had some good times, but it was time for me to move on. He walked me to my car, and as I drove off in my Mitsubishi Galant, *Pretty Wings* by Maxwell played in the background while he waved goodbye. It sounds like a soap opera with a horrible script, but this dramatic scene happened to me. Still, a moment that once brought me tears of sadness now brings tears of laughter. I set high expectations for someone who didn't even believe they deserved to be with me.

Looking back, I'm not upset that he didn't make my birthday party. I just can't believe I allowed his absence to steal my joy. There were people in my life there to celebrate me, and his disappearance shouldn't have mattered. This moment taught me that if someone who claims to care for me fails to show up for something they know is significant to me without any explanation, they don't deserve to be in my life.

REFLECTION

To the ladies (and fellas) reading this. Someone's absence should not prevent you from celebrating and living your life. It's never your job to convince someone why they should want to be with your fabulous self because it lessens your value. Not to mention the man was not her husband, so looking for him is a huge NO. Only a wife is responsible for her husband and his safety, and his absence is, is her concern! As much as it sucks, people are free to flake as they please. It's up to you how you want to proceed with that flake.

For the men reading this, a no call/no show is a massive disappointment because it implies that you are not a man of your word. Whether you care about someone a lot or not, consistently flaking on what you say you are going to do only trains you as a man to be unreliable. The best thing to do is not mislead someone on, and define the lines as friends. You never know who will end up being significant to you, and it's better not to burn any bridges.

CRUSH TO CRUSHED

When I have a crush on someone, I am a completely different person. This cool, down-to-earth woman with class turns into a giddy schoolgirl. It was no different when I met Christopher. I was automatically attracted to this handsome and funny man. He had a crisp fade and the juiciest lips I had ever seen. Did I mention he was chocolate? Oooh, I love a chocolate man! We met at a show where he was performing, and after his set, I was eager to let him know how talented he was. We exchanged numbers, and I couldn't wait to learn more about him. Instead of texting or calling, the giddy schoolgirl in me led me to do what most crazed millennials do: I went straight to his Instagram page.

As I scrolled, I began to like and fantasize about him even more. He was funny and also an amazing father of two beautiful children, and he had so much style. As I scrolled through his Instagram page and he sang my favorite old R&B songs on his posts, I thought, *oh my gosh, is this my future boo?* Instead of showing my interest in Christopher, I found myself drawn to events he would perform at. We eventually became friends. Whenever I was around him, I became that giddy schoolgirl. I didn't dare to tell him how much I liked him. After a random text exchange, he asked me if I was flirting with him. When he blew my cover, I had no choice but to step back into my form as the cool, down-to-earth woman with class. It was time to let my feelings known.

Christopher and I had busy schedules but were able to take some time to meet up. Our first date consisted of lunch filled with cocktails and great conversation. I learned more about him beyond his Instagram page. After a few more fun, casual dates, I started to like Christopher even more. Whenever I looked at him, all I could think was, *He needs a good woman in his life.* I was attracted to him, but I also looked at him as a friend, and I could trust sharing my feelings. After a brief encounter at an Ethiopian restaurant, I was now eager to share my feelings with my funny future boo. Still shy but ready to share, I sent him a text that said, *I think you're really dope, and you need a good woman in your life.* I still can't believe I had the guts to say something so bold. Thank God for text messages.

As the bubbles popped up in my iMessage, I began to have bubble guts. Oh gosh! What was he about to say? Does my funny future boo feel the same way? My iPhone alert went off to let me know I had a new message, and I was eager to see his response. I slowly opened my phone, and my bubble guts went from zero to 100 as I read his message. *Naw, I'm not ready for all of that. Somebody else will do you better.*

REFLECTION—ERIKA

Hearing something like this can be a bruise to the ego. My cousin Terrance often asks, "But did he ruin your life?" Ask yourself this question when you get disappointed by a potential bae. This woman fantasized about this man. In her eyes, he seemed like the perfect guy, but he did not share the mutual idea. Even if it's hard, you can't help but respect someone who can be honest and say, "I'm not ready," while suggesting that someone else do you better.

MY FIRST HEARTBREAK

Davis and I grew up together in a small town outside of Detroit, Michigan. Our families were close, and we spent a lot of time together. What I remember most about Davis in my younger years are his piercing eyes. He had the kind of eyes that every woman prays for with eyelashes to match. Davis was my first male best friend.

In third or fourth grade, I overheard my mom talking to her friend about one of her co-workers who was in an arranged marriage.

"What's an arranged marriage?" I inquired

"If me, your dad and Davis' parents said that you two had to get married when you grow up, that would be an arranged marriage," she answered.

I believe this moment is what made me think that Davis would be my husband one day. My mom planted a seed when she used that example. Davis and I continued to be close during our adolescent years. Our relationship was strictly platonic until we briefly dated during our freshman year in high school. It felt weird to me, so odd that I had my best friend break up with him for me. Crazy right? But I didn't know any better at the time. Davis and I continued our friendship. When a girl named Lisa transferred to our school at the beginning of our senior year, it was love at first sight for her and Davis.

Seeing Davis in a relationship with someone else made him more attractive to me. We continued spending time together. When he was not with Lisa, he was hanging out with me. The three of us never hung out together, and he told me Lisa complained about not knowing his female best friend. I avoided hanging out with the two of them because I felt it would just blow over. I believed that Davis would be my husband one day. My thoughts were, it just wasn't our time, so what's the point of getting to know his girlfriend?

Davis and Lisa ended up going to the same college. They dated on and off during their undergraduate studies. When we were home for the summer, Davis and I were like two peas in a pod. I didn't mention Lisa at all. People even started to think that we were an item. We never confirmed or denied anything. We just continued on with our friendship.

After college, Davis and Lisa took a break. As I was preparing for graduate school, I didn't have much contact with Davis as well. We talked every once in a while. I began dating people, but in the back of my mind, I knew Davis was the one for me. One day while heading to class, Davis called me. I was so excited to hear from him because it had been a couple of months since we last talked. I told him what was going on in my world. When I finished updating him, the next three words he said changed my entire world.

"I'm getting married," he told me.

They were not the three words I was looking to hear. I still can't describe the feeling I had when Davis told me this news. I felt paralyzed. The vision I had for us died at that very moment. After a long pause, I managed to say, "Congratulations."

He told me that he and Lisa worked things out and decided to get married. Davis also said to me that I would soon be receiving a wedding invitation in the mail. My body was numb for the next few days. I was still in shock. Davis was getting married, and he wanted me to attend the wedding?

As his friend, I put my feelings aside and supported him on his wedding day. With our families being so close, they would be there anyway. A few of our childhood friends attended as well, and it made it easier to stomach. When the pastor asked if there were any objections, one of my friends nudged me, and we giggled a bit. They were trying to create a real-life scene from *Brown Sugar*. But this wasn't a movie. It was real life, and my dream of being with Davis was no longer realistic.

REFLECTION

Sometimes, things just don't work out like we imagined they would, and sometimes it is because we blew it. As much as we would love to believe greater will come later, we ask you don't gamble much with good people. In our youth, some more than others develop a habit of taking others for granted. We never know how Davis felt about her in return, but we know it's not a good idea to think people will always be there. Some say nice guys finish last, but we say they get married.

BABY, BYE

If you look up the definition of a down chick on the internet, you will see a description of me. I have always made it my priority to bring my best in my relationships. Once, I was deeply in a love groove with my bae Garson. For two and a half years, our relationship moved in a way that showed great promise.

Garson knew I was a loyal woman from day one. Early on in our relationship, his grandmother became very ill. She was dealing with life in a way that no granny should. As she lay in her hospital bed, I would clip her toenails for her. Yes, you read that correctly. While rubbing her legs with lotion during one visit, I noticed her toenails were turning black. My immediate reaction was to clip them. This gesture went beyond me having a love for her grandson. It's just who I am.

With a heart like that, I never expected to experience what I did when I returned from my birthday soirée with friends in NYC. After I touched down in my hometown, Garson asked if we could meet for lunch at our favorite spot. Of course, I accepted the invitation and made my way to see my guy and chow down on some delectable bites. I pulled up to the restaurant and noticed Garson's fancy Harley outside. It was all shiny and bright, like my expectations for our future.

I walked in and saw Garson and was very happy to see him. At this point in our relationship, I felt there was nowhere for us to go but up. We were practically living together. I got along with his mother, and his friends thought I was perfect for him. Unfortunately, what transpired shortly after I ordered my glass of wine was a daymare. For those who don't know, a "daymare" is a horrible scenario you experience during the day while you're awake. As I sat at the table looking at Garson, I could tell something was weighing heavily on his heart. I knew Garson inside and out. We were great friends, and I saw his flaws and knew them well. And by the "Usher" look on his face, I could tell he had a confession.

The bartender brought my glass of wine in what seemed to be slow motion. Now, I'm sure my merlot was delivered in real-time, but everything in that setting got blurry for me. It seemed as though I was in a scene from the *Matrix* where I was dodging invisible bullets.

I asked Garson, flat out, "Is everything ok?"

"Man Peanut, did you have a good birthday?" he replied.

I looked at him dumbfounded because who wouldn't have a blast in NYC shopping, eating, and celebrating life with her girls? "Yes, it was off the chain. What's up with you?"

"I'm good, but I need to tell you something." He said.

"Well, as long as you're not telling me you got a baby on the way, we're cool," I joked. Instead of looking like he just heard a funny joke, Garson looked ashamed and disgusted.

"Man Peanut, I actually do have a baby, and he's been here for a while now. He's almost one."

Wait. A. Damn. Moment. So, my corny joke was a reality, and it belonged to me? Now, this was super wild like an episode of Black Mirror, and I completely lost control of myself. What I was hearing was nowhere near sensible in my mind. I couldn't rationalize when he even had the time to procreate. We were literally together 98% of the time. Still, with that leftover 2%, he managed to have sex with someone else unprotected and release his seed. He composed a life with someone who couldn't care less about his granny's toenails, his mama, understand his weird sense of humor, support his future dreams, his vintage car fetish, and his overall health and happiness.

I slipped into a series of rage that released anger so aggressive and distorted that I'm sure Garson was clueless about what move to make next. I screamed. I yelled and took my shoes off because anything that touched me made my skin sizzle. My feelings were ablaze, and my heart was left deeply bruised. I can't recall anything else from that day because it was all a collection of deceit and betrayal, which my mind refused to replay.

While I never, in my years of dating, felt such deep and intense emotional pain, I didn't let it stop me from being a loving woman and desiring true love I was worthy to receive. I made peace with Garson some months after the "big reveal." It benefitted my life in such incredible ways. By not holding on to that anger toward him, I could move on without any baggage and scars. It helped me enter into the most beautiful relationship of my life with my husband.

CHAPTER 4
FOND MEMORIES

Woman Dating Confession: *Some guys came into my life for a reason and a season, but they helped create some of the fondest memories I have ever had.*

As we travel through time, we often have moments that run across our minds and make us smile, laugh to ourselves, and reflect. We hear so often that even if you've had a string of questionable dating stories, there are some great times sprinkled in the mix of madness. The thing with dating is that every date is not going to be a hit and lead to you meeting your spouse at the end of the aisle. It's safe to assume that each person you date will not leave a lasting or pleasant impression on you, but for those who made the cut, you are indeed something special. We appreciate you!

THE MASKED KISSER

I was working as a hostess during a Masquerade Ball for a group of Howard University Alumni. My job was to seat all of the award recipients and their guests. I came in a black strapless dress and a mask. Suddenly, through the crowd, walked in a 6'6, snicker thick man in a crush, red velvet, custom-fit blazer. His teeth were as white as a bar of dove soap.

He instantly took my breath away when he put his hand on my shoulder and said, "I'm Dave, a guest of Tony Clay's." I was startled as I didn't see his name on the list. I didn't even have a table for Tony Clay. My stomach began to tighten because whoever Tony Clay was, he hadn't yet arrived. Now, I had to find a creative way to tell this man he was not on the list. I looked up at Dave, who stood patiently, smiling at me. As he waited, he made it his business to tell me he was a former NFL player. I looked him up and down as I began to picture the calve muscles underneath his suit.

I think he saw all of my teeth as I smiled back at him and said, "You're good. Follow me." He followed my lead as I went upstairs to find a table for Tony Clay and his beautiful guest. Dave grabbed my hand and thanked me for all of my help. He told me he would hold the table down until his entire party arrived.

As I walked back down the stairs, Tony Clay was just arriving with his 12 other guests. I walked the party to their table where Dave and Tony greeted each other with a handshake and hug. Dave told Tony how proud he was of him and that he was glad he could make it out to support. He then turned my way and informed Tony that I had been an amazing hostess all night. Tony said, "Oh, yea?"

Dave said, "Yes."

I replied to both of them, "I'm glad you and your guests are here. Please let me know if you need anything else."

Dave replied, "Yea, make sure you come back." He picked me up and kissed me on the cheek. As he gently put me down, he told me he wanted to see what I looked like under my mask. With his M&M skin tone pressed to my face, I melted like butter. I never uncovered my face, and I never found out Dave's last name. But, he made my night. Every woman loves to be picked and admired. This wasn't a date but definitely, a moment to remember.

STREET KING

When I was in graduate school, I would drive home after class every Thursday night to enjoy the weekend with my friends and family. It was a two-hour drive, but anything was better than spending the weekend in a small town in Indiana. One Friday night, while at the club with some friends, I met this guy named Cory. He was a bit older than me, and he was a street dude. I usually wasn't attracted to this type of guy, but I really enjoyed our initial conversation.

Cory was impressed when he found out I was in grad school. He told me that most of the women he knew barely made it out of the hood. Cory was in the street but very smart. I could tell that he was a well-respected man. I was away at school most of the time. Therefore, I didn't see any harm in being cool with Cory. He would call me during the week while I was at school and ask me about everything I was studying. He was intrigued and often told me he was proud of me. He even wanted to know what books I was reading.

I talked to Cory for a few months, and whenever I was home, he would meet me where I was and buy drinks for my friends and me. Because he was a street dude, I made it a point to only meet up with him in public. When the weekend was over, I would head back to school while he went back to doing whatever he did during the week. One night while meeting Cory with my friends at the club, I ended up extremely intoxicated. I somehow got separated from my friends. I wasn't in my right mind when Cory told me I could stay at his place. All I remember is him taking my keys and driving me to his high-rise along the lakefront. I have no idea where that place is to this day.

I woke up the next morning, and that's when my good sense kicked in. *Where are you, and who are you with?* I asked myself. Unlike any other guy, anything I expected didn't happen. Cory had given me ginger ale and charged my phone. He had slept on the sofa in his living room while I was in his bed. It goes to show you that you really can't judge a book by its cover. At that moment, I understood why he was so well respected. This super street dude turned out to be one of the nicest and considerate men I had ever encountered. Granted, I didn't know how deep in the streets he was, so I was reluctant to ride around in a car with him. But beyond that, he was always looking out for me 110%. Much more than I can say about some of the white-collar, so-called gentlemen I have run across. I wish I didn't lose touch with Cory. He was a stand-up dude.

YOU'RE A GOOD WOMAN

I was at an event with a very elite group of Black professionals. They were a bunch of snobs and uptight people, but the affair was still lovely. I was in attendance with a couple of friends, and we met a group of guys that seemed cool. We ended up exchanging info for networking purposes. One of the guys I connected with was named Larry. He inquired about one of my friends, and I told him I would try to make something happen. Larry wasn't the best-looking guy, and I knew my friend wouldn't find him attractive, but I told him I would see what I could do.

He invited me to an event one day and asked me to bring my friend. She couldn't make it, so I brought my cousin, and Larry brought one of his friends.

Now, Larry's friend was FINE. I'm talking about Blair Underwood fine. I exchanged info with him, but nothing came of it. Larry and I continued to hang out. We would go out to eat or go to the movies and various events. Although I wasn't physically attracted to Larry, his personality was superb.

He was also a boss. One day I met him at his house to ride to an event together. Before we headed out, he gave me a tour and told me he was buying the home next door. His goal was to buy the block eventually. A Black man with a plan. Yes! He automatically became more attractive.

Larry and I never flirted, and I didn't think he was interested until he invited me to be his plus one at a wedding in Puerto Rico. We ended up not going because his schedule changed due to work. He wanted to make it up to me and asked if we could go somewhere the following weekend. He told me to pick the location, and we could go wherever I wanted to go. I chose San Francisco because I had never been to the Bay Area. We left on a Thursday and stayed there until Sunday. We had an incredible time going out to eat, riding the trolleys, and discovering the city. When we headed back to the airport, I told him, "Thank you so much. I enjoyed myself."

He replied, "You're a good woman. You deserve it." Being reminded that I'm a good woman was continued motivation for me. Although it didn't work out between the two of us, it showed me that men notice a good woman. Even if it doesn't work out, they know. Always remember this when you're in the dating game because you never know who's taking notice of the amazing woman that you are. Men notice a good woman, and the right one for you will snatch you up when it's time.

DISNEYLAND

Once, I worked at a job where I was in charge of planning a red-carpet fundraiser during the holiday season. I planned this particular event for about four years up until I quit my job. The next year, I partnered with one of the celebrities from the previous fundraiser to host another holiday event. I made sure that I was extra cute that day because you never know who you will meet at these types of events. In my mind, I thought I would make some new business contacts. One of my friends whom I invited brought two guests. As one of the hosts, I went around to greet guests and let them know the purpose of the fundraiser. A guy who was with my colleague engaged me in conversation.

The dating scene in Los Angeles is bizarre. Some people are only interested in you by what you do for a living. So, I wasn't expecting to meet anybody I would be interested in on a personal level. As I talked to the guy who had engaged in conversation with me, I could tell that he was a little friendlier than the other guests. He was professional but borderline flirting. I asked where he was from, and he told me he was from Baltimore. It began to make sense why he was so down-to-earth. I thought he was a transplant, but he was visiting.

When I found out that he didn't live in Los Angeles, I said, "Oh, so you're just going to tease me? I meet a handsome man, and of course, he doesn't even live here." I couldn't believe those words came out of my mouth because I'm generally shy about flirting. He told me he would be around for the next few days. He was going to Vegas for a couple of days then was planning to head back to Los Angeles before going back home. Then he asked if I had any plans that following Monday. I was planning to go to Disneyland because I had a pass and had only been there once. I wanted to see how it was during the holidays, and that was the only day I would be able to go. Most would be planning to go with a group, but I was planning on going by myself.

Still, I asked if he wanted to go. I didn't think he would take me up on my offer because we had just met. He did. He told me he would hit me up when he was back from Vegas. With me being from Chicago, I knew there was Garrett Popcorn in Vegas. I joked and told him if he happened to see it, he should feel free to bring me some back.

The day before Disney, he hit me up via text to make sure we were still on. He told me he would pick me up the next day. He was a little late due to driving straight from Vegas, but he apologized for that. When I got in the car, he gave me a large tin of Garrett Popcorn. You would have thought we already knew each other. From the moment I got in the car, we talked about a little bit of everything. Even when we were waiting in line for rides, there was no awkward silence. Instead of forcing a conversation, I suggested that we play Blebrity, a game app on my phone. We had a good time.

While in the car headed back from Disney, I told him my plans for the holiday season. My family and I were spending Christmas in Miami, after which I would head to Orlando to visit my aunt. Ironically, he was planning to be in Orlando at the same time. He was going to visit some of his frat brothers before driving to Atlanta for New Year's Eve. When he told me he was going on a road trip, I told him I wanted to go. Again, this usually is out of my comfort zone, but I was in one of those moments where I just wanted to live my best life. I told him I had a friend that lived there, and I could stay with her. She was also throwing an NYE party, so I figured it would be perfect.

Three weeks after Disney, we were on a road trip from Orlando to Atlanta. I guess you could say this was our second date. We had a great time talking and listening to music. I'm that person that will judge you based on your playlist, so I requested that we listened to his. The drive to Atlanta was about six hours, so we learned more about each other during that time. When he dropped me off at my friend's, he headed to his frat brother's house. The next day, we brought in the new year together at my friend's party. On New Year's Day, we went to the Old Lady Gang to make sure we ate our greens and black-eyed peas for the new year. While this never blossomed into a relationship, it was one of the best couple of dates I ever had. For anyone who is still in the dating game, I suggest that you have fun when you get the chance.

CHAPTER 5
HE TRIED IT

Woman Dating Confession: *I remember running into a guy I met at a party. He tried to act brand new like he didn't know me. When my cousin noticed this, she said, "Look at him with his tired ass suit on!' From that day forward, he was known as TAS (Tired Ass Suit) because he tried it!*

Now and again, we will come across a handsome, slick-talking, eloquent, cologne wearing man who is also crafty with his hands. As these men seem to appeal to all of our senses, they often lack a core ingredient that prevents them from being keepers, and it is usually good intentions. Guys like the ones we described understand the appeal they have and tend to use it to their advantage. When this happens, we can fall for the Okie Dokie, pull a Casper the Ghost, and disappear or use it as the opportunity to help them learn.

As women, we've heard it time and time again: A man will go as far as you let him. We believe this to be true. If the direction he is heading does not suit you, be sure to let him know. If you tell him "no" enough, it may encourage him to reflect on his shortcomings, and this self-reflection promotes his growth. Keeping your head in the dating game means you may endure some people who will truly test your patience. You can't control whether someone tries to pull a fast one on you, but you can manage your reaction. Let's see how some of our girls reacted when they were tested during their dating experiences.

MAKING THE BED

When I first moved to LA, I met Darren, a handsome, tall, and chocolate-skinned man. We had so much in common. We talked on the phone for about a month. Our schedules weren't meshing well, so it took about a month to go out.

Darren hit me up the night we decided to go to dinner and said, "Hey, I'm exhausted. I just got off of work. Do you mind just meeting me at the house?" Now, I typically don't have a first date at someone's house, but we talked for about a month, and I felt like I could trust him. When I arrived at his place, I asked where I should park. He said, "You should park down the street in case you decide to stay the night." I just laughed out loud. I thought to myself that this dude thought he was slick.

I said, "Okay. Well, can you come and get in the car with me? I don't know how far down I will have to park, and I don't want to walk by myself." So, I picked him up, and we went to park the car. After this, we walked back to his place. This guy had cooked an entire four-course meal. He had baked salmon, corn, mashed potatoes, bread, and had some champagne. Confused, I looked at him. He had said he was tired, yet he had time to cook a huge meal. Like, okay, you're also trying to do the most with champagne and strawberries.

When we finished dinner, we sat on the couch to watch TV, and Darren could not keep his hands off me. I hadn't been with a guy in a minute, so the touching from his large hands made me a little weak. He kissed me, grabbed me, and in my head, I was thinking, *I'm going to give it to him. No, you can't.* I had been celibate for about three and a half years at that point. So, I was pretty much on my square about not giving in to my sexual desires. I was drinking hella wine. It appeared that he intended to get me drunk.

I kept peeing since I was drinking so much wine. On the way to the bathroom, I had to pass the bedroom. I noticed the bed wasn't made. It wasn't a big deal, but I peeped it. Later, Darren told me he had to go to the bathroom and would be right back. When I had to pee for the fourth time, I walked past the bedroom and saw that his bed was made.

I'm like, *Oooohh, he's trying to get ready for the takedown?* When I went back to the couch and started kissing me, I said, "You know what? I gotta go." Darren made it clear that he wasn't ready for me to leave. He grabbed me and tried pulling me toward his newly made-up bed. I grabbed him and tried pulling him toward the door. We were literally playing tug of war. This dude put my hand on his crotch so I could feel his penis. He was PACKING. I said, "Ooh, Jesus! I gotta go, Darren." He asked what I was scared of. I told him I wasn't afraid of nothing; I needed to go. He finally gave in and let me go before he walked me to my car. I didn't talk to him much after that.

Years later, he met one of my friends through me. He was all up in my face but ended up exchanging numbers with my friend. Darren told her, "Oh, your friend's cool, but I want to get to know you." I thought that was interesting. She knew my story with him. I didn't want him and told her that it was cool if she wanted to talk to him. They did briefly, and he did some silly stuff with her too. He slides in my DM now and again. He's still handsome, and I'm still uninterested. Now, he's in his early to mid-40s and is still doing the same thing. I guess he's still trying to find someone else he can make his bed for.

REFLECTION

This story right here is hilarious. It's funny (and sad) to see the desperate measures a man will take to try to woo a woman into his bedroom. Darren didn't seem to have much game and was trying to find the fastest way to get in our sister friend's pants. This is why he made a four-course meal when he was "too sleepy" to go out to dinner. We are glad this didn't work out because he was quick to switch up when he wanted to do the same thing with her friend. Good try, brothaman!

HEY, BABE

I met this attractive guy at a Hollywood event, and we hit it off immediately. He worked with a well-known artist in the music industry and was accompanying her. This guy was in town from New York for a week. He presented himself to be a God-fearing, smart, ambitious dad who was hard working. Overall, he seemed like a good dude. We began talking multiple times every day. It was less than a week, and he had already started calling me "babe" and would say things like, "You're gonna be mine."

I'd flirt back and say, "Oh, you're quite sure of yourself, huh."

His rebuttal was, "I'm intentional about who I spend my time getting to know, and based on what I know about you, you have the characteristics of the type of woman I'd consider being with." He had the best conversation and a way of making me feel comfortable with being vulnerable. I was enjoying talking to him.

We planned to meet up for dinner right after the BET awards for our first date. He ended up not being able to meet because he had to work with his client. He told me that the following day would be better, and I said that was fine. We agreed to do brunch. I let him know I had a workout class and that I would call him once I finished. The following day, after my class, I called him. No answer. I called a couple of hours later—still, no response. His not answering was strange because, for an entire week, we spoke multiple times every day.

Six hours passed, and I texted him and said, *Hey, not sure what happened to you today, and I hope you're okay. I'm very disappointed that I didn't hear from you. Have a safe trip back home. It was nice meeting and talking to you. Take care.*

Ten minutes later, I got a phone call from him telling me he didn't get in until 7:00 am because he was in the studio with his client. He explained that when he got back to the hotel, he crashed, then woke up at 2:30 pm and had errands. He apologized and told me that everything was out of his control. In the conversation, he said my name wrong. I quickly corrected him. See, never trust a guy that only calls you babe. He calls everybody he's talking to "babe" because he doesn't want to mix names up. The guy tried to get me to meet him for a drink, but I told him I already had plans and hoped he had a safe trip back to New York. Boy, BYE!

REFLECTION

Fellas, here's a quick tip. A lot of grown women who have just met, you will look at you sideways when you hit them with the "hey, babe" or "good morning, beautiful." Honestly, some may ask what is wrong with these terms because they are endearing. Because these words are used so often and insincerely, it has killed a lot of women's desire to hear it. These terms of endearment, at this point, should be saved for the special woman in your life. When you use these phrases too soon, we don't feel special because we perceive that you probably address all women with these terms. We just look at it as a potential red flag. So, in this case, this guy used "babe" so he wouldn't have to remember our friend's name. Good thing she deleted him from her contacts before things progressed.

HOW SWEET IS THE TEA?

I was dating this guy I grew up with, and he was in town visiting for the weekend. When he arrived, we went to a sandwich shop. At the shop, I spotted this guy Shannon—a flamboyant gay man—who made my costumes for all of my pageants. He would also tell me about his connections in the LGBT community whenever I went to him for fittings. When I got out of the car with my date, Shannon immediately recognized him and said, "Hey! How are you doing? You look like a million bucks." The two of them were quite gingerly, and I began wondering what their connection was. I didn't ask, but it set off an alarm for me.

My date and I went out that night and stayed out until around 3:00 am. Since we were now hungry, I decided to pull up in the drive-thru at Crystal, a fast-food restaurant down south that you go to when nothing else is open. The guy taking our order was very flamboyant, just like Shannon. When we got to the window, he leaned out and started talking in a flirtatious way. I noticed he was not looking at me, but my date. My date leaned over me and caught the man's gaze in the window. "I have a question, how sweet is the tea?" He asked.

The guy in the window giggled. There was definitely something going on over me. I'm like, *"Wait a minute! What is going on here? Is he gay?"* I felt like something was up. When our food arrived, my date and the guy were giggling at each other. And they were bantering after the inquisition of how sweet the tea was. We had our food for a while, but we were still at the drive-thru window for some strange reason, and I could not help but notice my date and the cashier gazing into each other's eyes. The tripped-out part about it was when my date received his iced tea; he decided it wasn't sweet enough and asked for something else.

REFLECTION

Okay, to each its own when it comes to your sexual orientation, however a huge issue in the dating community is down-low people. Men used to say that they did not mind their women being bisexual; however, when their women left these men for other women, things got just as real for men. We do not support people who bring this deception into other people's lives. The down-low and in the closet community have brought much devastation to the dating scene. This has been a factor in the rise of HIV and STD cases, specifically in the Black community, as if the numbers of available men are not low enough.

GHOSTED BY A FRAT BOY

It was 11:45 pm on a Saturday when I got a call from this guy in a particular fraternity that shall remain nameless. His name was Lamont, and we hung out a few times with mutual friends. When I picked up the phone, he said, "I don't know if I'll make it home because I've been drinking. Can I come to your house and crash?"

In my head, I thought, *Self, do you want to let this man come to your house? You've known him for less than 90 days. He could be crazy.* Then I thought about all of the mutual friends Lamont and I knew and thought, *You know what, Shawn or Kelly wouldn't be hanging out with somebody that's crazy.* I decided to go ahead and tell him he could slide through. But let me be clear; it was off the strength of my friendships that I allowed Lamont to come to the crib.

When I let Lamont know he is welcome to crash, he said, "Bet. You know, I've been trying to get up with you since we met anyway? What's your address? I'm on my way." My doorbell rang 20 minutes later. I opened the door, and a glassy-eyed Lamont stumbled through my door, smelling like a bottle of Courvoisier. He plopped down on my sofa and said, "So, what's up?"

His speech was slurred. "Where is your room? I'm trying to lay down," he continued. Lamont got up from the sofa and proceeded to walk around my house while I followed right behind him. He pushed my room door open and said, "Yes!"

I told Lamont, "I know you don't think you are sleeping in my bed. I am not cleaning up any vomit if you start to feel sick. Also, since you've walked all through my house, you now know where the bathroom is. You will also be sleeping on the sofa." I grabbed a sheet and blanket from my linen closet and had Lamont follow me back to the sofa.

He said, "Are you for real?"

I said, "Yes. Does this look like a face that says I'm playing?"

"Man, whatever," Lamont said while taking the blanket and pillow.

I told him, "I'm going to get you some water because I'm sure you didn't drink any while you were out." I asked if he had anything to eat to help soak up some of the alcohol.

He said, "I had a little Italian Fiesta pizza that the bruhs had at the party."

I brought him two bottles of water and said, "Please don't throw up on my sofa. If you need anything, I'm in my room."

I wasn't in my room for a good 30 seconds before Lamont yelled out, "I can't come and get in the bed with you?"

Again, in my head, I was like, *this is only the second or third time I've seen you, and your drunk ass is trying to finesse your way to my bed. You're cute or whatever, but I ain't goin'*.I yelled back, "Nah. I'll see you in the morning." Five minutes after his outburst, all I could hear was Lamont snoring.

I came out of my room in the morning, and he was still sleeping on the sofa. I decide to get some breakfast started. I figured he would have slept the alcohol off, and maybe we would have an opportunity to get to know each other. I started making grits and bacon. Just as I was finishing making the pancakes, Lamont said, "Are those pancakes I smell?"

I replied, "Yes." Lamont got up and went to the bathroom. As I was cracking the eggs, he came out of the bathroom. I asked how he was feeling, and Lamont told me he felt much better than the night before. He headed back to the sofa. About 15 seconds later, Lamont was standing behind me in the doorway of the kitchen. I asked, "Are you okay?"

He said, "Yes. Imma take the trash out."

Oh, okay. He's trying to be a gentleman. I thought to myself. I thanked him and let him know the trash bin was downstairs on the side of the house. I was just about finished and asked, "Do you eat cheese on your eggs?"

Lamont told me, "Yes," as he headed out with my trash.

After ten minutes, I began to wonder if Lamont got lost. When I called him, the phone went straight to voicemail. I took the food off the stove and turned the oven off, so I could make sure he didn't get lost. I put my shoes on to go outside. This fool had left my back door wide open and was nowhere to be found by the trash bins. I called him back to back to back and finally, after getting no answer, I left him a voicemail and sent a text. In the full spirit of Iesha from the movie *Poetic Justice,* I yelled into the phone. "You left my entire door open. Fool! Anybody could have come into my house and something could have happened to me."

When I hung up, I sent a text and said, "That's the thanks I get after I allowed your drunk ass to come and spend the night at my house. I better never see you out on the street, or imma have my brothers and every cousin I have on the Southside of Chicago to beat your ass. You might be cute with your El Debarge lookin' drunk ass, but you still short. Do you hear me? YOU'RE SHORT!" I learned a valuable lesson. Don't let strangers in your house even if you have mutual friends. Their fraternity does not validate their character any more than a badge validates the police.

REFLECTION

First of all, Lamont, if you could make it to our girl's house to crash, you could have made it to your home to sleep. It seems that as the sun came up, you were reminded why you came to her house in the first place and realized you were unsuccessful. Soon as you gained your memory, you also lost the courage you got from the alcohol to tell this woman that you were leaving. Being that drunk was a safety risk for you and our homegirl, and she still looked out for you on the strength of the two of your mutual friends.

As a side note, every gesture is not gentle. If the man were indeed a gentleman, he would not have asked to crash at a woman's house he was interested in, in a drunken stupor. Like himself, he knew the trash needed to be taken out and used it as an excuse to flee the scene. Back to Lamont. Clearly, you were salty because you went to our friend's house with intentions to have sex but saw it was nothing happening, but hey, thanks for taking out her trash.

PHILOSOPHY OR ANATOMY?

I had mostly honors courses during my sophomore year in college. Philosophy 101 was the toughest. The only thing that made it worthwhile was the striking senior with black wavy hair. Truthfully, he made it easier to stomach the class. During a pop quiz, I noticed him staring at me from afar. After class, he walked up to me and spat his game. He asked if I needed help studying. I guess my frustration with the course was written all over my face.

Of course, I took him up on his offer. He was a sight to look at and wanted to help me. I played it safe and had him meet me at my house during a time my mom would be home. We eventually started hanging out beyond our tutoring sessions. My mother and aunts thought he was handsome and such a nice young man. He was charming and often told me how cute I was. He said he loved my innocent demeanor and that I reminded him of a little princess. What attracted him the most was that I was more ladylike than most girls he knew.

One day after class, he invited me to his apartment to study. I had known him for a while, and my family met him, so I didn't see any harm. I told him I would meet him later on that day. I was so excited as I grabbed my books and headed to his house, ready to study. When I arrived, you wouldn't believe what happened. This dude opened the door in a white terry cloth robe. Weird, right? Well, wait until you hear this. This mug opened his robe, and he was naked. *Ummmm, are we studying philosophy or anatomy?* I politely turned in the other direction and headed home. He was a lousy tutor, anyway, I was still getting a D. I dropped the class and him.

My mom inquired why he didn't come around anymore. I tried to give her a general explanation, so I told her I just didn't like him like that. But when she said, "Y'all don't be wanting the ones that want y'all," I had to tell her the truth. When she learned the real reason why I dropped pretty boy Floyd, she was shocked and said, "Girl, I ain't raise no fool!" Yeah, mom, do you still think he's a gentleman?

REFLECTION—ERIKA

We can't reflect on this story without pointing out that this is my mom's experience. Yes, guys were trying it in the '70s and centuries before that. Anyway, mom, this guy had "creep" written all over him. Because you were young and fascinated with his fineness, he thought he could pull a fast one on you. But Granny ain't raise no fool. You ran and never looked back.

I want to point out that he referred to you as a "pretty princess." I found this kind of odd that he related someone in their college-age to something that seemed so childish. But we will thank Pretty Boy Floyd. You kept your head in the game and eventually met my dad, the love of your life.

Some guys will try to prey on girls who they perceive to be naive. Unfortunately, some girls have not been able to dodge these kinds of men, which has led to harrowing memories. If you are one of the women healing from someone who tried to play on your innocence, we pray for your healing and hope that you experience the kind of love God has for you.

DON'T WANT TO MEET YOUR MAMA

While I was in law school, I joined match.com during spring break. I met a guy with a decent sense of humor and was just a cool guy all around. Our first encounter turned into multiple dates that I enjoyed. As Memorial Day approached, he asked me what my plans were. I told him I usually hung out with my family. He told me his family had a ranch outside of the city, and they always spent time there during Memorial Day weekend. He recalled a time when I told him I was interested in learning how to ride a horse, so he said this would be a perfect time.

My new friend asked me if I wanted to join him and his family. I declined because I felt we weren't that serious. We had recently met, and I was just enjoying his company. Since we decided not to spend Memorial Day weekend together, he invited me to brunch a week before. While we were at lunch, he seemed antsy the entire time. It was odd because I was used to his calm, laid-back demeanor. When we placed our order, the waitress let us know that the freshly squeezed orange juice would take a while. My date ordered some anyway. We ate and had a good time. We were at our table for a little over an hour when the waitress asked if there was anything else we wanted before bringing our bill. When he ordered another glass of freshly squeezed orange juice, I found it unusual. The first glass took over 30 minutes to be prepared. I wondered why he would order more when it was time to go. It seemed like he was stalling.

I asked him what was going on. He said, "Oh, you must be in a hurry. I didn't want to tell you, but I'm waiting for someone."

I said, "Someone like who?" He began to stutter then told me he invited his mom to the restaurant. I asked, "To have breakfast?" He explained that he told her to come after breakfast to meet me. He felt that if I met her, maybe I would feel more comfortable coming for Memorial Day. He also told me that I would love her because we were in the same sorority. While he explained himself, he kept looking out the window, hoping she would arrive. I was upset because he had blindsided me, and was trying to make me stay by letting me know his mom was my soror. Well, sorry, soror, I had to go. I politely excused myself from the table and told him to holla at me after Memorial Day weekend.

REFLECTION

For all the guys reading this, we want you to know that most women, who are not in a serious relationship with you, may have reservations in meeting your family right away. Most of the women we know are only interested in this hazing process when we see the relationship is heading in a serious direction. As women who have grilled other women who have come into our family members' lives, we are only willing to go through this process for someone we genuinely care about and are sure of a future with them.

Until then, we are more interested in meeting your friends because they tell us more about who you are. Considering you selected these people to be in your life, they are most likely whom you seek counsel. Now, we don't speak for all women when we say this, and there will be women who would be excited and flattered to meet your mother early on, and sometimes you meet on a random and unintentional occurrence. The bottom line is, don't blindside us into meeting your mom before it's time.

BORDERLINE GORGEOUS

Sunday mornings are always a delight for me. I spend most of them by heading to the house of the Lord to receive an inspirational word before beginning my work week. As summer was approaching, I began attending the early morning service. It made it easier for me to be on time for brunch with my girlfriends. I thought making it to the church by 9:00 am would be a challenge, but there was a handsome usher who made it easier for me to roll out of bed.

"He's borderline gorgeous," I said to my girls over brunch. You know, the guy that is not fine but very handsome. He was not entirely gorgeous, just on the cusp. My friends and I always came up with funny ways to describe our latest crushes. Whenever we called a guy "ugly cute," it meant he was cute with a dash of ugly. Anyway, Borderline Gorgeous was caramel with light green eyes and had an evident love for the Lord. He greeted me every Sunday morning with a smile. He would occasionally engage me in small talk about how much he enjoyed the pastor's sermon. I developed a slight crush on him.

I figured he was just kind. Numerous women were falling all over him and trying to become his chosen girl. He had his pick of the litter. When I ran into Borderline Gorgeous at a picnic, I found out that he had been eyeing me. We engaged in small talk, and he asked if we could hang out someday soon. I eagerly gave him my number and was ecstatic when he called a few days later.

Borderline Gorgeous had just remodeled his home and invited me to check out his new firepit in his backyard. I knew him from church, so I figured why not. When I arrived at his house, he kept telling me he couldn't believe I picked up his call. It sounded like he was crushing on me just as hard. I was slightly flattered. I followed my crush to the backyard. When he asked if I was hungry, I told him no but would take some water. He went into the house, and when he returned, he had a bottle of water for me and a soda and a bag of chips for himself. I couldn't help but laugh to myself as I watched this grown man eat a bag of chips that came from a variety pack. He looked so goofy as he ate out of this little bitty bag. He began making small, awkward talk. I always envisioned him as cool and put together but was surprised that his conversation sounded like someone was speaking to him out of an earpiece and telling him what to say. I figured it was just nervous energy.

Thankfully, he suggested that we watch a movie. After watching the enjoyable film, I realized it was getting late. He told me I was welcome to stay if I didn't feel like driving home. I was tired and agreed to this impromptu slumber party. After falling asleep on his couch, I woke up to him trying to pull a fast one. He grabbed my hand and put it down his pants. All I could think was, "*Where is the rest of it?*" I was so embarrassed for him. I tried to sleep as he continued to randomly attempt to wake me up in the middle of the night. I was curled in a ball as if to say, *Oh noooo, churchman! I thought you were going to be cool.* It seemed like the sun was taking forever to rise. When it did, I was ready to dash. Before leaving, Borderline Gorgeous asked if I wanted breakfast. I politely declined and told him I had a busy Saturday.

He called me a few days later and asked if I wanted to hang out again. I declined and let him know work had picked up. He continued to call and text, and I always hit him with the same excuses. I even began attending the 11:00 am service again. Brunch would have to wait. I did an excellent job dodging him until I ran into him at the Chicago House picnic. He asked when we would hang again. I let him know that work was keeping me extremely busy. Summer ended, and I stopped receiving calls from my former crush.

One day, while walking into the 11:00 am service, someone tapped me on my shoulder. I turned around, and it was Borderline Gorgeous. He was leaving the 9:00 am service but spotted me and wanted to say hello. He asked if I wanted to join him and a group of friends at his house for Monday Night Football. Since there would be people there, I cut him some slack. I arrived at his house the next day with snacks and quickly noticed I was the only guest. Now I got upset and thought, *Man, this is some BS.* I was looking forward to mixing in with people and potentially leaving at halftime.

When the game began, Borderline Gorgeous went into another room. Out of nowhere, loud music began to play. He was playing 80s music in the middle of 2015. Suddenly, *Fire & Desire* by Rick James and Teena Marie started to play. This man walked out butt naked, little penis and all. I laughed so hard right in his face. I found it remarkable that as old as he was, nobody had told him to put that little fella away. I told him I didn't want him to be confused because nothing was going to happen. I walked out of the door and laughed the entire way home.

REFLECTION

Here's a message to those who seem to forget that beauty is only skin deep, looks may get a person in the door, but it's their character and personality that keeps them there. This is the perfect example of why it's sometimes useful to leave a crush as just that, a crush. As for Mr. Borderline Gorgeous, no matter how fine you appear to be, it's hard for anyone to take you seriously if you expose your genitals to a person who had not proven herself to be interested in intimacy.

Borderline Gorgeous also makes us think about the people we meet in church and how everyone is not always who they seem to be. We touched on this a little earlier in the Smooth Operator's story, but what about the guys who are active servants in the church and self-proclaimed men of God? The deacons, trustees, and even pastors portray a very different character behind closed doors.

One of our good girlfriends was dating a very religious guy. He would criticize Christians for going to church on Sunday instead of observing the Sabbath on Saturday. But he was ready to get into her pants every chance he got. It's just an example of the many men and women whose only involvement with the Lord is when it is convenient for them and make excuses for moving outside of God's will. The moral of the story is, meeting a man in the church is not a guarantee that he won't try it.

ALWAYS KEEP A DIME

Before I get into this story, I have to let you know that the year was 1975. I was excited because I was finally going out on a date with my biggest crush. Y'all, he was so attractive to me. All the girls on my block had a crush on him too. We would sit outside my house on the steps, talking about how handsome he was. Imagine how I felt when I was the lucky girl he asked out on a date.

Before I left, my big brother, who thought he knew all the ins and outs about dating, said, "Here is a dime if you need to call me."

Of course, my smart mouth said, "I don't need your dime!" I snatched it out of his hand. My date pulled up outside the house. When I headed out, I did a Gloria walk from the movie *Waiting to Exhale* as he watched me make my way to the car. I got in, *Reasons* by Earth, Wind, and Fire was blaring out of the speakers of his El Dorado. *Oh yeah, my type of guy!* I asked him where we were going, and he said it was a surprise. *A surprise? How sweet.* I sat back, cheesing my butt off and smiling ear to ear. I watched every turn and wondered what the surprise was when we pull up at this dinky hotel. "Ohhh, so we're going to a party?" I asked.

He replied, "Oh, it's going to be a party, alright. Just me and you."

"What?" I replied, ready to go through the roof.

He said, "You heard me."

I not-so-politely said, "Well, you got the wrong one. You can take me home."

He says, "I don't think so."

I jumped out of the car, and he sped off. Do you know what I was doing at that moment? Digging in the bottom of my purse, trying to find that dime.

REFLECTION

We cracked up laughing at this story because it sounds like a scene from a comedic television show. Like Frat Boy, homeboy was out as soon as he found out he wasn't getting any action. We can hear the screeches from his tires. And as we pointed out earlier, men were even trying it back in the day.

The best way to know the character of a man is to see how he reacts when he finds out he isn't getting some anytime soon, if ever. If he wants to dodge because you won't give in to his advances, let him go and consider it a blessing. A man who is not capable of entertaining you outside of sex shows you his level of interest and maturity.

We want to point out that the sister girl was initially not prepared to make that phone call. When you are treading through your dating journey, it is crucial to be prepared for any foolishness and take necessary safety measures. Keep someone on speed dial, and don't go anywhere if you don't know how to get yourself back. For example, it's not uncommon for a man to want to take you on a nice trip when you are just dating. If you ever accept such an invitation, it would be smart to have enough money in your bank account to make it back home. You never want to be stuck in a situation that you can't get out of. It is best to drive your car if you need to leave unexpectedly and avoid any potentially dangerous situation. Anything can pop off.

THE UGLY FRIEND ZONE

A friend of mine introduced me to this guy a few years ago. He was super smart, a ball of fun, and had it going on. The only problem was that I just wasn't attracted to him. There was no chemistry on my end, but he was very interested in me. He would hit me up to take me out. After two wine flights at a wine bar, I wasn't attracted enough even to want to kiss him. Thankfully,

I didn't have to let him down because he ended up taking a job in another state. He would come home every once in a while, and we would hang out. As I said, he was a ball of fun; I just wasn't attracted to him.

He continued to keep in touch via social media. One day, he sent me a DM with heart eyes as his way of starting a conversation. He told me he was thinking about moving back because he had a job offer on the table. He didn't know if he was going to accept it, but if I told him to move back, he would be on the first plane smoking. I strongly encouraged him not to make any decisions based on how he wanted our relationship to go, but to let the Lord guide his footsteps.

He decided to take the job, and this opened the door for us to communicate more frequently. I still wasn't attracted to him, but I decided to give him a chance. I even gave myself a pep talk. "You say you want a good man, but when presented to you, you're not giving him a chance because you're not physically attracted to him?" One day at dinner, he asked what I was looking for in a relationship. I told him I was dating with intention and not looking to date just for fun. Being around him helped me look past the lack of physical attraction enough to kiss him. One day during an intense make-out session, he decided to let me know his D was mine if I wanted it.

Our relationship seemed to be heading in a serious direction, and I asked if he wanted to accompany me to a gala I was planning. He told me he would love to be on my arm that night. We coordinated outfits, and I was excited for him to be my plus one. A day before the event, he called me. He started the conversation by saying, "You know, we are always cool." I knew something was up by the tone of his voice. He went on to say, "You know I would never blindside you. I respect you too much." He proceeded to tell me he had recently started talking to this girl, and some of her family members would be at the gala.

"Excuse me, my gala?" At this point, I wondered who this woman was and why it was so vital for him to tell me. He explained that they had just started talking. I was left me wondering, *what were we doing then?* This man had been chasing me for years, and I finally decided to give him a chance even though I was far from attracted to him. He also knew I was dating with a purpose and intentional. We weren't in a committed relationship, but I was under the impression that we were headed somewhere. I told myself it wasn't that serious due to us not being committed. I contemplated telling him not to come but moved forward with the plans.

We had a room together the night of the gala. He showed up extremely late. I was having a good time with my friends, doing me. He arrived when it was time to eat, and our interaction was extremely awkward. Drinks were flowing, and after a festive night, the two of us headed to our room. He thought he's about to finally get some action.

"No, you're not getting any here. You better call that chick you just met."

When we woke up the next morning, he said, "I guess I better take this walk of shame. Even though we didn't do anything, I know your friends will be in the lobby when I leave."

"You can take the walk of shame, but we both know nothing happened." I told him. At this point, I didn't have any more time to waste or play games. That was that, and he kept it rolling. Two weeks went by, and he called me out of the blue.

He asked, "How is my friend doing?" Well look at that, this ugly guy just friend-zoned me. I was now just a homie even though he had been telling me his D was mine only a few weeks before.

REFLECTION

There will be times when someone is interested in you, and you just aren't attracted to them. From what we gather in this story, our friend was willing to look beyond the physical, to find a deeper connection. It just turns out that it didn't work out in her favor. Sometimes we are willing to give people a chance because we don't want to be superficial. However, a lack of good looks doesn't signify humility. We understand relationships are much more profound than physical attraction, but you shouldn't have to force it.

CHAPTER 6
LOVE MADE A FOOL OF ME

You're just a lover out to score, I know that I should be looking for more, what could it be in you I see, what could it be...oh love, oh love, stop making a fool of me.

— DENIECE WILLIAMS, *SILLY*

Have you ever seen one of your confident, intelligent friends ignore all the warnings in their relationship, leaving you wondering how she could be such a fool? On the outside looking in, you see every sign that should have her running to the hills. But instead, she makes up excuses for his unacceptable behavior. Have you been that woman in a relationship where you knew something wasn't right, but for some reason, you kept giving the guy chance after chance? If this has been you, don't be embarrassed. It has happened to the best of us.

Sometimes, the oxytocin also referred to as the "love hormone," leads us into situations that we wouldn't usually put up with if we were in our right state of mind. According to research, oxytocin helps us become more accepting of others. One of the ways it's stimulated is during sex. When it's released, it creates lots of trust between you and your partner. It can also be released through an emotional connection.

Another word for this connection is a soul tie. A soul tie is a heavy yoke to a person designed only for marriage and commitment. Often, people do foolish things because their souls are tied to a stranger. Sometimes we can't prevent "fake love" from pulling the wool over our eyes. It can be hard to snap out of it and become available for the person you can trust when that soul tie is finally broken. So, keep all of this in mind as we dive into the next set of stories.

CLAUDE THE FRAUD

When I turned 20, I moved to a new city. I was there for a month or so when I met this guy who seemed super polite and sweet. We started talking and went out on a few dates, and I was starting to really, really like him. He drove a black Volkswagen Jetta. One day, he was supposed to pick me up for a movie date. He called and told me he was having car trouble. I told him it was okay, and I could drive.

On our next date, I noticed a spare tire on his car. I figured he recently had a flat or something. While driving, he said, "I hate to do this, but I'm kind of going through some stuff, and I need to get my car fixed." He asked to borrow money from me. Usually, that's a red flag, but since I saw for myself that he was having car trouble and we were spending a lot of time together, I told him, "Okay, sure." I asked how much, and he said he needed $700. I said, "Oh, that's a lot of money." I didn't have a lot of money. I was a 20-year-old waitress and was making a living off tips. However, my young and naive self said, "Okay, fine." I let him borrow it, and he promised to pay me back in two weeks.

Two weeks rolled around, and he returned my loan via check. He told me he wanted to make sure he paid me back in time and got the money from his aunt. He told me how much he appreciated me for helping him out. I was glad to know that he was a man of his word, and I felt I could trust him. I went to deposit the money into my bank through the ATM, and the funds were immediately available. I liked him even more because I deemed him trustworthy. Two days later, I got a call from the bank saying it was a fraudulent check. Someone had stolen the checking account and was writing bad checks to me. They told me I needed to return the money, or I would be prosecuted. I had already spent some of the money and tried to explain the situation.

When I went to call this guy to let him know what happened, his number had suddenly changed, and I couldn't get a hold of him. I was floored. I went and made a police report which I took to the bank and explained. We were able to work something out where I didn't have to pay back all of the money.

A year went by, and I hadn't seen or heard from the guy. I was working at a new restaurant. One day while at work, he walked in with another girl. I walked past and looked at him. He looked like he had seen a ghost. He got up and went to the bathroom area. I went to his date and said, "You better run as fast as you can. He's a scammer." I wish I had said more, but I was at work and didn't want any drama.

REFLECTION

Ah! The heart of a woman is, by God's design, extremely warm and giving. We are nurturers, and it goes beyond the bond we hold with our children and starts first with the man of our affections. We are sure that this is true as it relates to this particular young woman's tale of scam and scram. This man not only deceived her in giving her that monopoly money check, but he also ran for the hills and avoided being corrected for his errors. Who changes their number when they've done wrong? A coward, a user, a weak man, that's who. Even children can stick around and receive a reprimand when they have misbehaved.

It was kind of our friend to loan money to her fraud bae, who was rolling through the city on a donut. We are guessing that she got caught up in the emotional side effects of the oxytocin. Unfortunately for her, he was not only a man-boy who was comfortable asking for money, but he was also a fraud. Most grown and responsible men feel uncomfortable asking their significant other for cash. If this happens early on in a relationship, it is a vital red flag.

THE SUPERVISOR

I worked at a new job for about eight months when my supervisor requested me as a friend on Facebook. I accepted it because I low-key had a crush on him. But he was my supervisor, so I didn't want to cross any boundaries. I also found out from a co-worker that he was dating another one of our superiors. They had been on and off for about 12 years. Shortly after he became my Facebook friend, he started commenting on my pictures. His comments were amiable, and he would say things like, "Hey sexy." I guess becoming Facebook friends made him comfortable with making small talk with me at work. One day, I had to call off sick. I didn't want to because it was a holiday and I didn't want to get in trouble for not coming into work. So, I messaged him on Facebook to find out the rules for calling off on a holiday. He told me not to worry about it because he would cover me.

After noticing he was absent from work for about two weeks, I reached out via messenger to make sure he was okay. He told me he was using his vacation days to take some time off and get some work done around his house. He told me he would love to see me and asked me out on a date. I was hesitant at first because of his on and off situation with the other supervisor. I was not trying to get caught up in a work triangle and mess up my coins. But apparently, they had no serious ties: no kids, house, nothing outside of the 12 years of being on and off. I decided I would see what this 6'4, dark chocolate man with a beautiful body was all about. We had a great connection at work, and I wanted to see what it would be like to spend some personal time together.

Our first official date was at Cooper's Hawk, a winery and restaurant in Orland Park, Illinois. He was a total gentleman, and we talked for hours. While enjoying a wine flight, we agreed to keep anything we do a secret. Two days later, we went on our second date. When he dropped me off, he called and talked to me for an hour. He told me he enjoyed our time and didn't want it to end. He asked me to come to his house to hang out. He lived about 10 minutes away, so I agreed.

When I arrived at his house, I was so nervous. He was fine, older, and my supervisor. He asked me if I wanted a drink, and I immediately accepted. I was impressed that he liked my favorite alcoholic beverage, Remy Martin. We started drinking, and I got a little drunk. We had sex, and I fell asleep at his house. I woke up with a bad hangover. I was so embarrassed because I threw up all over the bathroom and felt like he wasn't going to talk to me anymore. Instead, he got up, cooked me breakfast, and made me feel better.

For the next two years, we spent a lot of time together and even went on trips. But we never spent any time with family or friends. I'm very family-oriented, and he wasn't. He had two older kids, but I had never been around his family and vice versa. I had invited him to stuff, but he would never show up.

So, I began putting pressure on him and asked him what we were doing and where we were going. He started talking about a future with me and said he would change. He said he wanted to meet my friends and family, and he wanted me to meet his. My 30th birthday rolled around, and we went out to dinner. We spent a day together, and he even met a couple of my friends. A couple of weeks later, I noticed he was beginning to act a little distant. I called him out on it and told him I felt he had been acting funny since I told him I wanted to get closer.

He told me, "No, I've just been busy." He blamed it on taking care of his mom and a bunch of other stuff. The next day, I received a call from a mutual friend telling me that she received a text message that my man was getting married to his ex-girlfriend from work. I didn't believe what I was hearing, so I hung up and called him immediately. He said, "No! It's not like that." He asked if he could come to my house and talk about it in person. He was at my place within the next 30 minutes. I will never forget this because it was a Friday and the wedding was taking place on Sunday. He turned his phone off and stayed with me for the whole weekend. We ate. We talked. We cried.

We made love and just tried to figure out what was going wrong in our relationship and if it was even something to resolve. I was trying to figure out when he had time to plan a wedding. It didn't seem formal. It was some last-minute stuff where a random group text was sent instead of a formal invitation. He told me he didn't plan the wedding, and she did all of the planning. "It's complicated. I can't go into it right now. It's something I have to do, but I do love you." Sunday came. It was the day of his wedding, and he was in my bed.

I told him, "Your wedding starts at 1:00 pm. Get up." He cried and said he didn't want to go. "Don't leave this lady at the altar. You need to be a man and tell her how you feel." He told me he didn't want to marry her. Another hour went by, and he was two hours late for his wedding. It took a lot in me, but I said, "You gotta go. You have to face it."

He finally left. Instead of calling the wedding off, he said, "I do." My co-worker texted me a picture of the newlyweds. The night of the wedding he was calling me, and I wouldn't answer. He started texting me, saying how sorry he was and hoped I would forgive him. He loved me but had to do what he had to do. Monday came, and I found out he had gone on a honeymoon to Vegas for a few days then to Mexico. When they returned, there was a mutual friend's birthday party, and they were both there. Once he saw me walk through the door, he left, but she was still there. At this moment, I realized not everyone at work knew about him and me, but a handful did. His new wife knew, but we never said anything to each other about it.

He had been texting me while I was still there. I ended up leaving the party. When I got home, he was sitting in front of my house and appeared very drunk. He asked if he could come in so we could talk. I said, "You've been married seven days, and you're back at my house." He spent the night at my house, but we didn't do anything. I just didn't want him to get hurt because he was drunk. The next morning, we discussed how things were going to be at work. About two weeks after they got married, the wife ended up quitting. I took a promotion at work, which allowed me not to see him. Although we worked for the same company, we weren't on the same schedule.

Six months into their marriage, he was still calling and texting me. I considered blocking him, but it was pointless because we worked at the same place. It was easy for him to get a hold of me. He ended up moving into an apartment while his wife was at work. He told me he left her to be with me. Like a fool, I went back to him. I accepted his apologies, and we were going to figure it out. He said he was filing for a divorce, but he never did. I found out he was still cheating. He had two other girls that he was entertaining. At that point, I was done. I cut the relationship off for good. For a year and a half, he went through a phase where he would just stalk me. He'd pop up at my house asking for forgiveness, telling me his life was in shambles because I wasn't a part of it.

Three years later, he still calls and texts. He has not moved back in, but they are still legally married. They spend holidays together. We still work at the same place, but I haven't seen him in almost a year, due to me getting a promotion in another department. I should have caught the red flags early.

One of those was that we dated for two years, and I never met anyone in his personal life.

Another red flag was the date nights were always far out in the suburbs. He would make it seem so romantic. We would drive 30-40 minutes away, but I never thought anything of it. We never did anything locally.

All of this sounds crazy. Based on this story, I should have dropped this guy immediately. Because of so many past hurts, I went through a phase in the healing process where I would ask him if there was something I did wrong or could have changed. I started having self-doubts because I truly loved this man even though he didn't love me. I am happy that I was finally able to get over him and move forward with my life.

REFLECTION

There are so many layers to this story; we don't even know who to address first. I guess we will start with Mr. Supervisor. First of all, sir, you are lazy and lack decent etiquette. Can you not snag anyone outside of your job? But that's not even the root of the issue. From the looks of this story, you sound like a master manipulator who could probably use professional help. Your manipulation skills were so strong that you had our friend questioning her worth and wondering what she could have done differently. You took her kindness for weakness and played on the fact that she was willing to entertain a dicey relationship.

Instead of trying to run game, we need you to read your work manual to see what the protocol is for having a relationship with your subordinates. Contacting an employee outside of work with messages like "hey sexy" is grounds for sexual harassment. If our friend had such an experience with you, we could only imagine what it's like for the woman who married you. This story screams low self-esteem at its finest. It sounds like you are fighting some demons, and you have brought other people to battle them with you.

You don't know what you want out of life. We are trying to figure out what would make you get married after spending the entire weekend with another woman that you supposedly love. In the words of Halle Berry in Boomerang, "*What do you know about love? What could you possibly know about love?*"

This story had RED FLAG all over it. You should never allow someone else's self-esteem to impact yours. Everybody is suspect in this story. Even the wife. How do you allow someone to marry you after being two hours late to your wedding? Who's really the mastermind in this operation? What type of mind control did this man have that caused two of his lovers to work together and never speak on this issue? Or was the man being controlled by the wife? We are all confused.

As for the young lady, red flag number one was the fact that he dated your supervisor on and off for twelve years. This scenario was already grounds for disaster. Of course, he didn't want to introduce you to his family or go on dates where anyone could see the two of you. He knew in the back of his mind that he was going to marry the other woman eventually. He saw a beautiful young woman such as yourself, and instead of letting you know someone could do you better, he attempted to ruin your life along with many others.

There are exceptions to the rule, but it seems pretty consistent that it's not a good idea to date someone from work. This entire situation could have been prevented if the relationship was strictly professional. But of course, like most of us, curiosity sometimes gets the best of us.

JAMAICAN ME CRAZY

When I moved from Detroit to LA, I lost a lot of weight and was feeling myself. I went to a club in Hollywood and noticed this handsome fellow staring at me. I told my girl, "Yo, he is fine." My weight loss had me coming into my own and feeling very confident. As he continued to gaze from across the room, he made his way to where I was. He approached me and introduced himself. I noticed he had an accent, so I asked where he was from. He said, "New York." I laughed because I knew he was lying. He had an island accent. Then he said, "Naw, I'm from Jamaica." We ended up exchanging phone numbers, and he pursued me instantly.

This man swept me off of my feet with his style and finesse. We spent a lot of time at each other's houses. I liked hanging out at his place because I was struggling in LA, he had a beautiful apartment, and I enjoyed his place much better. He would cook for me, and we would dance and just chill. He taught me how to slow wind, and it excited my spirit. One thing eventually led to another, and we ended up sleeping together. This man turned me OUT. He taught me all kinds of tricks in the bedroom.

As I continued to go over to his place, things suddenly became weird. It turns out he had a whole girlfriend, and I was the side girl. I didn't like that at all, but my nose was so wide open that I continued to see him. Soon after, I discovered he did some unsavory things to make a living. He pushed drugs across the country. Did that stop me from messing with him? Nope! I covered for him a few times and even let him con me out of my money. It was all sorts of madness. While all of these things were unraveling, I found out he was targeting White women to love and marry him, so he could legally stay in the United States. It sounded like an episode from 90-day Fiancé. That was the last straw that yanked me back into my senses.

REFLECTION

Oooh chile, this Jamaican hottie must have put a spell on you! To be mesmerized to the point that you helped cover-up for this man as he pushed drugs across the country? We are just going to thank the good Lord that you saw enough worth in yourself to run and never look back eventually.

CHAPTER 7
MARRIED MEN

"Boy there you go, you're telling me that you love me.
But you belong to another girl who loves you."
I'm So Into You, SWV

Here's the scenario, you meet a man, and it's been such a long time since you've felt such a strong connection if ever before. Everything about him is perfect, except for one compelling fact, he's married. You tell yourself, he's not a bad guy, he's just in a complicated situation. You even feel sorry for him and pray that the two of you will one day be together. I mean, after all, you are his soulmate, so leaving his wife should be a no brainer. Right?

Many classy, confident, and beautiful women have been suckered to believe that God sent them somebody else's husband. The moment you find yourself connecting with someone married, run, Forrest, run. There are lots of married men who have disrupted the hearts of single women without any intention other than pleasing themselves. They will tell you any and everything to get what they want or keep you around until they know what they want to do about their "unhappy" marriage.

Some of these married men have sex with multiple women, then go home to their wives and families and have no intention of ever leaving.

Others find just one person to engage with and open up the heart of that individual. Instead of addressing their issues head-on, they will engage in everything that allows them to ignore their problem even if that means finding vulnerable women to keep them occupied. Before you know it, you will be providing them with the things missing in their marriage, whether it's sexual or emotional.

Sadly, millions of people in the world are in marriages that God did not ordain. As single people, we have to understand that this is not our burden to carry. It's important to come to this realization because if you are single, there may be a day when a married person will attempt to fill a void with you. Don't allow an unhappy, unavailable married man to distract and pull you away from the person God has for you. The stories in this chapter are funny, but jaw-dropping because we can't believe some of these people had the nerve. Let's see how our friends handled these sticky situations.

THE RING DIDN'T MEAN A THING

South Beach in Miami has its share of tourists looking to leave all of their troubles at home. As a native, I normally stay away from the debauchery that takes place there. One day, however, I broke my rule when accepting a lunch invitation from my former colleague visiting from New York. While leaving the restaurant, a group of handsome men from Louisiana attempted to flirt with us.

"Excuse me, miss. You are beautiful." I looked up to see a short but cute, bald, caramel-skinned man who seemed to be in his mid-40s.

"Thank you," I replied as I tried to make a fast exit to the door.

"Are you in a rush, beautiful?" He asked.

Here we go with this "hey beautiful," I thought. After telling him I was trying to make my way home, he began to engage me in small talk.

"I would love to take you out before I leave." He said.

"I'm not sure if I will be back in the area," I told him.

"I don't mind meeting you somewhere else. I've been to Miami often, but I've never stepped outside of the tourist area." He was cute, and I was newly single, so I figured, why not? Mr. Louisiana was only in town for a couple of days. I gave him the location to one of my favorite Cuban spots.

We had so much fun during our lunch date that we roamed the neighborhood for a few hours and learned more about each other. With excitement, he showed me pictures of his daughters back at home. He gushed as he talked about his kids and pit-bull, whom he deemed his number one companion. While showing me a photo of him and his youngest child, I noticed he was pictured with a ring on his left finger.

"You're married?" I asked him.

"No, I'm not. I've recently divorced. It's an old picture."

I shared with him that I had recently gotten out of a relationship. I enjoyed this date so much that we lost track of time. Before we knew it, it was 7:00 pm, and it was time for him to head back to South Beach to hang out with his guys. He walked me to my car, hugged me and whispered in my ear, "Would you like to meet me at my hotel later on? I would love to taste you."

"Thanks for the invitation, but I will have to pass." I chuckled as I thought to myself, *this man just met me. He hasn't even gotten a kiss, and now he's talking about he wants to taste me?*

"Well, I'd love for you to meet my boys and me for breakfast before I leave tomorrow. Feel free to bring a friend." He replied.

We met up for breakfast the next day, and I brought my friend. The entire time, he was very flirty and touchy-feely with me. He told everyone how much he enjoyed spending time with me, and he wanted to eat my booty the night before, but I declined his invitation. I looked across the table at my friend, and gave her a look that said, *Is he out of his mind?*

Before we parted ways, Mr. Louisiana told me he wanted to keep in touch with me and hopefully fly me out to see him soon. I didn't have the energy to tell him this would probably be our last time seeing each other. I had a great time, but I wasn't interested in a long-distance bae or him for the obvious reasons.

The next day, I received a selfie of Mr. Louisiana throwing up the peace sign with a message that told me he enjoyed our time together. I couldn't help but notice he had on the same ring that was in the picture with his daughter.

What's up with the bling-bling? I texted back.

He texted back to tell me his divorce is still fresh, and he puts his ring on sometimes because he's still sad about it.

Yea, okay, I texted back. I was not bothered because I knew I wasn't planning on seeing this man again. But I wasn't surprised when he called me two minutes later to explain. In less than 10 minutes, Mr. Louisiana gave me his entire life story that included the details of his divorce.

When he finished, I replied, "Well, I was just asking because it doesn't make sense for a divorced man to continue wearing his ring."

My reply must have stirred up some emotions because that's when he got defensive. "You want me to tell you I'm married? Fine! I'm married. My wife dropped me off at the airport."

I pointed out that he wanted me to come to visit him. I was curious to know how he was going to pull that off. Mr. Louisiana went into detail about how he would have sent his wife on vacation or rented an Airbnb and claimed it as his home. I ended this conversation, thankful that I had dodged a professional cheater with a mapped-out plan of attack. Not to mention, he was ready to do sexual things that I am not sure I would ever be mature enough for and then go home to kiss his wife and kids.

REFLECTION

Mr. Ring Don't Mean a Thing. You could have easily gone in the "you tried it" chapter. Clearly, that's what you did. We are curious to know how guys like you can be so comfortable with putting your mouth on the private parts of a woman you have known for less than 48 hours then go home to your family like you are an honorable man? Three words: you are nasty. And you're not the only one. It's disappointing, to say the least, because marriage is honorable and this man lacks discretion, loyalty, and we could keep going but why waste time?

When you meet a man on vacation or while he's on a business trip before you tread further, make sure to find out his marital and relationship status. We don't mean finding out by just asking. This story shows us that men will lie about whether or not they are married. Make sure his words and actions align. The truth eventually comes out because it's tough to hide such a committed relationship as a marriage.

NIESHA

If someone were to ask me what sight annoys me to no end, I would immediately tell them it's seeing a married man not wearing his ring. Everyone has their thoughts about it, but it's disrespectful to me. No matter what excuse I've heard surrounding the topic, it lacks intelligence because the man not wearing the ring is more exemplary of his inability to honor God. Being ring-less is the ultimate display of this. More importantly, his lack of wearing a ring is a symbol of his disrespect. If I sound like I'm overreacting or slightly tripping, it matters not to me because these facts are valid. The purpose of our wedding rings is to represent the infinite unity we share with our spouse. God created marriage as a sacred covenant to be honored and upheld by both husband and wife. If you don't wear your ring, how will anyone in public visibly know that you are off-limits? They won't, and you know this, and this will allow the unnecessary potential for onlookers to engage in possibilities that you should not entertain as a married person.

I have heard the argument that wearing a ring doesn't define whether your spouse loves and respects you, and I call BS. As a married woman, it brings me much joy that my king doesn't ever want to appear to be in the land when he isn't. Why would anyone care to appear single when they made vows before God and loved ones unless they are not true to the commitment of those vows consistently? Marriage is not a temperamental type of experience that you only acknowledge when you feel good about it. Wearing your ring represents respect for your "till death do us part" partner. It solidifies your maturity in the love you profess to have for the one who stays stuck to you like peanut butter and jelly.

MARRIED ON THE LOW

My 35th birthday was a night to remember. I reserved a table at one of my favorite clubs and invited some of my closest girlfriends. I was feeling really flirty in a white bodycon dress. I had lost ten extra pounds for this moment and was happy to show it off. While dancing and enjoying every moment, in walked this tall and well-dressed man. He was wearing a tailored blue suit, a white-collar shirt, a black tie, and was easy on the eyes. He was turning heads in the room, including mine. We made eye contact, and from there, a conversation started. When he found out it was my birthday, he and his friends retreated to my section. His friends entertained my friends, and they paid for all of our drinks the entire night. When it was time for my girls and me to hit up the next spot, he asked if he could take me out to celebrate my birthday. I gave him my number, and he called me a few days later to see if I wanted to hang out.

We didn't have your ordinary dinner and movie date. We went to a club. Apparently, he was the man because we were able to skip the line. We walked straight up to the bouncer, and he let us in. I found out he was a well-respected police officer. It was during the summer, so we spent a lot of time going to clubs. About a month into talking, he spent the night. From there, our relationship started growing. He had three kids: two sons who were 21 and 16, and a 12-year-old daughter. His children were in his care during the summer. I wasn't ready to meet anyone's kids, so I never went to his house. We always met at my house or somewhere in his neighborhood.

There were times when I would meet him at the gym, which was a block from his house, and we would work out or go running in the area. I embraced that. Five months into the relationship, one of my girlfriends called and asked, "Who is this new guy you're dating? You are spending a lot of time with him." I told her how he was so good to me. He was a real sweetheart. She asked for a picture, so I sent it. He had no shame in taking pics with me. We were also Facebook friends. When I sent my friend the pictures, she responded and said, "I know him; that's my friend's husband."

I said, "No! Are you sure? This guy is not married. He can't be married." We spent too much time together. He spent multiple nights with me. I listed everything we had been doing over the last few months. Two days before, we had engaged in unprotected sex, and it was his initiating. I didn't want to, but he did. He said we were official. We talked about all the risks, and he also had a vasectomy, so kids or STDs I did not view as a consideration. He even asked to be exclusive two days before I heard about him potentially being married.

She told me, "They were just on a family vacation. They took the kids to Florida."

I said, "Yea, he was talking to me all week." He sent me pictures of him and the kids and even sent me naked pics from the hotel room. He told me the kids had their suite across from him.

She said, "I don't know how he was able to do that." I was so shocked and outdone. I asked her not to say anything to his wife because I wanted to talk to him first. She agreed to let me handle it because she didn't want to get involved. I called him immediately and found out it was true. He told me they had been married over 20 years and were high school sweethearts. She was a stay-at-home mom. Of course, he made up all these excuses about how he was not happy, which is why he spent so much time with me. I asked him why he didn't wear his wedding ring. He told me he didn't like wearing it.

After apologizing for not telling me, he said he would leave his wife to be with me. I laughed and told him I heard that before. I said, "I'm too old to be a married man's side chick." He wasn't honest initially, so I was not about to go any further with this man. Being willing to leave a marriage of 20 years for someone he recently met made me look at him sideways, and I thought he was just looking for a reason to go.

After I told him we were done, he started stalking me and coming to my house. I would walk out of my house, and he would be outside. I would pull up, and he would be outside. He would call over and over. I blocked him from all forms of contact. He eventually stopped stalking me.

As I reflect on this situation, the only mistake I feel I made was not going to his house. Other than that, there really weren't red flags. If it weren't for me talking to a friend, I would have never found out.

REFLECTION

First of all, what's up with all of these married stalkers? Although our friend in this story feels the only mistake she made was not going to this man's house, it was the biggest mistake. As nosey as we are, we are shocked by the fact that there are women who don't necessarily care about going to a man's house. You are reading a book by two women who will go down the rabbit hole of information. We are trying to go to your house, politely excuse ourselves, and head to the restroom straight to the medicine cabinet to conduct research. Don't judge us. We aren't the only ones who have partaken in such behavior.

As women, we naturally want to know everything about the man we are seeing. We also want to know if there are any traces of another woman. One of the best ways to find out is to go to his house and hang around his people. Especially his kids. They will spill all the tea.

On the other hand, we are happy that our friend decided to leave this guy alone. Even if he told you he was leaving his wife of 20 years. It probably wasn't going to happen, and even if it was, he had already proven to be untrustworthy. Many married men will also say that they are unhappy and will paint their wives as lazy, crazy, and everything in between. What you have to remember is that wife has her side of the story too. If a man is in a relationship with a woman he pretty much describes as unworthy, it's a direct reflection of who he is. No matter how much he likes to think that he has outgrown his partner if he is still there, they are both on the same level. And if you decide to entertain such a guy, it is a direct reflection of you. We are glad our friend in this situation saw that she was on the winning side of all of this and excused herself from the ghetto games. This man was trying to play with her heart.

TABLE FOR THREE

I met this guy named Eric, who asked me on a date after a few phone conversations. Eric met me at a decent restaurant in downtown Seattle on a packed summer night in July. Looking back, I think it must have been something in my spirit that let me know this was no cause for excitement because, despite the ambiance, I arrived wearing jeans, flats, and a graphic t-shirt. However, Eric came ready to impress and had on a fitted shirt revealing his muscles, with slacks, loafers, and choker style chained necklace. He ordered a glass of wine and engaged in deep conversation. As we were talking and enjoying the moment, things suddenly took a drastic turn.

A woman walked towards us whose boldness I could sense without her speaking and preceded to sit down at our table. She was smiling at us with beautiful teeth and deep-set brown eyes. I looked at Eric and noticed the disgruntled look on his face. I instantly knew this was an ambush, and this woman was here to crash our date. Before I could ask him who she was, she asked the same question of me.

I sat there in silence, waiting to see what he was going to say to this woman. However, he sat there like a mute, and she then directed her attention towards me. She said, "Hello, I am Naomi, Eric's wife."

Seemingly as soon as she spoke, Eric got upset, and they began to argue. Naomi told him she was sick of his lies and deceit, and the way he responded to her was unbelievable. He began to yell and was extremely disrespectful. The more offenses Eric hurled at his wife, you would have thought she had hit him over his head. In that very second, I thought to myself it was only a matter of time that he would have tried to dish me the same treatment. I sat as long as I could, but I felt the anger of his words burning in my chest as if they were intended for me. I could no longer endure his disrespect of his wife and blurted out "Stop talking to her like that, what allegiance do you have to me to be talking to your wife that way, I ain't nobody to you."

Eric looked at me in shock but not without attempting to explain his point and minimize his wife. The more he continued running his mouth, the more I felt my face twist up in disdain. Naomi began shaking her head in disbelief. She was muted by her surprise of being defended by her husband's potential fling. In mid-sentence, I stopped talking as I noticed my anger prevented me from seeing we had made a scene. I took it as a cue to excuse myself from the table, but not before I told Eric's wife I was sorry she had to endure him. From that day forward, I said not one more peep to Eric and walked out of the restaurant.

Hours later that night, after I got out of the tub, my phone rang from an unknown number. I answered, and the woman on the other end said, "Hey, this is Naomi, Eric's wife. I just want to say thank you for what you said."

After an unexpected two-hour conversation discussing the drama of the day, time would reveal later that Eric's deceit was a blessing, and I gained a friend in an unorthodox way. Yep, you guessed it, after 13 years and Naomi's quick divorce she has remained one of my closest friends to this present day.

REFLECTION

We love this story so much because there are too many married men out here disrespecting their wives. A lot of cheating men will complain about their wives, and as we previously stated, you don't know the wives' side of the story. In this case, our friend became privy to the wife and concluded this man, as many of the elders say, "wasn't worth a pot to pee in."

We are glad that our friend did not allow this man to disrespect his wife and ultimately put this clown in his place. Many women get caught up in their desires, forget to be sisterly, and disrespect another woman right along with the man. But it's important to pay attention to your intuition because from sis' feelings of not being really into the date; it eventually proved to have been for a reason. It's easy for the man to complain about his woman when she is not around to defend herself. But always remember, if he has a story, you better believe she has one too. Don't break girl code for the sake of having a man. He will probably give you as much of a headache as he is giving her.

SEPARATED

Every Friday, there was a happy hour at this Mexican restaurant in Cincinnati, Ohio. One night, I spotted this handsome guy across the room, and I noticed him checking me out too. I asked a friend of mine if she knew him and she told me that he was separated. I didn't care if he was separated; I wasn't interested in talking to someone who was married.

I ended up going to the same happy hour a week later, and that's when my friend told me the guy I spotted had asked about me. He was there with his friends, and this time, he approached me. I wasn't interested until he told me he was going through a divorce, so I took his word and gave him my number. We dated for about three years. Actually, I can't even say we dated because he was married the entire time and talking about getting a divorce.

I ended up moving away, but I came back often to visit. Whenever I was in town, I stayed at his house. The last time I visited, I was with him for about three or four days. On an early Saturday morning, while lying in bed, we heard banging on the door. It was his wife, and she entered the house before he had a chance to answer. He ran downstairs, and I could hear them arguing. It was chaotic.

I just stayed in bed because there was nowhere else to go. I figured he would handle it. Next thing I know, I heard someone coming up the steps and into the bedroom. His wife looked me in the face and said, "Uh, who are you?" She turned around and walked out. She yelled at him and said, "Who the f*ck is in our bed?"

I got up and started getting dressed. Just then, the wife's pregnant sister came upstairs. She came up to me and said, "Bitch, who are you?"

I stood up and said, "Don't worry about who I am."

She said, "Bitch, you don't need to be here."

I said, "You gonna hit me?" I knew she wasn't going to do anything because she was pregnant. She went back downstairs, where my married boyfriend and his wife were still in a heated argument. The police ended up coming, and I stayed upstairs until the drama ended. When it was all over, he came to apologize to me. He told me she was crazy and seriously done, even though his wife wasn't over it. You know, stuff guilty men say when they get caught up in something.

He's the person I regret dating the most, and I was so in love with him. Now that I know real love, I wasn't really in love with him like I thought I was. As my best friend says, sometimes you have to go through something like that to appreciate the person that was handpicked for you.

REFLECTION

This story is the perfect example of how you can be drawn to a situation that you usually would not entertain. In the beginning, our friend said that a separated man was still a married man. It's easy to say it until you end up in a situation where a guy catches your interest and shares his side of the story. As women, we can't afford to be involved with any type of married man emotionally or physically. It's just not worth it. Because we are naturally nurturing, situations like this will have you doing all the things for a married man you should be doing for a fully available man who is committed to you.

Even if he wanted to, no married man could be fully responsible for your heart. When things hit the fan, and most of the time they do, this type of man will throw it up in your face that you knew he was married. You will be left feeling silly that you ever caught feelings. Please take it from us and make yourself available for the full blessing that is ready to come your way.

While we understand that married people go through their share of troubles, the honorable thing to do is close one chapter before opening another. Unfortunately, you will more than likely be the one to initiate this move because most of the married men, like those described in these stories, will go as far as you let them. A relationship should be avoided until the ink is dry on the divorce papers. Thankfully, our friend didn't stay too long after the reality hit her in the face.

MY WIFE IS STILL ALIVE

While hosting a group of colleagues at a Dallas Mavericks game, I encountered an older Caucasian guy. He was not my type per se, but he was successful, lots of fun, and full of wisdom. We talked, laughed, and exchanged contact information during halftime. It was refreshing to meet someone so full of life, and I was excited to add him to my professional network.

He reached out the same night to see if I would join him for dinner the next day at a five-star restaurant. Afterward, we went to a venue a few doors away. There was music playing, so we hit the dance floor. We stepped into the place and became the life of the party. The two of us looked odd but compelling together. Here was this older energetic White man with this young and vibrant African American woman. We were both dressed nicely, and people kept walking up and complimenting us. They enjoyed our energy and were drawn to us.

This night sparked a budding friendship. Over time, I learned he was a widower. He told me his wife passed away due to complications from a car accident. He had a son and a daughter around my age. I took a liking to him as a caring person. He also wanted to know all about me and was supportive of my vision and dreams. Whenever he came to town, we would spend time with each other and hang out. Every blue moon, we would meet up in another city. He even met my family at a pre-Fourth of July event. They laughed because we looked so odd together, but they thought he was real nice.

One day, we were at dinner, his phone kept vibrating, and he followed up via text. It wasn't the first time that his phone would go off, and he followed up via text. He wasn't my man, so I ignored it. But of course, curiosity got the best of me.

I told him, "Let me see your phone." He didn't hesitate and handed it over. I looked at the text, and it was from another lady that was going out of town with him. She asked if he was going to pay for her power bill. I wasn't upset because this was just my friend, but it was clear to me that he was entertaining other women.

Soon after this encounter, I unexpectedly received a long text from him that said, "My wife is not dead. She's still alive. I've been caring for her, and it feels like she's dead because she is not the same woman she used to be due to her illness." He went on to say how much he cared about me and didn't want to hurt me. At that point, I was speechless because our friendship was built on a lie. I viewed him as an awesome man who took care of his wife before she died. Now he was letting me know she was still alive.

I ended the friendship immediately. For days, he begged me to talk. I agreed to go to dinner because I understand how it feels when someone won't let you explain yourself. During dinner, he broke down and said he was sorry and never wanted to hurt me.

I told him I accepted his apology but didn't want to hang out with him again. When we parted ways, he followed up with a text implying that he wanted me to be his mistress. I was in awe. This experience taught me that you have to ask the right questions. Don't just ask men if they are in a relationship. Ask them if they are married. Ask them if their wife is dead but really alive. Ask them everything. Some of these people will still lie. But you won't get the answers you need without asking questions. So, that's my story of the married man with a dead wife that was still alive.

REFLECTION

Mr. My Wife is Still Alive. We don't even know where to begin with you. Our jaws are still dropping. Like, this happened in real life and not a distasteful screenplay? We don't know if we are amazed that you lied about your wife's condition or because you tried to prey on our single friend. Here's a message to men who are cut from a similar cloth. Single doesn't mean desperate. Some men believe that just because a woman is riding solo, and the pickings are slim, she's up for anything because she is lonely and craving male attention. It's the exact opposite. Most women are single by choice and have learned to enjoy their singlehood. They know they could be married, but they choose not to settle. For you to think she would take you up on the offer to be her sugar daddy, you had another thing coming.

In an ideal world, we would like to ask all the questions, but a lot of times, no matter what you ask, you only know until you find out. In this situation, the only thing our friend could control was her reaction. She did right by leaving this married douchebag alone.

CHAPTER 8
AGE AIN'T NOTHING BUT A NUMBER—OR IS IT?

Woman Dating Confession: *As a woman in her mid-30s, I like that I can date a 25-year-old man or his 50-year-old father. The dating pool is pretty broad, that's if you're open to dating out of your age bracket.*

A lot of younger men are into older women. If they flirt with or pursue you, try not to hit them with, "Oh, you're so adorable" or "You're the same age as my little brother." Keep in mind that a 28-year-old man is still a grown man. Who cares if he's younger than you? Younger men are fun to date because they have lots of energy and will try hard to impress you and make it known they are mature enough to date you. At the same time, keep in mind that a man's brain isn't fully developed until 25. Sometimes, you will be reminded of this when dating younger. So, choose your youngin' wisely.

As far as dating older men is concerned, they are fun too. If you get a good one, you might enjoy yourself. They don't have to prove to you they are a grown man because they are. And you will see it in every way. They are wise and love to take care of their woman. If you are a single lady reading this and have only been open to your age bracket, we challenge you to go a little younger or older. Give it a try and let us know what happens. In the meantime, we have a couple of stories from our friends who found that age is nothing but a number.

YOUNG AND TENDER

When I met George, he was 18, and I was 21. He was wrapping up the second semester of his freshman year in college, and I was preparing for graduation. A group of his friends approached my friends and me while at a party one night. All of them were quite handsome. Because they were three years our junior, we referred to them as "YT"—young and tender. Each of us jokingly picked which guy would be our YT. George made sure that I knew he would be mine. He even had the courage to ask for my number. Because he was bolder than some of the seniors I knew, I gave it to him. When one of my friends saw us exchanging numbers, it was over. When we left the party, I was the joke for the rest of the night. "I see she likes them young," one of them laughed.

I was a little embarrassed that I connected with my YT, but not enough to reject his request to hang out when he called me a couple of days later. We had about three weeks left in the semester, and it was starting to become warm outside. George met me outside of my dorm. He said his friends were enjoying the weather by having water gunfights. Instead of playing childish games, George preferred hanging out with me. George and I walked to McDonald's, where he proudly told me to get whatever I wanted.

I tried to ignore the fact that George liked me mainly because he was so much younger. I told myself he didn't like me; we were just friends. When you're in your 30s and 40s, a three-year difference isn't that bad. But when you're in college, it seems like you're a decade apart, especially if the woman is the older of the two.

George drove for two hours to attend my graduation party. When I opened up the card he gave me, three pictures fell out. One was a group picture from the night we met, another was of the two of us, and the last one was a solo picture from his high school prom. Some of my friends were with me when I opened up my card. Of course, they had mad jokes. George and I hung out a lot during the summer after I graduated. He even kissed me on the lips once. But I still told myself he didn't really like me, again because I did not want to date someone younger.

When I finally got over George's age, he had become distant. I guess he was tired of me ignoring all of his hints. I told him I felt the same way, but it was too late. He ended up getting a girlfriend he eventually married. The funny thing is, she was older than me.

REFLECTION

In college, a three-year difference can seem like a lot. But when you get into the world, it's not. There's a stigma against women who date younger men. They are called cougars or sugar mamas. If a younger man approaches you, it's a compliment, and you should take it as such. Don't let what others think to stop your happiness and influence your decision. Some men just like older women, and it has nothing to do with you. As you can see with this story, Young and Tender still ended up with someone older. It's in our DNA to overthink. Don't knock something until you try it. If you meet a nice man and, despite his age, seems to be mature, there's nothing wrong with getting to know him.

YOUNG GRANDMA

When I moved to Houston, I found a spot that had live music. I was in my early 30s, but you could find me kicking it with the old heads from time to time. After work one Friday, I went with one of my friends to my new favorite spot. While we were there, she introduced me to some of her friends, including an older gentleman. At first glance, I couldn't tell he was almost 30 years older than me. He was older, very polished, and well respected.

When we connected, I had no intentions other than having him in my network. The more I ran into him, the more I began to love his personality and style. After a while, we created a beautiful friendship and started hanging out. I guess you can say we were dating. It was different because I didn't think I would date a man as old as he was. I was just drawn to him.

He had children as well as grandchildren. His grandchildren took a liking to me, and I would spend time with them when they were visiting. I was enjoying time with this man until one day when I got my wakeup call. We were hanging out, and one of the grandkids referred to me as grandma. I thought he was joking. I was young, and being called grandma didn't sit right with me. I didn't even have a child of my own, let alone a grandchild. That was when I checked myself. I was dating an older person who could technically be my granddaddy. This situation made me immediately put him in the friend-zone.

We are still friends, and I'm grateful to have met him because I gained wisdom and knowledge from his friendship. Dating an older man has its perks, but if you are looking for a man you can grow with, you may not want to entertain someone old enough to be your granddaddy.

LOST ROOTS

I once dated a man that was 18 years older than me. We were both in bike clubs and met at a social gathering. We were attracted to each other and spent a lot of time together. I felt a strong connection with him, and our relationship evolved with no hiccups. We met each other's family. We spent holidays together and talked a lot about our future. We were very spiritually connected and often prayed together.

Everything was going well until his coworkers invited him to some kind of convention. He returned excited about the Black Power movement. While there, he watched *Hidden Colors,* a movie series that showed the history of Black culture. He was there for a few hours and came back home to tell me about it. He became very passionate to the point where he was obsessed. He started purchasing a bunch of history books about the movement. I loved that he wanted all of the knowledge, but as he became pro-Black, he began to judge me. He asked that I stopped hanging out with my White friends and told me I was no longer allowed to wear my weave because it represented the European aspect taking away from my Black heritage. He told me I needed to be more natural, and I didn't need to wear makeup or get my nails done. He wanted me to be natural from head to toe. I had no problem with that; I am natural today. But, I don't see anything wrong with putting on some clothes and enhancing my beauty.

Things went left when he started telling me there was no God, and I was praying to the White man. He told me all my White friends were devils. He said they weren't my real friends, and I wasn't supposed to trust them. It became overbearing to the point where I told him I couldn't do it. He wanted to dictate the clothes I wore when, for three years, it was never an issue. While in a heated argument, I said, "You're 46 years old. What did these people do to you?" I felt like he was part of a cult or something. I couldn't fathom how this grown man could be converted so quickly. He was totally against spending any more holidays together and would call it the "White man holiday." Finally, I had enough. I told him I couldn't be with him anymore.

We broke up. A few years later, I found out his son ended up marrying a White woman, and his daughter married a White guy, and he had grandkids. His kids told him if he wanted to be part of their life, he had to respect their significant others. He did because he wanted to be in his kids' lives. The grandkids changed him. He started celebrating holidays and relaxed a little bit. Four years after we broke up, he called and apologized for everything he did. He said he was in a bad space and didn't know exactly what went wrong. He told me we would have married me a long time ago if he didn't go through that phase. Now, he believes in God and isn't anti-White anymore. I consider him to be a good friend and keep in touch. He reaches out to say hello during birthdays and holidays.

REFLECTION

Maybe a mid-life crisis or a man lost looking for his roots, either way, this man ran our friend away with his newfound herd mentality. Age does not necessarily mean maturity, but in this case, it was not maturity but someone who had a shaky spiritual foundation. As much as we encourage learning, all learning is not created equal and can break meaningful relationships if everyone is not committed to the same teachings. It is never good to criticize someone who did not sign up for that walk. Don't neglect to lead your partner gently. It won't matter if you are correct in what you learn or not if you are leading out of a condemning spirit.

NOT READY FOR LOVE

In high school, I was a b-girl from my oversized polo sweater and gap bootcut jeans down to my Adidas shell toes. My favorite pastime was meeting up with my friends and throwing some graffiti on an abandoned wall or cheering my peers on in ciphers as they would battle rap. It sounds like a scene out of a movie, but this was my real life. Around this time, I met Rashad. He was the most refreshing and funniest person I had ever met. We were young but more advanced than our peers as it related to our work ethic and finances. Both of us had great jobs in downtown Brooklyn.

When I met Rashad, I was already crushing on someone else. It did not prevent us from being friends. When senior prom came around, Rashad accompanied me. One of the greatest moments of our lives. The vibe was so fun and amazingly cool as we were taking over for the 99 and 2000's. That night, he let me know that he was starting to develop feelings for me outside of our platonic zone. I thought it was nice but not something I was willing to entertain at that time. I wanted to ensure that our friendship remained solid and authentic through and through. I loved him dearly but just as my friend.

Fast forward to the fall, and we were both beginning our college careers at schools in the city. It was an electric vibe in the city and obviously among me and my longtime friend Rashad. We went from just being super cool to hanging out after classes and going to eateries around town, to hanging out at his family's beautiful home. I quietly became a fixture in his home and what a comfortable place it was to be. His parents and sister were some of my favorite people to be around. As my feelings for Rashad began to develop, so did my desire to become a part of his world full-time.

We decided to make it official, and it felt like the skies had opened up to us. We were unstoppable in the force we had become. We loved hard, and it was evident that the saying is true that best friends make some of the best lovers. Sure, we were young, but you really couldn't tell me that we weren't going to go far together in life. The loyalty that Rashad showed me was something out of the best love story and most beautiful sonnet.

Keep in mind that for me, this was never supposed to be. I never planned on being submerged in the space of warm fuzzies and hearts with this man. However, at that time, it was indeed the only place I wanted to be outside of my home. As young love sometimes goes, our good thing came crashing down and fast when it did. An argument here and there, bratty and selfish ways, his need to get his point across, and just a heap of petty on both of our ends caused us to drift apart. During this time, I decided what would be best for me was to visit my best friend Tenise at her university. I knew she would give the good vibes I needed. When in a funk, after turning to Jesus, time with my bestie was ALWAYS a good idea.

How the story unfolds is like one out of a perfect movie that you would see twice in theaters and then purchase on Amazon Prime. Tenise and I went to a party in the yard of her school, and it was just incredible seeing people come together in the name of good music. While hanging with my girls, I spotted a guy who was checking on me. He was handsome, but I didn't entertain it because although Rashad and I weren't on the best of terms, we were still a couple.

The DJ that night was on fire! *Cupid* by 112 began to play as this cutie walked over my way. We briefly spoke and discovered we had a mutual friend. Once we had that "it's a small world" convo, he introduced himself as Anthony and asked me for my phone number. I immediately shared with him that I was in a relationship and visiting my best friend, so I dubbed him. As we were getting ready to leave the party, Anthony stopped me again and gave me his number. I took it but had no intention of ever seeing him again.

Back in Brooklyn, I knew that Rashad and I were at a crossroads in our relationship. We were either sinking or swimming. While I wanted to ride the wave with him, I felt at times that we were just floating in life, playing it safe. We were young and had our lives ahead of us, but were we meant to do life together? Also, I couldn't get Anthony out of my thoughts. After about three weeks of going back and forth in my mind about what to do next, I put my big girl panties on and made my decision. I told Rashad we should break up and go our separate ways. As we sat in my car and had this awkward conversation, I saw the sadness in his eyes that I had never witnessed before. No one looks amazing when they're getting dumped, but at that moment, I felt I committed a crime of the heart. Rashad got out of the car. He yelled at me and told me how much he loved me and never wanted us to end. I felt crushed. In my young mind, I thought it was better to break up than to cheat, especially when I was with such a loyal guy.

Fast forward again, and I decided to see what Anthony was talking about, and we ended up dating for a few years. However, Rashad and his love for me was never far from my mind. I later discovered that Rashad's love was rare, pure, and timeless.

REFLECTION

To be young and recognize that you would rather leave someone than cheat, is commendable. Either way, the person's feelings end up hurt, but at least it's because their girl was honest. We all have our taste of the "one who got away." It's always good to treat people valuable because you don't know how things will end up happening in the future. Sometimes we take people's emotions for granted because we are young and feel like we're not ready. However, you never know if that opportunity will ever come up again. This lesson doesn't come with age, but with maturity.

CHAPTER 9
DODGING BULLETS

Woman Dating Confession: *It's so funny when you think about all the things you wanted, and all the ones you thought for sure were going be your forever bae, only to find out later on that you dodged a major bullet.*

The heartache and disappointments we experience from ignoring red flags do not compare to what you are being protected from. Sometimes, a heartbreak will turn out to be one of the best things that ever happened. It can be hard to see that you have dodged a major bullet in a moment of disappointment. Breakups are tough, but a lot of times, they turn out to be a blessing. The two of us can speak our truth and say that if we hadn't dodged a few bullets back in the day, we wouldn't be the happy and confident women we are today. We may have had our hearts broken, but God spared us from relationships that could have been more painful had we stayed in them.

CAMOUFLAGE

Back in the day, while working at this popular retail store, this handsome, chocolate man walked through the door, and I thought to myself, *he's adorable.* He shopped around, and while he didn't buy anything in particular, we enjoyed discussing travels and destinations. No numbers were exchanged. I was in a committed relationship. He left the store, and I thought that it was just another day when a cool gentleman pops in my job.

Fast forward, two years later, I was living in a new city and state. I was heading into work, feeling incredibly amazing and super cute. When we ladies get our eyebrows threaded, lip gloss is popping, and hair is big and bouncy, you really can't tell us NOTHING. I had on my favorite camouflage jacket and gave all the good vibes going up the escalator when I spotted the adorable chocolate drop from my old gig. He had on a camouflage jacket as well. *God, I see what you're doing.* I thought to myself. I mean, he had to be showing up in the destiny department. We met in one state and ran into each other in another state, only to be wearing pretty much the same outfit. This had to be God.

We both couldn't believe that we were living in entirely different locations and ran into each other. We laughed about it, and this time, we exchanged numbers. After our first hangout, it was clear that we both wanted to try out a relationship. We exclusively dated for seven months, but within those months, you talk about a sister being on edge. Funny how someone you see on the surface to be a good look, really is not, and GOD will let you rock with what you thought was a "good idea."

While we enjoyed fun times, like me throwing him an intimate birthday party that included balloons and tequila, we also had some extremely whack moments. One moment, in particular, was when I was convinced in my heart that he was cheating on me while I was at a BBQ. He told me that he would meet me at my homegirl's apartment. Four hours passed, and I was still waiting for him to arrive. I headed home to decide if I should carry on or drop him. While deciding against my better judgment and plenty of denial on his end of any outside canoodling, I gave him some extended time. After dating for almost seven months, the final straw came when I finally received an invite to his house. Eternally I felt it was super crazy that he never asked me over to his place, but I soon discovered why.

After surveying his place and discussing why he was sleeping on a mattress and not a bed, I took a stroll to the restroom. Out of curiosity, I surveyed the medicine cabinet and bathroom drawers to see what I could find. Sure enough, when I went snooping, I found a maxi pad and got the answer I needed. I walked out of the bathroom and out of his life for good. I knew that decision was the perfect one for me indeed. Something in my spirit let me know I was dodging a bullet.

REFLECTION

It's funny how we can use small superficial signs to think that we have found the one. How could it not be for me? Did we not run into each other in a completely different city wearing the same outfit? As women, we grew up on fairytales. So, it's normal for us to have this way of thinking. Something in our friend's spirit told her that this wasn't the relationship for her, making her dodge a bullet early on.

THANK YOU RICK

In high school, almost every girl I knew had a crush on Rick. He was tall, lanky, fair-skinned, and had the biggest Kool-Aid smile. He transferred to our school during my sophomore year. Also, he accompanied me to our homecoming. We never dated but remained good friends. Rick and I lost touch after graduation but reconnected at a wedding of one of our mutual high school friends. We were so happy to see each other and found out that we both lived in the same city.

While dancing together at our friend's wedding reception, Rick asked if I would go on a date with him when I returned home. We went on a date and had so much fun catching up and reminiscing about the good ol' days. The two of us continued to hang out at least once a week. While eating at our favorite pizza place, Rick asked me to be his girl. He was so smooth, and our chemistry was good, so it was easy to agree.

I don't know if it was because we gave it a title, but when we decided to become an item, things changed. As a couple, I expected to see Rick more, but actually, it was the exact opposite. I heard less from him. My reaction to his distance took me to another place in my mind. After several unanswered calls and text messages, I left multiple voicemails inquiring to where he had gone.

In an attempt to get things back on track, I invited him to attend a concert with me. He accepted my invitation. At the end of the performance, we got into a heated argument on our way back to Rick's house. As we yelled at each other, I followed Rick to his apartment building. When we reached the top of the stairs, he slammed the door in my face before I made it to the door behind him.

To this day, I have no idea how I had the strength to head back to my car and drive home. I was devastated. Rick wouldn't return my calls and ultimately moved on with his life. That was the last time we spoke. One of the toughest moments in life, but looking back, it could've been worse. What I had experienced were early signs of a potentially emotionally or physically abusive relationship. Slamming the door in my face was the best thing Rick could have ever done for me. Thank you, Rick.

REFLECTION

Thank you, Rick is such a peculiar story because he initiated the relationship. For whatever reason, he pulled back. It's easy to want to pursue something with someone you are familiar with, but just because you have a history, doesn't mean you should bring them in your future. Sometimes you have to let your past pass by you.

The fact that this person was able to thank Rick for slamming the door in her face says a lot. She was able to recognize her worth and realized that if someone could be as disrespectful as slamming the door in her face, what else could he potentially do? The rejection from this painful experience was probably unbearable. But we are thankful that man's rejection is God's protection.

DADDY DOLLAZ

I was in my early 20s and at the club with my girls. It was during a time where I worked hard all week so I could enjoy the weekend. My friends and I were always the ones who attracted a group of guys wanting to pay for our drinks and invite us into the VIP section. All we had to do was show up. We never paid an entry fee or waited in line because the bouncers loved us. When my girls and I got together, none of us had to come out of our pockets. Not because we couldn't afford to. There was just always some guy trying to holler at one of us.

On this particular night, I was excited because I had just passed my boards and became a registered nurse. Drinks were flowing, and my girls bragged to everyone that I was the smart one out of the group. The DJ played all of my jams, and I was on the dance floor, enjoying myself and minding my own business. While I was doing one of my dance moves, someone grabbed me by the waist and started dancing. Another song came on, and we continued dancing. We danced to three or four songs before he introduced himself. "My name is Devon, but you can call me Daddy Dollaz." He kissed me on my hand. I laughed as I looked at this light-skinned, iced-out, chubby man with hair that showed he wore his doo-rag every night.

Daddy Dollaz asked if I want another drink, and I accepted his offer. While at the bar, he told me he wanted to take me out to celebrate me passing my exam. I took his number and called him about a week later to go out. I didn't see anything serious coming out of it but figured it would be fun. Daddy Dollaz took me where a lot of hood guys love to go, Pappadeaux. He told me I could order whatever I wanted—music to my ears. One of the reasons I loved going out with thick guys is because I didn't have to be cute with it. I could eat as much as I wanted without being judged about the food going to my beautiful and curvy waist.

Daddy Dollaz did what a lot of other guys didn't. He made me laugh and had contagious energy. He made me feel like a real woman. He was a street guy but had goals to start his own business, and I tried to encourage him. I thought Daddy Dollaz was going to be a quick season in my life. That was until the two blue lines showed up on a pregnancy test.

Five years later, I was at the courthouse with Daddy "No Dollaz," fighting for child support. All of those fun times went out the window when it was time to handle a real-life situation. I should have listened to my cousin, who told me to "never date anyone whose ass is bigger than yours." After our child came, he showed his entire ass. He became abusive and condescending. Our tumultuous relationship ended, but a beautiful human entered into the world.

REFLECTION

It's crazy to think about how you can go from dancing with a potential bae in the club to the courthouse with that same person who once made you laugh sitting across the table at Pappadeaux. That's life. You can't dodge every bullet. When life gets real, that's when people's real characteristics come out. Unfortunately, many people didn't find out the core of a person until they were bonded with them through children or marriage. We believe God can get the glory out of any situation. Thankfully a beautiful child was born that is loved and celebrated.

GOODNIGHT, DADDY

"Your network is your net worth." I would tell myself while navigating through traffic at least twice a week to attend multiple networking events. One happy hour, in particular, was accompanied by a host of successful and handsome men. While at the bar, I met a guy, my friend eventually nicknamed the Fake Steve Urkel. What's worse than the real Steve Urkel? A fake one. The only reason you don't know his real name is due to the sake of legalities. If I had it my way, this fool would be on dontdateemgirl.com.

There was nothing smooth about Fake Steve Urkel. He was as nerdy as they come. However, his résumé seemed quite impressive. He graduated from Syracuse University. He worked at a million-dollar real estate company and owned a condo in Santa Monica. At least that's what he told me. At the time, I was interested in learning more about real estate, so we exchanged numbers.

Fake Steve Urkel followed up with me the next day via an email with all kinds of typos. (Red flag #1). We scheduled a meeting to talk about real estate opportunities. I was quite impressed as I arrived at his office in Beverly Hills to speak with him and his business partner. They gave me advice on the current real estate market and provided tips to clean up my credit report.

A few days later, Steve invited me to dinner. Still nerdy as ever, but I was attracted to his story. Supposedly, he went from rags to riches. He once lived out of his car and now had a condo in Santa Monica and multiple properties. All of this financial success before the age of 30, and he gave all the credit to the Lord. *Successful and loves the Lord! Jackpot!*

With a full belly and a few glasses of wine, you couldn't tell me that this man was not a boss. I inquired about his love life, and Fake Steve Urkel told me he was single after being cheated on by his ex. He had trust issues when it came to relationships. Steve used this same excuse when I asked why he had yet to invite me to his condo. I mean, a decked-out condo in Santa Monica is something most Black men would want to show off. I've met men who were excited about the little pad in their mother's garage. So why was Fake Steve Urkel so secretive about where he lived? I just didn't get it. He had been to my place several times.

"You probably have a wife and kids," I joked over dinner at Fogo De Chao.

"No, I'm just a private person. I will invite you to my place one day. I'm just not ready."

I continued to enjoy my time with Fake Steve Urkel.

When he requested me as a friend on Facebook, I used it to conduct research. I scrolled through his page to see what I could find. The year was 2016, and by the time I made it to 2014, I noticed a status that made me raise my eyebrows. *Facebook family, what are you thankful for? I'm thankful for my beautiful wife and daughter.* Was I being punked? I laughed so hard until my belly ached. Then I picked up the phone and sent him a text.

Do you have a wife and daughter? I texted

He FaceTimed me immediately. "Let me explain." He went on to tell me about the ex who cheated on him. "We were never married, but we referred to each other as husband and wife. She has a kid. She's not mine biologically, but I claim her as mine."

Fake Steve Urkel picked up the phone to clarify immediately, so I thought he must be telling the truth. I was aware of the red flags but was not ready for it to end. As time went on, I didn't think twice about Fake Steve Urkel's "fake family."

One day, while on the phone with Steve, he told me he had just arrived at his sister's house and was about to hang out with his nephew. I could hear the child on the other end, trying to engage Fake Steve Urkel. He kept responding with words like "Okay, nephew" and "Sit down, nephew." We were on the phone for about an hour when he said, "Goodnight, nephew." That's when the voice on the other end said, "Goodnight, daddy."

REFLECTION

Sis, what did Fake Steve Urkel do to make you stay in this crazy situation so long? You knew about the red flags but continued to allow him in your life. We think that love made a fool out of you too. As soon as Fake Steve Urkel gave you that bogus story about his fake wife and child, that was your cue to leave. He had the perfect opportunity to let you know of this situation when you inquired about his love life. Lots of guys raise children who aren't biologically theirs but claim them as their own. You dodged a bullet with Fake Steve Urkel, but there is a child somewhere in the world who doesn't know the truth about her fake father. That's worse than any bullet you could have dodged. We see why you would want to expose this man on dontdateemgirl.com.

AFRICAN KING WITH A DREAM

It was New Year's Eve, and instead of being bored at home, I put on a sexy black dress and accompanied my neighbor to a house party. When I spotted a 5'11, man from Nigeria, with dimples and a smile to match, I made it my business to introduce myself. I don't say this lightly when I tell you that this man was FINE.

He sat on the couch next to me, and it was an instant connection. We had so much in common. Both of us were in the same field of work, and we had similar goals. By the end of the night, I was confident I had met my

African king. Maybe it was the champagne from the midnight toast that boosted my confidence, but when it was time to leave, I gave him my number and put my name in his phone as, "The One."

The beginning of 2017 was spent with my African king. It was a VIBE! I would visit him for home-cooked meals, movie nights, and we would exchange business ideas off each other. I enjoyed spending time with him. When he came over with his 9-year old son to watch the fireworks for the 4th of July, it sealed the deal. My family was in town visiting, and when my African king walked in the door, he was wearing one of my shirts from my apparel company. He was fun, fine, and supporting my business. I became even more attracted to him, and to see him as a father was the icing on the cake.

What did I do? I embraced that baby boy and showcased my skills as an incredible stepmother. My friends and family laughed as my African king's son kept referring to me as auntie. It was their culture's tradition to refer to women as auntie instead of miss or ma'am. As his new auntie, I immediately gained his son's affection by sneaking him some pork. The little boy told me, "My dad doesn't eat pork, but I do!"

A few days later, we were cruising down the highway headed to the San Diego Zoo. I packed some lunches, loaded up the car, and headed down the freeway with my African king, his son, and my little cousin whom I picked up on the way. I had to make sure future stepson had someone to play with. Spending time with my African king and his son at the zoo was a sure sign that he could potentially be the one. On our way home, while listening to Davido, my king told me how much he appreciated me finding an activity for him and his son. He thanked me for a warm couple of days and admired how patient I was at the zoo and that I came fully prepared to take on the day. He put his hand in mine, and as we drove into the sunset, I began to see this man in my future.

While sitting on his couch, eating a bowl of jollof rice one day, I shared my feelings for my African king. He went on to tell me that he wasn't ready for a committed relationship until he was financially stable.

Imagine my surprise when a few weeks later, I saw him posted on Instagram with his new blushing bride. I will never forget the feeling I had when this picture showed up in my social media feed. It was like a knife in my heart. My African king married? I didn't see this coming. I immediately blocked him from every form of contact and tried to forget that he ever came into my life.

Less than a month after I saw his post, I received an email from my former African king asking me to call him. Damn! I forgot to block dude from my email. I called him to see what he could possibly want.

"Why did you block me?" he asked me.

"Um, because you got married out of the blue. Just a couple of months ago, you weren't even ready for a serious relationship."

"She got pregnant, so I married her." He said matter-of-factly.

As I hung up the phone, I was sad but grateful that this counterfeit of an African King was not my problem. I was even more grateful not to be the woman he claimed to have only married because she was pregnant.

REFLECTION

It's so funny how we can imagine ourselves in a life that's not meant for us. Unfortunately, some of our dating journeys will involve seeing some of the people we like get boo'd up or married to someone else. It's a bruise to the ego, but if it were meant for you, you'd have it. We're sorry to say this because we are all about bigging up our male counterparts. But this guy doesn't sound like a king. He sounds like a fraud. If he had any kind of integrity, he would have let this young lady know that he was getting married.

In the end, she dodged a major bullet. This guy lied about being in a relationship and claims he only committed to his wife because there was a child involved. What an insult to the child and their mother. Even if he just said this to make our friend feel better, he is out in the world telling people that the only reason he married his wife is because she was pregnant with his child—key characteristics of a narcissist. Not to mention, he sounded like a user. He took our friend's kindness for granted and missed out on a good thing. We just pray he gets it together for his wife and family.

YAHOO PERSONALS

Way before match.com and all the dating apps, there was Yahoo Personals. I was about 25 or 26 and was making my way through the dating scene. I had never tried Yahoo Personals but decided to give it a try. After a couple of conversations with a guy I matched with, we decided to meet at a restaurant. As I reflect, there were red flags based on our phone conversations. He was from Virginia, and I thought that was cool because I'm from Maryland. Before we met in person, he told me that his ex-girlfriend left him for a woman. It was very evident that he was still very bitter about it. He said a few negative things about gay people and women like her. I figured he was just mad.

The day we were supposed to meet, I asked my friend and roommate to come with me until he showed up. Online dating wasn't famous yet, so they agreed to be there in case he turned out to be crazy. When he showed up, I introduced him to my friends before we went to our table. He barely spoke to them and came off very cold. My two friends were White, and I got the impression that he wasn't too fond of White people. Still, I thought he didn't need to be rude. We got our table, and things seemed to be going cool until he started talking about how he made a lot of money because he worked in the music business. It seemed like he was bragging. When the server brought the bill, he looked at it, put it down, and said he had to go to the bathroom. While he was in the bathroom, I took my debit card out to pay for my meal. I looked at it more as we were meeting up rather than an actual date. I was still feeling him out.

He came back and saw my card on the table and flipped out. When he sat down, he asked, "What is this?" I told him since this was our first meeting, I figured I would pay. He asked, "So you think I can't afford it? You are one of those independent women who think you don't need a man? Didn't I say before I went to the bathroom that I got this?"

I started looking around to see if anyone could hear him going off on me. I was stunned. Then he said, "If we go to the movies, you gonna pay for your ticket? That's alright. You're gonna learn." As he went on, all I could see was Ike Turner in a scene from *What's Love Gotta Do with It.* He yelled, "I got money, you think I don't have money?" Then he took out a wad of cash. I tried to explain that I wasn't trying to offend him. He finally came back to his senses, but I was ready to go. He acted as nothing happened and asked if he could drive me to my car. I told him I was okay and could walk, but he wouldn't leave it alone.

I told him, "Fine. You can drop me off at my car." He safely got me to my car. But as I drove off, he was staring at me with this creepy look on his face. Soon after, he texted me and asked if I wanted to go on another date. I was honest and told him I didn't think we were compatible and wasn't interested in going out again. He wrote back, *Cool, I understand.* That was on a Saturday and the following Monday, I had turned off my phone because I was on jury duty. When I turned it back on during lunch, my phone was blowing up with text messages and voicemails. This dude was calling and texting me back to back while I was in court. He texted me, telling me he didn't understand why I didn't want to go out with him again.

His messages said things like, *we had a great time, you're just one of those independent women.* In a very long text, he told me he didn't agree we weren't compatible and wanted to know what my problem was.

I didn't text him back; I called him. "Look, I don't think we are compatible. It's not up for discussion, and I don't want to go out with you again." I told him firmly. That's when he started screaming at me.

He kept alluding to me being one of these independent women and referenced his ex. He told me, "You don't feel like you need a man and that's what's wrong with you women. You are going to be alone."

I was pissed and argued back. I could barely get a word in, so finally, I said, "F*@# you" and hung up. He kept texting and telling me I just want a weak man like Urkel. I called my sister because I was so upset. She asked why I was entertaining him anymore. He was crazy. She was right; I immediately stopped entertaining his madness. That was my first online dating experience, and boy did I dodge a huge bullet with that one.

REFLECTION

There's not much to say in this reflection because it is evident that multiple bullets were dodged in this story. However, we want to take out the time to cancel any word curses that have been spoken upon our friend and other single people. Unfortunately, you may come across people who say you will be single and alone forever. Words are powerful, and we come against the negativity that has been spoken to people during their season of singleness.

CHAPTER 10
THE WAIT

But they that wait on the Lord shall renew their strength; they shall mount up with wings as eagles; they shall run, and not be weary, and they shall walk, and not faint.

—ISAIAH 40:31

NIESHA

A few months after Papi Chulo had his last glance of my silhouette strutting out the door, I was in New York, really getting into the groove of things. I was single, and this time around, I was ready to mingle. The New York grind was not smooth, but I had landed a decent job and found a sweet spot in Brooklyn. I was beginning to enjoy my life on the East Coast. On a random weekend, I decided to fly home to Chicago and visit some friends and family. One of my first visits was with my best friend Rian at her condo. While in the lobby, I discovered a rather fly chap working at the front desk. I wasn't in a rush, so I made a quick stop for some glance exchanges and introduced myself to this young man. We ended up exchanging contact info before I headed upstairs to see my friend. When I told Rian about my encounter with her handsome doorman, she immediately began to roast him and proceeded to tell me what kind of car he drove.

"Don't waste your time on his ass. Look where he works." She told me while sipping her rosé.

"Dang, why are you lighting this man up?" I asked her. Rian saw a scrub, but me, I saw a working man.

As I was leaving that night from a good sip and chow with Rian, the doorman ended his shift. He asked if I would like to walk and talk. It was a beautiful summer evening, and the sun was setting, so I figured why not. On our walk, I found out that he was finishing medical school, and the doorman gig was to support him and his daughter. He was smart and a great father? See, this is what I was trying to tell Rian. He had potential. I didn't usually go for the guy with kids, that's just my personal preference. But, I was willing to break one of my dating commandments and explore a relationship with somebody's daddy.

I engaged in yet another long-distance relationship and made a lot of effort to visit him because I wanted to give my best. My new chap never came to visit me in New York and continuously used his busy schedule as an excuse not to. I didn't trip; I made it back to Chicago as often as I could to enjoy my new man and provide emotional support during his last semester in medical school. I enjoyed our time together so much that I overlooked many items that went against my dating commandments, like his bad breath. It was extremely vile. So vile that I had to kiss him holding my breath. As things got more serious, this man I will now refer to as Dr. Boo Boo Breath informed me that our relationship would no longer work unless I relocated to Chicago. I let him know that was not happening. About a week after Valentine's Day, he dumped me.

I cringe at the remembrance of his breath, but Dr. Boo Boo Breath's abrupt exit was the set-up of a lifetime. Immediately after getting dumped, I did my routine of deleting all of my pictures, text threads, and cried my eyes out for a few days while on the phone with E. I blocked him on every form of contact. After noticing he was blocked, he tried to reach out to me on the Bible App. That didn't work either because, at this point, I was starting to recognize a personal pattern and was ready to change the narrative for my love life. I had enough! A few days later, God got me all the way together.

THE SPIRITUAL WHOOPING

NIESHA

My heart hurt so badly after this incident. It was like a build-up from every heartbreak I had ever experienced, and I was tired. I had given so much of myself in exchange for what? A man who exhibited some great potential? I was over dating potential that never manifested into real goodness that was consistent. I was stressing over someone who was putting forth a baby's pinch of effort. I was working daily to become the absolute best version of myself but was supporting the dreams of someone who didn't think enough of me to make any sacrifices. This heartbreak felt like a bad whooping, worse than the ones your granny or mama could ever lay on you. You think a whooping with a coach belt hurt? Try one that hits your mind, body, heart, soul, and spirit, and you have no choice but to take it. I took mine on a bench in Crown Heights, Brooklyn, and it led me to choose celibacy in my dating life.

ERIKA

At this point, Niesha had been in New York for about three years. All of her disappointments were coming from men in Chicago. Now, don't get me wrong. We love a Harold's Chicken-eating man from the Chi. There's nothing like connecting with someone from the same stomping grounds as you. However, she didn't live there anymore, and it was time to move forward and explore the pool of down-to-earth men of God living on the East Coast. After her incident with Dr. Boo Boo Breath, I had a dream about Niesha that prompted me to send her a copy of *The Wait* by Devon Franklin and Meagan Good. It's easy to decide to be celibate, but the practice can be a struggle, especially when you reach your prime. I sent this book to Niesha and encouraged her while praying that God would honor her obedience. And that he did! It was incredible to witness.

Niesha

When I opened the mail to see my copy of *The Wait,* I cried. I knew it was God telling me to surrender to him fully, and if I was to stay in the dating game, I had to do it His way. I wrote a celibacy prayer and asked God to hook me up with all 64 things on my "future king's list." I was ready for a mate that was genuine to the core and loved me for the person God created me to be. After that spiritual whooping, being obedient wasn't that hard. I became excited that my love life was in God's hands and was confident that he would hook me up royally and loyally in a massive way. I thought about all I had to gain and the heartache I was being spared from by doing it His way.

A funny but very critical moment in my purposeful dating journey took place when I was visiting my dear friend David. We were all in his living room, laughing, and just enjoying good company and vibes. My spirit was tapped while I was sitting among my friends, and I immediately got up and went to the bathroom. Once I was in the small intimate space between the sink and the tub, I placed my hand over my womb and began to pray to GOD. I thanked him for sparing my life and keeping me free from anything that would bring any baggage to my future spouse. I had to thank my Father in that very moment for keeping His promise to me in Psalm 34:22. I had to praise Him and ask that He continue to cover me in all ways. Let me say to you that He went above and beyond. God powerfully answered my prayer. I dated myself for seven months before I got back into the ring again. I wanted my future soulmate to get the very best version of me, so I let God work on making me that woman, and wow, HE DID THAT! I don't regret anything leading up to this point because Dr. Boo Boo Breath, along with Papi Chulo and a few others, were the catalyst to strengthening my relationship with God and getting in position for the love blessing I was praying and preparing for. Thank you, Ninjas!

Erika

To witness this story up close and personal was such a blessing for me. When Niesha decided to surrender to God's perfect will for her life, she was at an age when most women became intimidated by their biological clocks. At a certain age, it can be challenging to trust God and His timing. I've seen many people take whatever they can get or become extremely discouraged about meeting their soulmates. I quickly noticed that when Niesha adjusted her standards accordingly and stopped overlooking what she didn't want all for the sake of potential, things began to change for her drastically. If she encountered a new man, she could quickly identify if they would be a time-waster. The counterfeit relationships she experienced got her to where she needed to be spiritually, forced her to change her patterns, and step outside of her comfort zone, which ultimately led to meeting the person God ordained for her.

CHAPTER 11
HOW I MET MY HUSBAND

"I wanna thank you, heavenly Father, for shining your light on me. You sent me someone who really loves me and not just my body."

—ALICIA MEYERS, *I WANNA THANK YOU*

In love, we all have taken our share of risks. As we said before, opening your heart up tp potentially be hurt is not an easy thing to do. But it's so worth it if you learn how to embrace your journey. Now that you've gone through the roller coaster ride of experiences in Part I, some of our favorite people want to share how they met their husbands. Stay tuned for Part II because their husbands want to let the world know how they knew their lady was the one. Let's start with Niesha's story.

COFFEE BEANS

The way I met Bryan was by no means ordinary, and I like that it wasn't because I had done away with everyday dating experiences. After my seven-month dating hiatus, E and I decided to try out this dating app called Coffee Meets Bagel for two weeks. The way this app works is, you get a certain amount of coffee beans per day. When you see someone you like, you use your coffee beans to say hello. When you run out of coffee beans, you have to wait until the next day for matches. We both had some pretty interesting bi-coastal dating stories to swap and weren't throwing in the towel just yet. I'm not sure who introduced the other to the app, but it came into play. We were just looking for some comic relief with the potential of love finding us. After my first week on the app, I was ready to chalk it up as a dud. I added that the man had to be a Christian, so my pickings were gonna be slim. I didn't care about that too much because I definitely wasn't dating a man who wasn't rocking with Christ. No, sir, no ma'am. That was my non-negotiable from day one, and I wasn't backing off that.

Going into the second week, a nice chocolate man with snow-white teeth and a huge bright smile appeared. I saw this brother and instantly thought, *he looks like a fun time.* I swiped through his pictures and enjoyed what I saw. I took a screenshot of his pic and sent it to E for her visual approval in pure best friend behavior, and she gave it right away.

"Oh, he looks like he's a cool dude." E told me. "He doesn't look like your type, and that's a good thing!" She said in her raspy voice. I prided myself on being a chubby chaser and tended to go for men in size and weight who were somewhat pre-exposed to diabetes and hypertension. Don't judge me because all of us have a distinct type of person they prefer dating. Since he didn't look like my "type," E proceeded to insist that I see what was up. I sent him some coffee beans to let him know that I was mutually interested in him, and we started to chat away.

While in conversation with Bryan via chat, this connection was different and so incredibly enjoyable. We quickly went to talking on the phone, and those conversations were lengthy, funny, and refreshing. One of my favorite conversations before our first date was about the expired almond milk, which Bryan had in his fridge. I couldn't believe that the expiration date was deep into the prior year, and I laughed so hard about this. He sent me a picture of the milk to confirm the date he told me, and I knew then that he was trustworthy. It sounds crazy, but that instance has proven to be true to this day.

As I prepared for our first date, which took place on October 30, 2016, after I got off work, I felt so good about finally meeting him. Funny enough, we decided a few days prior that 5:45 pm would be a good time to meet. However, he never confirmed the time on the actual day. He said that he was waiting to hear from me and wanted to know if I needed to reschedule. I quickly said no. It was drizzling outside, but I wasn't deterred from seeing him. I jumped on the F train and headed to LES Sweet Chicks to meet my online bae.

As I was walking to the restaurant, I was on the phone with my sis Ciana. I told her that if I ended up getting catfished, I needed her to call me in 10 minutes to give me an exit. We both laughed and hung up. For some reason, I never got the nervous butterflies in my stomach as I got closer to my destination because I felt God's hand. I knew he was gonna block any type of wackness from me, and I was confident that Bryan would indeed be sucker-free. As I turned the block and took some steps forward, I saw this decadent man who looked just like his profile picture. JESUS! JESUS! JESUS! Thank you! I ran laps in my mind with praise because this was the too-good-to-be-true moment that my Father orchestrated for me. I was like, "Ooh la la!"

He opened the door for me, and we were quickly seated without any awkward energy. Bryan instantly felt like home to my spirit. He asked me if I wanted a drink, and I said no. He then replied, "That's cool, but I'm going to have something." I busted up laughing. I thought he was too cool and decided to get a Sweet Chick, which consists of my favorite tequila and watermelon juice. After exchanging some good stories and hearing each other's likes and dislikes, I came out of the gate with a lot of information about myself. An average man would've probably run and left me with the tab.

I explained to Bryan that I recently had a lumpectomy done on my right boob, and I was still recovering. I showed him a digital copy of my medical report that confirmed that I was disease-free and healthy. I also shared that I had some debt and that I was securing moneybags at my current employer, but they were currently petite. I told him that I love to shop, spend money in person and online, and travel. I shared that I hadn't filed my taxes for the past two years and that my savings account was malnourished. I told him I had only-child syndrome sometimes and was absolutely a daddy's girl and mama's baby. I wanted to be honest from the start and let him know everything I believed he would feel was a red flag. I wanted to be transparent to receive that in return from him. If it meant that I never saw him again, then so be it. It also gave us both the chance not to waste each other's time.

The game-changer of what I revealed next was the Hiroshima of our date, and that was the fact that I was celibate until marriage. I told him that there was absolutely no way that I was not going to stay committed to the promise I made to God and that it was so cool if he wasn't on board. In laughing but being very serious, I let Bryan know that no cock before the rock was my motto on this new journey I was flourishing on, and it felt great. Bryan gave me a sexy smirk and pushed back from the table as he proceeded to walk toward the door. He turned back around so fast, and we just broke into laughter as we recognized that this date was different for both of us. Bryan told me that he appreciated knowing my raw truths and never experienced anything like that before on a first date or date.

After our date ended and he walked me to the subway, he placed his arm around my shoulder. My heart immediately knew that he was my person. I could've told him then that I loved him and would have meant it 10000%. In the words of my sister Susie, "when you know, you just know." The rest is sweet history. Six months later, we were engaged to be married.

MY KING AND DREAM

The year was 2012, and I was in the city of angels following my dreams. Unknowingly, I had already crossed paths with my future husband as strangers in the same room. We met two years later at my 30th birthday party on June 9, 2014. Our mutual friend Leo invited him to my party, and once I announced going to Ghana on the microphone, he saw this as a segue to start a conversation. He introduced himself as Ahmadou and told me he wanted to hear about the trip when I returned.

Two months passed, and I came home to a message from Ahmadou on Facebook. He wanted to know about my trip and asked if I wanted to share the details over brunch. I accepted. After all, I had lots of pictures and stories to share. A week after our brunch, Ahmadou invited me to an LA Kings game. I politely declined and told him I was getting my hair done. Hey, two-strand twists can take hours. Instead of being offended or discouraged, he asked me to go out the next day to an art event. I told him I had already RSVP'd and would see him there.

Ahmadou asked, "Wouldn't it be more fun if we went together?" Now, anyone who knows me knows that I don't go to events with guys I don't know that well. I didn't want to network with the burden of introducing someone without a history or title. Plus, some people just don't know how to act. Still, I agreed to go out with him but was certain this was not a date.

He offered to pick me up. When I came outside, he was standing by his car. He opened my door and complimented me on how nice I looked. At the event, I noticed that he knew half the room, and I knew the other half. I kept asking myself, who am I with right now? He kept introducing me to people as Naledi (pronounced Ny-Lady). Of course, they all heard My Lady, and once I pointed that out to him, he laughed and kept it going all night. Ahmadou enjoyed the misunderstanding that all of these people were hearing. There were about 30 pieces of art on the walls. Halfway through the night, he asked me to go around to each art piece where he would guess the name (we had a cheat card from check-in), and I was to tell him how the art made me feel. I was hesitant at first. I didn't want to appear as if I was on a very public date. But after the third piece of art, I laughed so hard and forgot we were at an event. It was just the two of us walking around the room for the next hour. It was a star-studded event, so artists like Nas and Goapele were also in the place, which was great. Once we left, we went to eat and talked for two more hours. 'Twas a date, after all.

UNINVITED GUESTS

"How did you meet?" Four words every couple is bound to get asked at some point in their relationship. While many couples meet online, through mutual friends, or even from being high school sweethearts, that is not our story. On June 7, 2014, William and his family gracefully laid his maternal grandmother to rest. I worked as a funeral director apprentice at the time, and I had the honor of working with his family during their time of grief. Who would ever think that you would meet the person you are going to spend the rest of your life with at a funeral? You know that saying, "Every love story is beautiful, but ours is my favorite?" Well, this love story is our favorite. It's different, unique, and it's ours!

William's mother made the introduction. She told me, "I might have a husband for you." I laughed it off and thought she couldn't be serious. During the visitation, William came into my office, and we began talking and learning about one another. Of course, he had to ask me what made me want to get into the funeral industry. I shared with him that it was my paternal grandmother's passing that made me realize that the funeral industry was my calling. I told him that many people think being a funeral director is weird, but I see it as rewarding. The next day at the funeral, William, along with the other pallbearers, formed a line for me to pin a flower on their suit jacket. When the time came to pin William's flower on, he said, "Make sure you don't stick me." He came off as a little shy, but I knew then that was his way of flirting with me.

"I will not stick you," I replied, "I am a pro."

At the end of the services, William asked me if it would be okay to stay in touch. I gave him my number, and he texted me later that night. *Hello, this is Will. If you ever want to talk, please feel free.* He texted me every day from that day forward. He never went a day without saying hi or asking how I was doing. One day, he told me that losing his grandmother was one of the most difficult things he's ever had to deal with, and he wanted to thank me for helping him get through one of the most challenging times of his life. "I feel like God took an angel and left me an angel," he said.

I once read a quote that states, *love, and death are two uninvited guests. When they come, nobody knows. But both do the same work. One takes heart, and the other one takes its beats.*

RIBBON IN THE SKY

I think it's true what people say that you never know if the person next to you, in front of you, or behind you could be your mate. That's what happened to me when I was an undergrad in college. I went out to be a little sister to a popular fraternity. I was the first to be interviewed because I had to go to my part-time job at Wendy's. When I arrived, there were six or seven members of the fraternity sitting around in the room waiting to interview me. The guy who was in charge of the process was nicknamed Bootsy. After greeting me, the first question he asked me was, "Are you nervous?"

I wanted to say, "What in the heck do you think? Of course, I am." But, I just smiled and said, "A little bit." I didn't know any of the young men or what the process would entail. Still, the interview went well, and I headed to work. When I got home later that evening, my roommate, who encouraged me to go out for this sister group, asked how it went. I told her it went well. I also told her about the interviewer Bootsy who had asked me if I was nervous. I said, "I don't know why he would ask me something obvious. There's something about him. He came across arrogant."

She said, "Oh, no. He's a really nice guy."

I told her, "He seemed arrogant to me."

The process started, and I officially became one of the little sisters about two weeks later. When it was complete, I had the opportunity to get to know Bootsy. We started hanging out with another one of my friends and his frat brother. We became close friends. As time went on, we started hanging out more and more. It was just fun. He was easy to talk to and made me laugh. There was a guy I was seeing, but when I hung out with him, it wasn't the same feeling I had with Bootsy. That's when I realized I was starting to feel him a bit. So, I stopped seeing the other guy and started dating Bootsy seriously. It was a good feeling. What made it more special was that we started as friends and knew each other well.

Thinking back to that particular day of the interview, who would have thought that the guy I thought was arrogant and asked me a stupid question would be my husband and the father of my two daughters? It's really true. You never know when or where you are going to meet your person. You could meet that person and hang out with them for an extended period as friends and not know what God has in store. Here we are 38 years later, and I'm still married to this guy who started as my friend, and today, he is still my best friend. He is my ribbon in the sky.

MY FOREVER SOULMATE

One of my friends I went to college with had a party for his birthday. Another friend Jasmine, who I also went to college with, was in attendance. We were all inside my friend's apartment, having a real good time, and I spotted this cutie across the room. I saw that he was with Jasmine, so I asked her, "who is that?"

She told me, "that's my Uncle Rob."

I found him to be cute and wanted to talk to him. For the first time in my entire life, I approached a guy. I walked straight up to Rob and said, "Hey, I'm Izoha." He introduced himself, chatted, exchanged numbers and fast forward to that Sunday or Monday, we were texting, and the exchanges were just amazing. We didn't talk on the phone during this time, only text, which was perfect for me because I love texting rather than talking on the phone. We were texting each other books, and I noticed off the top that Rob could spell, and he knew how to use punctuation. Although we were only texting, I could actually hear his voice from just meeting him that one time. We were just having bomb text conversations that it was as if we already knew each other before.

We felt comfortable, and there were no awkward moments, so we finally decided to link up for a date. I think this was on a Thursday that we planned to meet. I was in Grad school, so we planned to meet after I got out of class that night. It was around 9:30 pm that he picked me up, which was the first thing I remembered because he had a car, which was one of my requirements.

He was very much a gentleman, opened the door for me, and had a playlist. Bruno Mars was playing, and the music selections were very good with a nice mix to them. I was living in the suburbs of Chicago and decided to go to a restaurant in Oak Park. It was a nice long ride, but there was never an awkward moment. It was so nice seeing him after our initial meeting. He looked the same way I remembered him from the party, and I had to thank GOD!! We just clicked; it was no denying that the feelings were mutual between us. Once at the restaurant, we ordered drinks, and I ordered a pizza too. We spent two, maybe three hours just talking like we've known each other forever. We discussed past relationships, what we were currently up to, looking forward to, and what we enjoyed doing in our free time.

Some time passed, and we begin to wrap up our date, and the waitress comes with the bill. Naturally, I was expecting him to pay, and I'm sitting there like whatever. He didn't say anything but whipped out a hot $20 bill. I knew that our tab was more than $20 because of the number of drinks between us and the pizza.

Then the date goes left. Rob asked me, "Do you have money for your stuff"?

I'm super offended like, *excuse me?* He invited me out for drinks. I shouldn't have to pay for anything. He asked me if I had my half for the bill, and in my Maya Wilkes from *Girlfriends* voice, I'm thinking, *oh hell no!* I was super salty. Anywhoo, he ended up telling me all he had was $20 and that he only anticipated paying for our drinks, and I had to pay the remaining difference.

I didn't want them to call the police on us for not paying, so I paid the remaining balance, and we left. We ended that date with me thinking this was the best date I ever had. We clicked so fricking much, and I talked to him like I knew him for years. I hate that it ended that way, which left a bad taste in my mouth, but we still hugged and said our goodbyes. I didn't know what was to come next honestly, but I was like we'll see what happens. I didn't want to have too high of hopes. However, I did enjoy myself so much in our time together.

He ended up texting me that he was so sorry and didn't know what to expect with our date. He also said he didn't know if the date would be worth his money or time, and to allow him to make it up to me. He asked if he could take me out again and pay for everything. On our second date, he paid for everything. We had just as much fun as we did on the first date. I feel like I knew he was the one on our first date actually, even though it didn't end the way I wanted it to or would've liked. We just had such a good time, and there was no way I couldn't give him another chance to see where it went and just be optimistic that this was as good as it seemed.

Despite the hiccup we had involving the bill, I felt super grateful that we had that good of a time because it was refreshing. After going on so many dates and talking to guys that were just blah to me, I was happy to meet someone who seemed like my real friend. A million things have happened since that date that showed me that he cares so much about me. He sees me for who I am and is always there to support me no matter the situation or circumstance. The amazing conversations that we started off having, we still have to this day. It's such a wonderful feeling for someone to know you without saying a word, and this is so true of Rob. I truly believe and know in my heart that he is my forever soulmate.

IT'S A FREE COUNTRY

I met my husband, Vernon, at the end of April 1998. I was still in high school. We attended a convention called the Black Family Conference, where minority students from area high schools talked about business and goal setting. He came up to me and introduced himself and asked my name and wanted to know what grade I was in. He also asked my birthday, which was strange because I never had someone in the first conversation, ask when my birthday was. He also asked if I had a boyfriend. I told him I did, but he was still determined and kept talking.

Eventually, we dispersed in different seminars, and the day went on. When we switched to a different one sometime in the afternoon, he walked in, and I was sitting down. Vernon saw the empty chair and asked, "Can I sit down next to you?"

I looked at him and said, "It's a free country." He went ahead and sat down. During the seminar where we talked about our future, they gave us paper plates for an activity. The plates were supposed to represent what we called our moons, and we had to write our goals and aspirations for the future. While we are sitting and writing, Vernon nudges me with his knee and shows me his paper plate. He had my name written down on it. Of course, it made me blush a little bit, but I tried to play it off.

We went to other seminars. After we finished, we had the end of the day wrap up, and we got ready to leave. Back then, we would try to figure out if we could leave with a number. I walked by Vernon and asked if he saw my friend. He said, "No, but can I get your number?"

I was thinking, *BAM!* In a calm voice, I said, "I will take yours."

He said, "oh, you must have a big brother or something."

I said, "something like that." It was really that my mom wouldn't let boys call me. I would have to call him. So then, I get his number, a few days go by, I call him. I couldn't remember who wrote the number down, but it was the wrong number. I tried not to let it get to my ego. Then one day, I saw his friend in the mall. His friend was a mutual friend of the family, and I knew him growing up.

I told him, "Oh yeah, he gave me the wrong number."

His friend said, "No, he didn't give you the wrong number; he would not do that." He gave me the right number, and I ended up calling him.

During our first conversation, we talked until the wee hours of the morning. Our goals, dreams, families, struggles, there were tears shed. It was different from any conversation I had with other teenage boys. I was young, but I knew this was different. Twenty-two years later, we are still together.

PART II
GUY'S EDITION

Man Dating Confession: *Men are simple creatures. It doesn't take a rocket scientist to figure us out.*

Initially, this book's intent was for women who wanted to share their funny and horrific dating stories. Thanks to our guy friends, we've come to realize that men kiss frogs too. Now, you have your share of scumbags. That's evident from the stories in Part I. Some incredible guys have been through similar situations with women, and we happen to know a few. Just like we invited the men to stay for the ladies' portion of the book, we ask you to do the same for them. With the same respect, please open your mind and hearts and listen to what they have to say. We want to highlight some common mistakes that women make during our dating and relationship experiences. Many times, when we've been dating for a while with no success, we're quick to say a few common phrases:

~ "It's no good men out there."

~ "All men are dogs."

~ "I can't trust no man."

Ladies, If you find yourself often spewing these phrases from your lips, you might be the common denominator in your unhappiness. This same goes for our male counterparts. The blessing is that it's not too late to cultivate some self-care and self-assessment habits to explore what's keeping you from the ideal relationship you desire and deserve. Regardless of what the majority thinks, guys have their fair share of moments that stretch them out of their comfort zones and have them on the receiving end of some foolish times. Enjoy!

CHAPTER 12
STRICTLY FOR LAUGHS

Man Dating Confession: *Men love a woman who will laugh at all of our jokes. Even if they are corny.*

Before digging into the deep conversations, we want to brighten the mood. Refill your glass of wine or favorite drink because these stories are hilarious. Some of these guys stepped out of their comfort zones, solely to provide you with a good laugh.

EGGTUATION

One afternoon at the grocery store, Ralphs, in North Hollywood to be exact, I spotted a bad chick that caught my attention. There are some women in life; you just can't pass on, and she was one of them. This hottie made me want to bring my best aisle game. When it comes to shooting your shot in the grocery store, it depends on the aisle. The aisle can give you the advantage to come correct with an approach. For example, a man can't be alpha in the vegetable aisle, and it was no way I was going to look like a beta male hollering in the produce section.

I couldn't bear the thought of her response. The meat aisle is an excellent section for light humor and recipe exchanges, but the middle aisle is where it all began. I decided to make my move when I saw her hit one of the middle aisles in the cereal section.

"Captain Crunch or Cinnamon Toast Crunch?" I knew this question would crack a smile from her.

"Cinnamon Toast Crunch," she replied

"Naw, I'm rocking with Captain Crunch," I told her.

We stood and debated long enough for me to know where she was from and what she did for a living. Within 10 minutes, I offered to cook for her. She quickly obliged. I told her it was under one condition: that she cooked for me in the morning. She knew I was implying that I wanted her to stay the night with me and seemed just as thrilled as I was for a sporadic encounter. We exchanged numbers and parted ways to continue our shopping. With excitement, I shifted gears since I was going to have company later. She was a bad chick, so I wanted to go all out. I know how women love a man that can cook, so on the menu was buttermilk chicken breast with roasted potatoes and corn. It was a special occasion, so I spared no expense to prove it. I topped it off with some Henny, of course!

The day leading up to seeing her was refreshing. It was like waiting 'til midnight to open a Christmas gift. When she pulled up to my apartment, it was showtime. I put on a movie while I wrapped up my meal. I set the dinner table up real nice and pulled out a chair for her to sit down. We talked while she gushed over the food and was impressed with the effort I put in. Things eventually led to the bedroom, and we had a good night. A very good night.

Morning came, and after a quickie, I was famished. I led her to the kitchen and showed her where everything was, and went to lay back down. I felt like a king as I laid in bed, waiting for my breakfast. She came into the room, excited for me to taste. I looked at the plate with a side-eye. "*What in the hell is this?*" I thought to myself. The bacon was burnt but salvageable, and the grits were harder than pool hall chalk. I hoped to God the other stuff was not eggs. Why would she even have two eggs on my plate: one scrambled and the other over easy? Who gives options like that? It made sense why I met her in the cereal aisle.

As she looked at me waiting for me to take my first bite, all I said was the first thing that came to mind. "Damn, babe, I don't even eat eggs. Never have." I was so glad I never told her how much I love eggs.

She rolled her eyes and replied, "So why do you have eggs in your fridge?"

Damn, she was right. I told her, "I rent out my place on Airbnb. I buy water and breakfast food for my guests. I'm trying to be a super host!"

She apologized for not asking for my preference and assuming that's what I liked. Her submissiveness was attractive, but honestly, she should have apologized for doing my eggs like that. They were so bad she needed to serve a weekend in jail for that mess.

I tried to put this horrible meal in the back of my mind because she had such a dope vibe. We hung out a couple of times after, but it was short-lived. She was a law student and a single mom. I wasn't looking for someone to debate with about how bad their child was. It was a bad combo for a bachelor, so in legal terms, that relationship was quickly dissolved.

But, my love for eggs remained. A couple of months later, I was out with some friends and decided to close out the night at the Standard Hotel to grab a bite. I ordered my favorite dish: steak and eggs. During loud laughs and jokes with the homies, I noticed the chick I met in the cereal aisle. I tried to refrain from making eye contact. Just my luck, she walked past my table. I was about to devour some of the most amazing eggs I have ever tasted, and her disposition was unforgettable. She looked as if she wanted to know what I was doing, like the audacity of me. Her eyes followed my hand, feeding my mouth. As I was about to take my first bite, she said, in a high-pitched voice, "I thought you didn't eat eggs, Joe!"

I was preparing to smooth it over and tell her I was just eating to soak up the liquor. Before I could respond, a random guy from another table yelled, "He didn't like YO eggs, bitch." I think I spat my food out. Every soul in there started laughing, and that was probably one of the funniest nights I can remember. She walked away, and that was the last time I saw her. I guess what I learned from the experience is that if a woman chooses Cinnamon Toast Crunch over Captain Crunch, run, Forrest Run.

THE MAD RAPPER

I met my ex-fiancée, Samantha, shortly after college. She was a waitress at a comedy show I attended with some friends. Samantha was polite, but everyone could tell she was extra friendly with me. She was very bold, and wrote her number down on a napkin and handed it to me before closing out our tab. We instantly connected. I soon learned that Samantha was working and finishing up her degree. When we weren't working, we were spending time together. I was fresh out of college, and she was attending school. We both had very youthful spirits. Some of my fondest moments with her were having freestyle battles after a drunk night out with friends. We were both garbage, but it always gave us a good laugh.

After about five years of being together, I decided to pop the question. My family was planning a cruise to the Bahamas, so I figured this would be the perfect time to propose. I recruited my older sister to help me orchestrate the proposal. Our cruise ship had a lot of family-friendly games to partake in, and one of them was the newlywed game. We planned for the workers on the cruise ship to recruit an unmarried couple to play the game. At the end of the game, I would get down on one knee. Everything went as planned, and Samantha was excited to take my hand in marriage.

When we returned from our cruise, things between Samantha and I became tense. I don't know what happened, but she started getting comfortable. She would call into work and go party with her friends. We started arguing more than ever. About a year into our engagement, I knew this was not going to work anymore. We were both guilty of not putting in 100%. I broke it off with Samantha and took a job in another state. I quickly adjusted to my new life and was happy that I decided to walk away from Samantha. I may not have been able to get out of it had I married her.

One day while working, my mother called me to ask what was wrong with Samantha. I wondered why something would be wrong. That's when she told me to check her Facebook page. I failed to mention earlier that when I was dating Samantha, she was an ordinary blonde White girl and was a nurse by the time we broke up. When I checked her page, she had cornrows down her back. I had never seen Samantha in any type of braids. But that's not what shocked me. She posted a live video of a freestyle rap that she made about me, and it was TRASH! I guess Samantha didn't realize it was trash because her friends were pumping her up. They commented about how she needed to record it as a track. About a week later, I received multiple phone calls from friends and family members, telling me that Samantha performed her song live in her dusty-ass cornrows. After our breakup, she went from being a nurse to pursuing a rap career. I guess Iggy Azalea better watch out.

R&B CRUSH

When I first moved to Los Angeles, I didn't know a lot of people. I landed a job at a well-known record label where we would get multiple phone calls from people trying to get a record deal for themselves or an artist they worked with. The calls came from famous movie directors or someone I would have never met if it weren't for this job.

My boss was always really busy, and I was able to connect to people on his behalf. While working, we got a phone call from a female R&B artist whose name I won't disclose. She wanted to meet with my boss, but he wasn't available. I took it upon myself and said, "I'll meet with you."

She said, "Okay. Come see me perform at R&B Live." R&B Live was a popular event for artists to showcase their talent. Some of the best people would perform, including this R&B artist. I agreed and was excited to meet up with her later on. She informed me that she would not be performing that night, but we could watch some of the performers. I was so nervous because she was my R&B crush. Mid conversation, she said, "I have to go to the restroom, I will be back." While I waited, she called me and said, "Come downstairs. there's another part of this venue I didn't know was down here."

I said, "Oh. Okay, cool." I went down the stairs, and it was empty. At that moment, she grabbed me and slammed me against the wall before tonguing me down. I couldn't believe I was getting tongued down by my R&B crush. All of a sudden, I heard a lot of stuff fall onto the ground. I looked down and thought, *what the hell!*

She said, "Oh my gosh, my pills." There were a bunch of pills, and she started putting them all in her mouth. She was popping small round pills, which she said were her medicine, but they weren't. My R&B crush was not only a show stopper, but she was also a pill popper.

GIRL FIGHT

I was in my early 20's and home from college for summer break. I ran into this hella cute girl at a house party, and we danced for a bit before I asked for her number. A few days later, I invited her out on a date. Since it was summertime in Chicago, I figured it was a great time to pick her up and see *Batman Begins* at Navy Pier.

Throughout the entire movie, we were hugged up. I could tell she liked me, and I was feeling her too. After the movie was over, we walked around Navy Pier. Some girls I went to high school with spotted us and came over to say hi. "What's up, Benny?" One of them said as they approached me and my date. Confused, my date looked at me because I hadn't told her my nickname was Benny. Before I could explain, the two girls started a conversation with me. They completely ignored the fact that I was with my date, typical hood girl stuff. I guess the conversation was too long for my date because she began huffing, puffing, and rolling her eyes. One of the girls noticed my date's attitude, looked at her, and said, "Bitch, I'll beat your ass."

My date mumbled something back, and the next thing I knew, the two girls were fighting my date.

I was frozen in disbelief before I shouted, "No, stop it!" My date reached out her hand for help as I tried to end the fight. I tried as hard as I could to help, but as a young man, I didn't want to hit a girl. The dissolution of this fight was pretty hard, but the fight eventually ended. After the beat down, I looked at my beautiful date, with smeared eyebrows across her forehead, plugs of hair missing from her bangs, and blood gushing from her lips. Imagine how awkward the ride home was.

STELLA GOT NO GROOVE

When I was 22, I went on my first cruise with my family. I had heard fun stories about cruises, so I was excited to go. Upon arrival, we met everyone for introductions. My sister had already made some friends and introduced me to all of the folks I didn't know. I met an older lady who seemed to be in her late 40s, and she was attractive. I was in a playful mood and ready to enjoy my vacation. She introduced herself as Tasha. She told me she was single and came off very flirty. When I flirted back, she told me she was just playing, and I was way too young.

I said, "You aren't too old for me. I would break your back." I was young, but confident I could hold my own. Everyone around us laughed. I was laughing but serious at the same time. A couple of days went by, and we kept running into each other on the ship. While sitting at one of the bars, we had a pleasant conversation. She had two kids who were way older than me. She was divorced and had been out of the game for a little minute. This woman made it clear that she was interested in me. When our cruise stopped in Ocho Rios, I took her on a date. We went to the water show and then for a walk. When we were headed back to the ship, I called my brother to see where he was. We shared a room, so I wanted to know his whereabouts because I planned on having company. When he told me that he would not be in the room for a while, I asked Tasha if she wanted to come with me.

I took her back to the room. We both knew what it was and didn't waste much time. I was excited about my first experience with an older woman. I thought maybe she would teach me a few tricks. It was the exact opposite; I was the one putting it on her. She was really into it and started making some loud sounds. It turns out that I could "break her back." It was fun at that moment, but after I achieved my goal, I wanted to go back to having fun on the cruise ship. Maybe even meet a young lady my age.

On the other hand, Tasha also enjoyed it and took me more seriously than I expected. We bumped into each other the next day. I didn't want to act like an ass because I still had to see her on the cruise ship, so I remained friendly. She invited me to her room, and thank goodness her roommate was in there. When Tasha introduced us, her roommate noticed I was way younger. It was very awkward. I made a clean exit, but during the rest of the cruise, she gave me stalker vibes. I would turn around, and out of the blue, she would be staring at me. Even my family members saw it. There were a few times when she asked my family where I was.

Even my dad said, "You must have put it on that lady." It was fun in that brief moment, but I wanted to focus on enjoying the cruise. I thought she was going to teach me some things, but I ended up teaching her. Like Stella, she was trying to get her groove back, but there wasn't much to work with.

WHY MUST I CHASE THE CAT

While in high school, my best friend was messing around with my girlfriend's friend. The two of them had a sleepover at my girl's house, and my boy and I planned to visit them when we knew everyone's parents would be asleep. We were young, horny, and ready. The plan was to go through the back door where my girl would have left the door unlocked. For some reason, I had her car keys in my pocket. About 1:00 am, we snuck out of my parents' house to head to my girl's. Instead of parking in front of the house, I parked down the street.

It was a predominantly White neighborhood, and we were two Black kids creeping in someone's backyard. We made our way to the back door. It just so happened that when we were walking out back, my girl's dad was in the kitchen getting a glass of water. We had no idea he saw us. While in the kitchen, all her dad sees were two Black guys walking in his backyard, so he called the cops. Since we had no idea what was going on, we tried to open the back door, but it was locked. This was before text messaging existed, so I called my girl to let her know I was trying to slip in, but there was no answer. She had seen her dad and didn't unlock the door. She was sitting there waiting with no way to signal us. We continued jiggling the back door, not knowing the cops were on their way.

All of a sudden, there were flashing lights in front of the yard. Still, we were oblivious to what was going on. We were just focusing on getting into the house. We walked around the house and tried to see the commotion. We saw the cops with flashlights, looking around. Then we spotted my girl's dad outside with them.

One of the officers said, "You two, come here!" We walked over, and the cops asked what was going on.

The dad pointed at me and said, "I know this guy." He turned to my boy and said, "But I don't know him."

Quick thinking on my part, I grabbed my girl's keys and said, "My girlfriend stays here. I was hoping she is up so I could give her the keys." I handed her keys to them.

The cop said, "Oh! you know you shouldn't be walking around like this at night."

Then my boy said to my girlfriend's dad, "Sir, I know you. I've been to your house numerous times." What he didn't know was, in addition to my friend trying to get with my girl's friend, he also had an encounter with her sister, who was also his daughter. We still laugh at the fact that we almost got arrested trying to chase after some cat.

TAKE ONE FOR THE TEAM

I met Renee in an AOL group chat in 2000 when I was 19. Her screen name was BAPS1482, which stood for Black American Princess and the date of her birthday. For the young people in the back, before you could slide into DMs, there was AOL. Depending on your interests, you could join a bunch of people you didn't know in a chat room. If you connected with someone, you could send them a private instant message. And guess what? There was no way to post or send pictures. You had to determine if you wanted to get to know someone based on the conversation.

That's precisely what happened with Renee. We would stay up until 1:00 or 2:00 in the morning, chatting about everything. She seemed cool. I didn't even need a picture to know that she was dope. After about three consecutive nights of messaging, Renee was comfortable enough to give me her number. When she answered the phone, she had one of the sexiest voices I'd ever heard. It was so soothing. Already, I could tell she was fine. We chatted on the phone and instant messenger for about two weeks before we decided to meet in person. She lived in the suburbs of Chicago but would be visiting her grandmother in the city. I came to find out that her granny stayed only five minutes away from me. Renee didn't have a cell phone at the time, so she gave me her grandmother's home number to reach her.

I was so excited to meet her in person that I called her on the exact day she told me she would be in Chicago. Her grandmother answered the phone, and as a gentleman, I politely introduced myself. When Renee got on the phone, I asked her if I could take her to the movies. She told me that she had to take a rain check because her cousin Cherell was in town visiting. I asked her how old Cherell was and when I found out she was 19, I told Renee I could bring a friend. Renee declined and asked if we could meet up before she went back home. I wanted to see her, so I insisted that she just bring her cousin along. After about five minutes of going back and forth, she agreed. I told her I would pick her up around 4:00 pm.

When we got off the phone, I called my friend Ray to see if he wanted to go on a double date. Ray was cool, and I knew the four of us would have a really good time together. He agreed to go, and that's when I realized this would be my first-time meeting Renee. I became excited and nervous all at once. I wanted to make sure I impressed her. I put on a throwback jersey and some jeans. I sprayed on my Issey Miyake cologne. When I was ready to go, I hopped in the car and put on Nelly's *Country Grammar* before heading to Ray's house. When I arrived in front of Ray's house, he was ready. He and his high school sweetheart had just broken up, so I knew he would be excited to meet someone new and shoot the breeze. After he jumped in the car, we made our way to see Renee and her cousin Cherell. We both contemplated what these young ladies would look like and prayed they were attractive.

When we pulled up to Renee's grandmother's house, Renee was already sitting outside. I knew it was her by the way she had described herself. She stood about 5'2, was chocolate, and had a beautiful smile. I walked up to her and looked her up and down. I admired her curves and was glad that I didn't experience what years later would be called a catfish. Renee seemed happy to see me but also had a concerned look on her face. "There's something I need to tell you." She said. I tried to figure out what could be so serious that it gave her this nervous look. "It's about my cousin who's coming." Before she could finish her next sentence, a very beautiful but pregnant Cherell came outside. Renee said, "This is why I was trying to reschedule. I didn't think your friend would want to go on a date with someone who is seven months pregnant."

When the three of us returned to the car, Ray looked at me, confused. As I opened the door to let Renee and Cherell in the car, I mouthed to Ray, "I had no idea."

Renee broke the awkwardness on the way to the movie by saying, "Don't worry, you're not the daddy." We all laughed.

Myself, Ray, Cherell, and somebody's baby mama headed to the movies. It turns out all of us had a great time. Cherell was pregnant but very cool. We didn't mind kicking it with her at all. When we dropped the two of them off, Ray and I had a good chuckle. "At least we know the kid is not mine." We laughed. I'm glad Ray took one for the team.

CHAPTER 13
SHE TRIED IT

Man Dating Confession: *Whether we like to admit it or not, we always know when we let a good one get away. Unfortunately, there are some women we don't mind leaving in the dust.*

Fellas, we can't stand to see a man who has been tried by a no-nothing, trifling woman who doesn't see your value. We understand that people are people, and sometimes as men, you get the short end of the stick too. The two of us have counseled our guy friends who have been discouraged from other potential relationships. All because a woman tried them.

Some women will take advantage of men because they don't know any better. But to whose expense? Unfortunately, are women that will take advantage of your kindness and test your masculinity by pulling you through emotional rings of fire, only to see how much affliction you can withstand. Making you want to throw in the towel altogether. That just isn't cool, or kind, and it shouldn't be deemed as normal.

Women are quick to call their bestie to vent when they feel like a guy treated their lives. Some of their delusional minds will have them thinking they can dish out garbage that should be received with open arms. When a woman tries it with you, this is also an opportunity for you to decide if you will go, Casper, the Ghost, or use this as an opportunity for growth in your relationship. Whatever you decide, we don't want you to miss out on a good woman all because you have been screwed over by someone who was never meant to be your queen.

PUFF PUFF I'LL PASS

Let me tell you about my worst date ever. I was a junior in college and was home for spring break. I went out with this girl I had dealings with whenever I came back. She asked if I wanted to go to the movies with her. My car was at school, so she had to pick me up. When she arrived, the girl I thought I was attracted to was dressed like a tomboy. Her clothes were wrinkled, and she was visibly high. I'm not a smoker but don't have anything against it, so it wasn't a deal-breaker.

When we got to the movies, we bumped into her ex-boyfriend and his date. I found this very strange. We got our snacks and headed into the theater. I forgot all about her ex until we saw him again while leaving out. He stopped my date and said, "Hey, you think you can give me and my date a ride home?" How he knew she drove us to the movies, I have no idea.

I thought she was going to decline, but she said, "sure." My date's ex and his date hopped in the back seat. The entire ride was just awkward. We dropped her ex's date off first. I sat there quiet and tried not to say much because it was night time, and I didn't want to take public transportation to get home. When we arrived at her ex's house, my date left me in the car and stepped out to smoke weed with her ex. I was in the car for about 20 minutes before she returned. My weed-head date got back in the car and began to drive me home. When we pulled up in front of my house, she proceeded to give me a goodnight kiss. That's when I curbed her. You will not waste my time smoking weed with your ex-boyfriend on a date with me.

REFLECTION

Miss Puff Puff I'll Pass, you were young, so we won't go in too hard. However, this makes us think about all the things women do that they wouldn't be able to handle if the tables were turned. For some of us, it's time to start treating men like you would want to be treated. Hopefully, by now, you have some class.

Why did you even invite this guy out? Were you trying to make your ex jealous? We are trying to figure out how you all ended up in the same movie at the same time. It sounds like maybe you knew he was going on a date, and you planned to make him jealous with your date, or vice versa. We are also confused about how you pulled two dudes in wrinkled clothing. We're just going to assume you had a bad day. However, it won't hurt you to get dressed and put some effort into making sure you looked nice for your date. For the guy who endured this madness, we are thankful that you have still kept your head in the game.

THE ARRANGEMENT

After 32 years of marriage, I separated and met a lovely lady on match.com. I was pretty new to the dating scene, and it was NOTHING like it was in the past. The lady and I chatted via text for a few days before we made plans to meet for lunch. At lunch, she looked amazing, just like her photos, and she had a great personality. She texted me to see if I wanted to come over to her place when I got off work that day. I replied *sure*, and to my surprise, she invited me back to her apartment after meeting so soon.

Being a gentleman, I called to see if I could bring her anything in particular. She asked me to stop at Whole Foods to pick up some goods, and I spent almost $100 on the few items she asked me for. I thought that was crazy, but "when in Rome." When she opened that door, I saw just why those groceries were worth picking up.

She greeted me with just a t-shirt and some panties on, and I lost it. I was totally off guard, and that was completely fine with me. Shortly after my arrival, we got into some action because we could not resist one another, and it lasted through the night. As I lay next to her in bed, I asked what her expectations from our connection were. Her response was bold and straightforward. She stated she was looking for an arrangement that involved her bills being paid, along with her rent and car note. I was blown away and clearly not the man for her.

REFLECTION

To our friend who is back in the game after 32 years, a lot has changed. Thankfully, you are fully aware that having a financial arrangement is not normal. First, we want to point out that you asked what her expectations were. These are conversations that a lot of men and women aren't having with each other. This woman isn't looking for a man. She's looking for a sugar daddy. If she is going to sell her goods for rent and a few bills, you don't want her anyway. She is selling to the highest bidder. Prostitutes left the streets, and now they're treading on the internet. Please don't allow this total disappointment to spoil it for the good woman you will encounter later, and trust us, you will.

For Ms. Arrangement, you don't have to sell your body to make ends meet. Don't prioritize your bills so high that it takes precedence over your safety. Many of us have had success stories from an online meeting, but there have been just as many tragedies as well. By the Lord's grace, nothing happened to you.

IN SEARCH OF MY BABY DADDY

Back in high school, I dated this White girl. I was the first Black guy she had sex with, so she always held a special place in her heart for me. I was the Black guy that made her never go back. While in the military, I flew home briefly to visit my family and friends before being deployed. I ran into the girl from high school, and she reminded me that I was the first Black guy she ever slept with. One thing led to another, and we were in the backseat of her car like we were teenagers again.

About a year later, I was at my house in Arizona, enjoying a sunny Saturday morning. I remember it like yesterday. It was around September, and I had my Marvin Gaye on as I cleaned my house while drinking some Titos. I was in a good mood as I picked up my phone and noticed I had a message on Facebook. It was the White girl from home, and she asked if I had time to talk. There's nothing that makes a man more nervous than telling him you need to talk. I tried to figure out what the heck she could want because we hadn't spoken since we last got busy in the back seat of my car.

I dialed her number, and she picked up. She said, "Well, you know my baby girl? I thought she was my boyfriend's kid, but we had a DNA test, and the results show that he's not the father." She went on to explain that I was the only other person she slept with besides him during the time she was conceived. My heart immediately dropped, and I sobered up quickly. I was confused because I used a condom. I know they aren't 100%, but it just didn't make sense. I had just finished a 12-month deployment. Before that, I was in and out of the field for six months. But since she said this was my kid, I told her I would be home in two weeks, and we could take a DNA test. I told her that if the baby were mine, I would take care of the sweet baby girl. She said there was no need for a DNA test. She already knew it was mine. Then she sent me a side-by-side picture of the baby and me *Maury* style. She was convinced that we looked alike. You are probably wondering how this broad got my baby picture. You guessed it, she found it on Facebook.

Things weren't adding up, so I reached out to one of my female friends. We did the math, and my friend said, "There's no way that could be your kid. Unless your sperm went down the drain and came to her house from Iraq."

While my friend and I talked about this, my cousin called me. "Boy, that's not your baby. She told two other dudes the same thing." He told me not to waste time doing a DNA test. We ended up finding out it was another childhood friend who is now a great father to the kid. He's the type of guy who will wife a chick after everyone has had their way with her. You may find that funny, but almost every group of guys has that friend. It's a running joke that you better get to a girl before he does. I'm glad he got to her first.

REFLECTION

Here's a movie trivia for you. ***Mom:*** *Children, what do you say when you meet a nice man?* ***Children:*** *Are you my daddy?* If you didn't know this is from *Don't Be a Menace in South Central While Drinking Your Juice in the Hood,* your Black card is revoked for the next 24 hours. Anyway, we just wanted to lighten the mood before we go in on Ms. In Search of My Baby Daddy.

This sounds like an episode out of *Paternity Court,* where you wanted to find a stable father for your child. You knew our friend had great military benefits and wanted in. We are just trying to figure out what world you live in where you think someone would claim your child before getting a paternity test. A side by side picture from Facebook is not equivalent. Just because you lack self-control doesn't mean you pin a kid on the man. Thankfully, this child has a great father because we aren't so sure about their mama. You really tried it.

BELLIGERENT BECKY

One of the worst experiences I ever had was while on a date. I went on a date, and I have to mention it was with a Caucasian woman because of how the story plays out. We met up and had a great time eating, drinking, and getting to know each other. We hung out for hours, and as the night progressed, we ended up at a gentlemen's club.

While at the club, she excused herself to go to the restroom. She told me she would be right back, so I sat at our table waiting. Ten minutes turned into 20, and 20 minutes turned into 30. While I waited, one of the ladies working at the club engaged me in conversation. Of course, she was just trying to get some money out of me, but I entertained her conversation since I had been waiting for so long.

My date returned and saw me talking to the lady. She got agitated and asked, "Why are you talking to her? I can't believe you would do this. It's so disrespectful." I was confused because she suggested that we go to this particular club. It was not uncommon for one of the workers to come and speak to me. We were at a strip club where it's their job to get me to pay for a dance. My date started accusing me of trying to date this girl. The worker became uncomfortable and walked away.

My date continued to flip out, and I reminded her that she left me for 30 minutes. The entire time, I didn't notice another woman standing behind her. Again, for the sake of the story, she was Caucasian as well. This woman jumped in the conversation and said, "She was with me."

I asked, "Who are you?"

She immediately started going off on me and replied, "It doesn't matter who I am. What are you doing? She looked at me and said, "you are so disrespectful." Then she turned to my date and said, "this is why you can't mess with Blacks." "I didn't know you were here with a Black."

"Whoa!" I responded. I had no idea who this woman was, but she was a racist. I told her, "I don't know who you are, but you're disrespectful. Please leave me alone." She continues to argue with me while my date says nothing. Thankfully, management overheard what was going on, and they ended up kicking the belligerent White woman out. They apologized to me and offered me free drinks and passes to come back.

I looked at my date and said, "Do you see what you caused? You left 30 minutes. A random person came back with you and disrespected me, but you did nothing." I thought my date was pretty cool up until this incident. At this point, I was disgusted. I never went back to the establishment or talked to her again.

REFLECTION

We almost left this story out of the book because it pushed our buttons. But we want to address conversations that need to be had, and this is one of them. As Black women writing this book, we want to make something very clear. We believe that everyone has the right to love whom they wish to. However, there is nothing more exciting than seeing a strong Black couple. When someone like Belligerent Becky has a chance to encounter a king from our tribe, we would appreciate it if you treat him with the utmost respect.

We also find this story interesting due to conversations we've had with Black men who feel like Black women aren't the easiest women to engage with. We can tell from this story that this is not always the case. For the sake of time, this is a conversation we will save for our podcast. But what we will say is that ignorance comes in all shapes, sizes, genders, and colors.

BROKE & HUNGRY

After about five dates, I took this girl Veronica out to Sunday brunch. It wasn't just any brunch; it was an expensive ocean-side brunch with all-you-can-eat seafood and bottomless mimosas. I spent about $300 for the two of us. I hit her up via text the next day to see how her day was going. She responded by texting, *I'm hungry.* I let her know that I had just eaten, but we could hit up a lounge or something. She suggested that we go to Post & Beam in Baldwin Hills, California. Not a high-end spot, but not cheap either.

When I got there, I was a bit irritated because she asked me to take her out to eat two days in a row. I'm not broke, but I just wanted to hang out. I ordered a small meal, and Veronica ordered a steak with some sides. When the server brought our food, she immediately began to smash. I didn't touch mine because I planned on taking it home for later since I wasn't hungry. When Veronica finished her food, she asked if she could have some of mine. I told her, "Sure." She began to go in on my plate. After attempting to take a third bite, my reflexes led me to push her hand away. She had her meal, and I wanted mine for later.

Veronica immediately got offended. She gave me a sour look and said, "Did you just push my hand out of the way? I would rather starve than have a man push my hand out of the way."

I told her, "First of all, you must be starving. Yesterday you ate a whole lot. Today you finished most of your food and still want mine." She was in medical school and only about 108 pounds. I asked her, "Are you not getting fed?" The way she was eating led me to believe she was a struggling student.

She got upset and was ready to go. I asked the waiter for the check and a box for my food. Veronica requested a box for the little food she had left.

On the way out, I went in for a hug and accidentally knocked her food out her hand. It hit the ground, but it was still in the case. Nothing fell out. I picked it up and gave it to her.

She said, "You're giving me this food? You think I'm going to eat this now?"

I said," It's still in the container. Nothing hit the ground."

Veronica was still upset and said, "No, you can just throw it away now."

She wasted the food I paid for just because the container hit the ground. After that date, I dropped her like a bad habit.

REFLECTION

Here's a secret to the nice guys. If you're trying to see if a chick is digging you, invite her to something inexpensive or non-food related. A museum or something you like to do and see if she will tag along. Some women will entertain you just to get a free meal. The best way to see if a woman is down to earth is by taking her on nice, cost-effective dates. As the relationship evolves, you can invest more of your time and money on high-quality dates.

Before paying for $300 brunches, get a feel for the woman's character first. We understand that this may be hard to do while sitting across the table from a pretty lady feeding her face. But every woman is not deserving. We know some men don't mind because they have it like that, and yes, we women love to eat. But, at a certain point, you want to find out if a woman digs you or the fact that you pick up the bill every time.

To our friend who endured this experience, this chick told you what she was on when she responded to your text by letting you know she was hungry. That was the sign that should have told you she only likes going out with you because you treat her to a free meal. At the very least, she could have asked how your day was going. A good-hearted woman who is into you most likely will not use you for a meal.

Now for you, Ms. Broke and Hungry, some nice men don't mind taking you out because they want to spend time with you. But no grown woman should have that expectation to lay on the shoulders of a gentleman who was just trying to get to know you a little better. It's not cool to be a user.

GOD TOLD ME YOU'RE MY HUSBAND

A few years ago, I moved to San Antonio from New Jersey to plant an extension of my church. A woman from the New Jersey church was going to fly in and help me with the ministry. Eventually, she would move and serve as a leader. Leading up to her trip, we talked on the phone and discussed plans for the church. When she arrived in San Antonio, we had a meeting over lunch.

We talked about where she would live, jobs, and her position in the church. All of a sudden, she hit me with, "You know why I'm coming to move down here, right?"

I said, "Yea! To do the Lord's work. I appreciate it, sis." I went on to tell her that it was really dope she was helping get the work done.

She looked at me and said, "No. I'm not coming down here just for that."

I said, "Well, I don't know, aside from you just having a heart for people and loving God."

She said, "Yea, that's all true. But I'm coming down because the Lord told me you are my husband, and I needed to support this work."

My fork and napkin dropped as I replied, "Come again?"

She said, "Yea, God told me that you are my husband in a dream. He instructed me to come help you build this work."

I was shocked and surprised. I said, "Okay."

She went on to say, "It came to me in a dream and a couple of visions." She even had the scripture for it, Proverbs 18:22. She said, "I believe you are my husband."

I told her, "I appreciate your honesty. However, it's interesting because if it concerns my life, I think that God would speak to me. God would reveal to me that you're my wife, too, don't you think?"

She said, "Yea, absolutely."

I said, "Well, that's the disconnect because I haven't gotten that memo yet. So, am I not connected to God? Did I miss out on something?" I wanted to get my memos. I just didn't get that one.

Dinner ended, and when she went back to New Jersey, I never heard from her again. It was good two weeks ago, so what changed? Why do people feel the need to get God involved outside of the other person having that same conviction? We were doing Bible study and exchanging scriptures, and she had motives. Because I didn't get the same dream that the Holy Spirit supposedly gave her, she went Ghost. This makes me think it wasn't the Holy Spirit that gave her the revelation. She probably had pizza the night before that crazy dream.

REFLECTION

Sigh! Woman of God. Where do we start? We know you probably read *The Wait* and heard how God told Meagan Good that Devon Franklin was her husband. We get it. With God, nothing is impossible. We could talk about this topic all day long. But for the sake of time, if God gives you this type of information, please keep it to yourself.

Like our brother said, he didn't get the same memo. This is an uncomfortable scenario because we have a lot of guy friends who have been told this, as well as female friends who feel like they know who their husband is. Some of them have never even encountered the man. In this case, we can't accuse the woman of really being a manipulator because people have had strange dreams they perceived were of God. However, if this was not the case, and she used God to manipulate the situation, shame on her! Maybe it was the embarrassment of him not feeling the same way, or him not getting the word from God too, that made her go Ghost after the encounter. But to ditch the work that she felt God was calling her to do says a lot about where her intentions were. Perhaps if she held her tongue, this could have been a love story. We will never know. In addition to the fact that the revelation was not mutual, and she abandoned the mission, we are left to conclude that her "revelation" never existed.

THE SNIPER

I met this girl on the Bumble App. She quickly gave me her number and insisted I come to visit her. She failed to tell me she was in the Army and lived on base. I picked her up, and when she came outside, I thanked the Lord that she looked exactly like her pictures. We went out to dinner and had a nice time.

After a hot and heavy make-out session in my car, she invited me inside. When we got into her house, there was a babysitter there. She failed to mention she had a kid during our date. (Red flag #1). The babysitter let my date know that her child was asleep. I was watching the whole ordeal thinking, *is she going to get it in with her child at home and we just met?* Truth be told, that was her problem. It was her responsibility and not mine. We were on the couch, kissing when she proceeded to say to me, "I'm going to wait 90 days before we sleep together." This was when Steve Harvey's book *Act Like a Lady, Think Like a Man* came out. She was referring to his manual that suggests waiting for 90-days to sleep with a man.

I told her I understood, but she continued to kiss me. She took my hand and led me to the bedroom. I told her, "Let's wait if that's what you want to do." Still, we did a little kissing and touching on the bed. She went down and did her thing without us having intercourse. I ended up staying the night, and we stayed up talking. In the morning, she told me, "Yea, I enjoy your company, but you're in competition with some other guys." I just shrugged my shoulders because this all sounded like hogwash to me. There was no competition capable of making me fret with concern. We continued to see each other for about a month, and I wasn't tripping about waiting because I had other chicks lined up. Keep in mind that she wanted to wait for the three months that Steve Harvey told her like he is a dating guru. After attending a work event together, we came back to her place for a nightcap. We got hot and heavy again. I stopped her and said, “Wait a minute. You want to wait.”

She said, “Forget that damn rule!” The next morning, she started pillow talking and revealed some interesting facts about me. She not only did some research on me, but she included my family too. She knew my cousin wrote a book and other details about the members of my family. She used the army database as her tool to investigate my entire life. (Red Flag #2). It’s crazy because I didn’t even know her last name during the time of these shenanigans. I returned the favor and started to do some digging of my own. She left to go to work and gave me a spare key, which granted me the access I wanted.

I saw her giving me a key to her place so soon as another red flag. While taking a shower, I saw a prescription medicine bottle. It had her full name on there. I Googled her name. It turns out she was married to an army sniper who was very good at hand tactical combat. I found him on Facebook, and he was currently traveling. According to his status, he would return to his family in a week. So, I had banged this girl, and her husband was coming home soon. She wasn’t going to tell me that she was married. I could have been murdered if he caught us in bed together. I had to cut it off immediately and scram. By the looks of her husband, I didn’t want any trouble. He was HUGE. I ended up telling her this was not going to work. I had fun, but if I had to do it again, I wouldn’t. Well, on second thought.

REFLECTION

Here’s the thing about delusional people and the stories they share and desire for you to believe. Once they exhibit a behavior that is not aligned to their words, you should know right away that they will not be capable of adding value to your journey. In this case, this lady was a liar through and through. She wasn't even aware of how crazy she appeared to a sane person.

Even when it came to the 90-day rule, what was the point of adding in those rules only to break them? The 90-day rule that Mr. Harvey spoke of involved no sexual moves, including oral sex, which is still sex. Here, we're able to see how this girl didn't know what she was doing, and her self-respect level was visibly tattered as we later discovered she was married. Since she's also a cheater, we can stop wasting ink on discussing her faults and forge ahead with this groove.

CHAPTER 14
AWKWARD MOMENTS

Man Dating Confession: *While on a date with this woman I immediately knew there wouldn't be a second date. She invited me to a concert that was going to take place a week later. I didn't have the guts to tell her I wasn't interested. Instead, I told her I had to take my grandmother to church that day.*

In dating, we all have our share of awkward moments. Some are more embarrassing than others. They aren't always fun at the moment, but give us something to talk about later. The guys in this chapter survived some very awkward moments in their dating life.

THE CRYING DATE

While out one night, I met a girl I found extremely attractive. We had a great conversation, but she was kind of hesitant to give me her number. She did anyway. We were texting a few days later, when she said, "You seem cool, but I have to be honest. I'm fresh off a breakup." She explained that she and her guy broke up a few months ago, and she still wasn't over it. I told her it was fine, and we could stay in contact as friends. I was always throwing parties, so I didn't see any harm in inviting her and her girls out. After she showed up to a couple of my events, I figured I would check the temperature to see if she would be down to go on a date. She agreed.

We went to Gyu-Kaku, a Japanese BBQ restaurant in Beverly Hills, where you can cook your food. While eating our food, she began to open up, and I was feeling her energy. That was until she started talking about her ex. She went on and on about how the breakup did a number on her. She seemed sad, so I said, "If you don't mind me asking, what happened?" This question must have done something to her soul because she immediately started crying. I'm not talking a few teardrops, she was balling crying. She told me that her ex got tired of her being quiet and antisocial. He wanted her to open up more. She was hysterical. People were walking by our table and looking at us. I was scared they were thinking she caught me cheating on her or something crazy.

She went into more detail about how they were in a three-year relationship, and she was supposed to be married by now. Then she said, "I'm approaching 30 and should be getting married, not single." I tried to console her and tell her it was okay, but she wasn't trying to hear me. She just kept crying hysterically at the table.

"It's obvious you aren't over this guy," I said to her. She told me she wasn't. Then I asked, "Although he dumped you, would you get back with him if he tried."

Her eyes lit up as she said, "Yea, I would. I would get back with him right now if he asked."

I thought, *why am I here?* That was one of the most awkward dates of my life. She ended up apologizing and even paid for our meal.

REFLECTION

This young lady did what too many grown folks are out here doing: dating with a broken heart. This type of dating is unfair to both parties involved. It's a common myth that the best way to get over someone is to get under someone else. This couldn't be further from the truth. One of the best ways to win in the dating game is to heal before entering a new relationship. Getting into relationships while your heart has not healed will do nothing but add to your brokenness. Things will come up in your new relationship, that you didn't address in the old one.

Both men and women have been guilty of this. Heartbreaks can take a while to get over. You owe it to yourself to heal properly before entering something new, even if it is lonely. Here are some signs to know if you are not healed, healthy, and whole before beginning a new relationship. When approaching a new relationship, you want to be emotionally healthy. Not perfect, but in a space where you won't blame your new person for your ex's mistakes. The good news is that God is close to the brokenhearted, and from our personal experience, His healing is superb, and nothing can compare. Besides crying on a date, here are some signs you aren't ready to get your head back in the dating game.

1. You can't stand the thought of being alone.
2. You try to date someone to suppress your sadness.
3. You still have emotional triggers that you need to address.
4. You rush new relationships and do too much too soon.
5. You don't feel like you have closure from your last relationship.
6. You're not over your ex.

CRAB BOIL

I ran into a girl I hadn't seen in a few years. When we initially met, the timing was terrible. I was in a relationship that was slowly dissolving. I ran into her again, and I figured this was the perfect time to see what was up. I called her to see if she'd like to go to dinner, and she accepted my invitation. To make sure she truly enjoyed herself, I asked where she would like to go. She told me she wanted seafood, so I suggested we go to a crab boil.

The date was going well as we caught each other up on our latest ventures in life. Before our food came out, she hit me with "So...where do you see this going?" I was caught off guard and let her know that I didn't think that far in advance. After all, it had been a while since I had seen her. I was just trying to catch up. After the date, I dropped her off and quickly followed up a week later to see when she would like to connect again. She replied with one of the longest texts I had ever read. I mean, it was so long it could have been a story in this book. She went on a tangent about how she was no longer interested in me. She told me she was ready to be in a relationship, and since I didn't know where I saw it going with her, she was not wasting her time.

I was quite baffled by her response. I told her, "To be honest, I was not even thinking about a relationship." It was quite astonishing because I had just reconnected with shorty, and she already wanted me to wife her. In no space in my mind did I think this was normal or feasible for me. Not to say she wasn't a nice woman, but coming on that aggressive made her less attractive. To keep it a buck, I thought she appeared desperate. For that reason, we no longer stayed in touch.

REFLECTION

To be honest, this is just an extreme of the standards we explain later that we believe that women need to have. The problem is, it was too early to ask this question. Upon this initial meeting, we encourage you to get to know the man before asking him where he thinks the relationship will go. In all honesty, sis you matter too, so take a good look at him first before you ask him a question you also are not sure about.

POP THE SEAL

One of my cousins and I are very close. We attended college on opposite ends of the state. We often kept in touch, and this girl Bianca who stayed on my cousin's floor, saw my picture and wanted to holler at me. I was planning to visit my cousin in a couple of weeks, so Bianca and I stayed in touch and talked over the phone. This was before you could video chat or text photos. So, I knew how she looked from her Black Planet page. In the words of Big Sean, *she was a seven in the face but a ten in the ASS.*

My friend and I drove five hours to visit my cousin at school. I had plans to meet Bianca and hopefully smash her. I was excited as I thought I was going to get it IN! As we laid up on the phone the night before, I made sure everything I said to her was sweet like honey. When I arrived, it was about 3:00 am. I said hi to my cousin and went straight to Bianca's room. When I got there, she had a face full of makeup, booty shorts, and a belly top. A shiny butterfly ring was hanging from her belly button.

Bull's eye, she was ready. She took my shirt off and started kissing all over me. She stripped down to her underwear, and I was ready to go. But the joke was on me. Come to find out, Bianca was a virgin. She wasn't trying to go. She was just teasing me and playing games. Normally, I didn't mess with virgins because I don't like the clinginess and attachment that comes with it. I figured I put this much work in, so I should go ahead and try. I spent the night trying to close out this deal. She wasn't going.

I tried talking her into some fellatio, and she still wasn't going. She started kissing me and left hater marks (hickeys) all over my neck. I'm like, *I have something for you to suck* on. I tried to guide her head in the direction I wanted her to go. But her neck resistance was on point. She wasn't going. I could see the night was a wash, so I gave up and went to sleep. I went back to my cousin's with hickeys all over my damn neck. Bianca wanted to make sure she marked me up so nobody else would try to holler the entire weekend. But it was a lesson learned. It turns out she was crazy anyway. I'm so glad I didn't pop the seal on that one.

REFLECTION

Okay, we have to discuss this as a learning moment. Especially for young people who may be reading this book. No matter how "ready" someone may seem, no means no. In the world of #metoo, it's essential to be careful of the kinds of situations we get in to. We might get a bad rep for saying this, but we will take our chances anyway. To bring change, we must have open conversations to point out growth opportunities for both parties involved.

Being the "everything but sex" girl is a bit of a tease. To strip all the way naked and then share that you are a virgin is setting yourself up for a potentially dangerous situation. As for the guy, if a woman says they don't want to have sex, don't keep pushing it. There's plenty of other ladies willing to say yes without much hesitation. The truth is that women are not objects, but in our hypersexualized world, it's hard to see that. In short, when it comes to sex, it's best to communicate your expectations early on. This situation could have been prevented if expectations were set before hitting the road. Because both parties weren't on the same, it created an awkward moment.

MICROPENIS

I was digging this chick, but she was hesitant to go out with me because of her friends' advice. After tons of conversations and much pursuing, she agreed to go on a date with me. I took her out to eat at a spot downtown. There was a live band and great food. After dinner, we went dancing at a lounge that was playing reggae. We spent the rest of our date grinding on the dance floor and continuing to indulge in multiple drinks.

We became hot and bothered and headed to her house. When we get to her place, we indulged in some outstanding sex. We stayed up laughing, talking and smoking weed until the sun came up. Around 7:00 am, I heard the front door open. My hot date didn't budge, so I asked if she had a roommate. She replied, "It's probably my kid's father." I hopped out of bed and got in defense mode, ready to fight if I needed to. The bedroom opened, and in came her baby's daddy. He stood about 6'4 tall, and I waited for the homey to bug up. Instead, he looked at her and fell to his knees.

"Why do you keep doing this to me? Why?" he screamed.

She looked down at him and said, "You know why."

He said, "You didn't care when we got back together."

At this point, I was spooked because I felt like I'm in a real-life *Trapped in the Closet* situation. Buddy continued to sob on the floor in a fetal position. When I got up to put my clothes on, she looked at him and said, "I can't get past your micropenis, I'm sorry."

After I was finally dressed, I stepped over buddy, who was blocking the door. When I got outside, I remembered I didn't drive. Now I was on her porch calling my guys and cabs to get home. The cab driver was about 15 minutes away, so I rolled another blunt. Baby dick came out of the crib sniffling and said, "Can I hit that blunt?" I'm like, "Sure." He began engaging me in conversation, and I started feeling sorry for him.

He asked if I needed a ride home, and I let him know I was waiting on a cab. He told me to save my money. The entire ride home, this guy told me how he had been messing with his baby mama since high school, and he was her first. He said that as soon as she saw more penises in porn, they watched together, she started treating him differently. When he dropped me off, I called my date from the night before and told her about the conversation. I was like, "WTF!" She confirmed the story and didn't care. It was such a crazy night. It was even wilder that the next day was Thanksgiving, and I was thankful that I didn't have a micropenis.

CHAPTER 15
CRAZY, DERANGED

"A crazy, deranged woman hates to see another woman smile at her man."

—MARTIN LAWRENCE, *YOU SO CRAZY*

As women, nothing ruffles our feathers like a man who is quick to call a woman crazy. Now, be careful if you meet a woman who says she isn't crazy. Most of us have a dash of it in us, and if you press certain buttons, you just may see what level of crazy your woman possesses. But deranged, that's another story. Not only are these women stalkers or abusers, but they are also unpredictable. You never know what will push their buttons.

When we saw *It's a Thin Line Between Love & Hate* while we were younger, we laughed at how Darnell had Brandi acting. We thought that she was crazy. We saw her stalk him, break into his house only to cook burnt bacon, and attempt to electrocute his new bae. In retrospect, we can understand Brandi's approach to being misled after warning Darnell about playing with her heart. He chose to lie to her, and paint a picture that he was unwilling to complete, with genuine care and concern for her soul. When he did that, she snapped.

Everyone has triggers regardless of if they openly speak on them, or not. However, sometimes folks don't need anything to set them off. It's just a matter of them being a little off their rocker. In that case, it causes things to get tricky. Our brothers in this chapter went through some things that we wish they hadn't encountered while keeping their heads in the game.

ONCE SHE WENT BLACK

I had never messed with a White girl in my life but was open to it after a four-hour conversation with a few of my homies. They would tell me all of the positive things White women were about. My first encounter was with a girl named Lindsay. We worked together. I was the first Black guy she dated, so we were in this new experience together. She became my work best friend. After this drunk night, we ended up having sex. We were on our way to becoming sex buddies until she told me that we had to stop or take our relationship seriously.

So, she became my girlfriend. She didn't like that I enjoyed partying and hanging out with my friends, mostly women. We were together for three months before she started switching up on me. Lindsay wanted me to stop hanging out with my friends. I told her she knew certain things about me initially, so she would accept them, or I was out. She continued to nag, so I broke up with her. Lindsay would blow my phone up and show up at my apartment unannounced. I became nervous and told God if He got me out of this stressful situation, I would never talk to her again. She finally left me alone, and everything was all good. When things were running smoothly, I got in a car accident and broke my arm. I couldn't do anything because it was a complete break. I had an arm I couldn't even feel. I started talking to Lindsay again because I needed someone to wash me up and bathe me. I was living the life and forgot how crazy she was. She was giving me showers, baths, and sex.

But of course, I started healing and doing the things she didn't like. I was going out again and hanging out with my female friends. On top of that, she started doing stuff I only heard White girls do: cocaine, acid, and tranquilizer pills. I told her she couldn't do that while with me. She said, "Well, you can't drink." I told her, "Drinking is regular. What you're doing is crazy. Weed is cool." She stopped doing drugs and demanded that I stop hanging out so much. I decided to break it off again. I had promised God that I wouldn't mess with her if He got me out of the previous situation, and here I was again.

When I tried to break it off, she threatened me with suicide. I'm like, *wow! she's really on some crazy shit.* I blocked her on everything, so she started sending my best friend messages. She would ask my friend to tell me to come over immediately. She would also have fake panic attacks. That was wild because I told God I wouldn't do it anymore, and on some BS when I was in need, I did it again. I was so nervous about her killing herself. She was from a hick town, and I didn't want her parents to come after me. Thankfully, the situation died down. Lindsay was the last White girl I dated.

REFLECTION

Before we reflect on this story, we want to point out that crazy, deranged women come in all races. Now, we really can't say that we feel sorry for our friend in this story. He went back a second time out of convenience, and when he no longer found use for her, he continued doing things that any woman would take issue with. This one just happened to be deranged, and the signs were there. Let's also remind you that you asked God to get her away but double-backed when you needed something. Let's explore the crazy, deranged signs ignored.

RED FLAG #1

Being sex buddies before deciding to have a relationship. They didn't get a chance to learn more about each other outside of work. That's until they spent a drunken night together that resulted in sex. The relationship started out of order and, as a result, ended in chaos.

RED FLAG #2

She was doing hard drugs. Dating someone who does hard drugs is a huge red flag. We all know the side effects of drugs, so we will skip the "say no to drugs" talk. Bottom line, this is a red flag.

RED FLAG #3

She was a stalker. Showing up unannounced is a huge red flag. It's always polite to give someone you don't live with a heads-up before showing up on their doorstep.

SUBTWEETS, BLEACH, AND CHICKEN FEET

During my sophomore year in college, I pledged a fraternity. The attention my line brothers and I received caused a lot of static between our girlfriends and us. One of my line brothers ended up breaking up with his girlfriend, who happened to be my girl's friend. Her friend thought that we all had a vendetta against the women we were dating. She told my girl some old news about me and another chick and tried to make it seem current. We broke up.

So, after the breakup, I began dating other girls. My ex and I reconciled and started dating again. This time, I wanted to take it slow because I was still hurt that she believed her friend over me. Since I wasn't in a rush to get back into the relationship, I let her know I was still seeing other people. Knowing that I was seeing other people, she would come to my apartment and leave random items on purpose. One day, we got into a heated argument, and she ended up airing her grievances with me on Twitter. She had various subtweets about me that didn't represent me in a good light. In one of her tweets, she accused me of letting another girl wear her clothes, which couldn't have been further from the truth. I told her another girl couldn't be wearing her stuff. But she refused to believe me.

That year, I became the president of my fraternity and was in charge of the parties. While planning a party, my ex-girl called and asked what I was doing. She began to question me about some things, and I told her because I didn't have anything to hide. I also cared about her. I let her know I was dealing with her but not at the level we were in our relationship before. That night after the party, I went to my room, and it had a weird chemical smell. I began wondering what in the world was going on. I looked around my room, and there were a bunch of my clothes on my bed. They all had tags on them because I hadn't worn them yet. One of the labels had a blotch spot where the price was smeared. There was another blot on my shirt and light spots on my floor. That's when I realized it was bleach.

I knocked on my roommate's door and asked him if anyone had been in my room. He told me that my ex-girlfriend came over to the house and said she had left something and came to get it. I asked if she had anything with her when she came, but he wasn't paying attention. I logged on Twitter and noticed she was subtweeting me and accusing me of letting a girl wear her clothes. I looked behind my door and saw the outfit that she thought I let someone else wear. Now I was furious because she came into my room and bleached my items, including brand new clothes. Probably about $3,000 worth of clothes were damaged, not counting the carpet. I went straight to her dorm with her clothes. I knocked on her door and caused a scene. Security came out, and I left her items with her. We didn't talk for a while. I cared for and loved her too much to try to do anything legally. I had to let that go. We still ended up getting back together. We just took some time to get back to a better point.

When we finally got back on track, she got upset with me again and accused me of talking to a girl in one of my classes. One day after arguing on the phone, I came outside, and there were raw chicken feet at my front door. I immediately knew it was her. She denied it at first but eventually admitted it. We ended up breaking up for good but still keep in contact from time to time. We can now talk and understand this was a time in life that we can now learn from.

REFLECTION

Now, this could have gone in the Love Made a Fool Out of Me chapter. But since it's a man's point of view, we had to add this to Crazy, Deranged. Like the song says, it's a thin line between love and hate. It's true, the sweetest woman in the world can be the meanest woman in the world if you make her that way. We are not saying our friend made this young lady a mean woman, but when a woman feels she has a valid reason for letting out her crazy, she will. In this case, she wanted to be back in a serious relationship with her guy, although he told her he still wanted to see other people. It sounds like she was not ready to receive this critical piece of information hence the subtweets and bleaching of the clothes.

When a woman loves someone, her level of crazy may go up a bit. Whether she's in a relationship or not. This story is a perfect example of how you don't know a woman's crazy level until you push her buttons. In this instance, she showed that when you mess with her emotions, she might try to put some voodoo curse on you by placing chicken feet at your door and bleaching your clothes. While she was just trying to get his attention, this is a form of witchcraft. This instance was not this serious, so we're afraid to know what she would do in a stickier situation.

BYE FELICIA

One Friday night, I met this girl named Felicia while at a club with some friends. She was kind of young, 22, to be exact. During our phone conversations, she talked mostly about her struggles with mental health. After realizing Felicia wasn't emotionally stable to date, I told her it was best to be friends. I wanted to help her from a Christian brother's point of view. She didn't like that idea and insisted that we go on a date and see where it went.

We planned a dinner date at a nice restaurant. Felicia got lost on her way to meet me, so I dropped her my location via iPhone. When this didn't help, I told her to sit still, and I would meet her at her location. It turned out she was right around the corner from the restaurant. When I greeted Felicia, she had this stupid look on her face and was completely silent. I asked, "Is everything okay?" Silence. "Are you hungry?" Silence. "Anything you want to talk about?" Dead silence.

When she finally started talking, Felicia began yelling at me about how upset she was that I left her in an unfamiliar place and could have been raped. I reassured her that she was lost in a nice neighborhood. She wasn't trying to hear me and abruptly walked off without saying a word.

I walked back to my car, thinking the date was over before it even started. As soon as I got in my car, Felicia called, and she started yelling at me again. I told her that I felt disrespected and didn't understand how it was my fault that she got lost. After almost an hour, she apologized and asked if we could continue with the date. I reluctantly agreed, but because we had wasted an hour, the restaurant was closed. I suggested that we grab a quick bite to eat then head to a sports bar.

It wasn't going too bad until she said, "I'm going to ask you a question, and I want a direct answer."

"Okay." I suspiciously said.

"Is there a chance of us being together with my mental health issues and me being so young?"

With a confused look on my face, I said, "It's too early to tell."

She responded, "that's not what I asked. answer the question." It was a yes or no question. But I answered the same way.

When she demanded I answer plainly, I told her, "as of now, no." She got quiet, and after about 30 minutes, we left. While driving Felicia back to her car, she started belittling me and calling me all kinds of expletives. When we arrived at her car, I told her I was not interested in seeing her again. That's when she threw water in my face and began hitting me. Before she got out of the car, Felicia poured water on my seat. She told me that I would be the reason she crashed on the way home. I drove away.

A few days later, Felicia called at 4:00 am to let me know she was at a hotel with a guy. They were in the middle of a fight, and she needed me to come to protect her. I said, "no, let the cops handle it." Of course, she called me out of my name and hung up. That's the last time we spoke. Bye, Felicia.

REFLECTION

Okay, we know that Felicia went crazy on this date. All signs showed that Felicia was not mentally stable to be in any type of relationship anytime soon or ever. Wanting to give her advice as a Christian brother is thoughtful, but you should never feel obligated to do so. Leave that for the professionals. Like some of our guy friends who are naturally nice guys, they go through experiences such as those described in this story.

As soon as she snapped the first time, that was your cue to leave. Felicia already showed herself to be mentally imbalanced on a date. If you would have left her in the parking lot, we wouldn't even have to read about her pouring water in your car seat or answering her 4:00 am call. Speaking of which, we are trying to figure out why would you even answer her call after knowing her mental state? Especially at 4:00 am. When it comes to dealing with someone who shows all signs that they are toxic, it's important to part ways immediately.

BLACK MAN IN AMERICA—A STORY OF PHYSICAL ABUSE

One of my co-workers and I discovered we had a connection and decided to explore it. This connection rapidly grew into an intimate relationship and progressed into a monogamous one. We lived about two minutes away from each other in the same neighborhood. My lease was ending, and so was hers. Our relationship seemed to be headed in the right direction, so we decided to move in together. I had never lived with a woman, and I was ready for this experience.

The first few months were cool, but after the year mark, she started showing her true colors. One day, I came home from work and made a quick bite to eat before watching a basketball game. I put my saucer in the sink and figured I would grab it later. I sat on the couch and turned on the game as I tried to unwind for the day. My girl came into the living room and mentioned the saucer in the sink. I let her know that I would get it later. After all, it was just one dish. She said, "No, you need to wash it now." I laughed because I thought she was joking.

As I laughed, she kept going on about it. I thought, *she needs to chill.* But I'm careful with my words because I know women hate it when men tell them to chill or relax. Before I knew it, my girl rushed toward me and muffed me in the head. I went into another room to watch the game, and she followed me there. I hit up my cousin and asked him to meet me at the bar.

She asked where I was going, and I told her. She followed me as I walked to the door.

That's when she said, "No, we ain't gonna have that in this house."

I laughed again, thinking to myself, *she must be joking, this can't be life.* As I walked out the door, I heard a swoosh sound go past my ear. She had thrown a bottle of Jameson at me before sprinting towards me to engage in a fight. Not wanting to hurt a woman, I pushed her off and held her down until she calmed down. This was the start of physical abuse from the hands of a woman.

When things were good, they were really good. But if I did something she didn't agree with, my girl became extremely aggressive. One day, we were at a lounge celebrating a friend's birthday. My girl got up to use the bathroom. I continued to enjoy myself and was within eye distance from where she was standing in line. A waitress came and tapped me on the shoulder. When I turned around, I was happy to see it was my childhood friend. We hugged and caught up for a couple of minutes. As she left the table, I looked up, and my girl was looking at me while waiting in line. She shook her head and looked at me with disgust. When she returned, she began accusing me of looking at my friend's butt and being flirty. I explained that we went to grade school together and hadn't seen each other in years. I told her I would introduce the two of them. She said, "I don't have to hear anything from that bitch."

I responded by saying, "Let's not get loud. we should continue to enjoy ourselves." I grabbed her hand to walk around, and the whole time she whispered obscenities in my ear. To make matters worse, she kept pinching me in my arm like I was her child. I turned around and said, "I'm out. Find a ride home." I headed out the door, and she trailed me. I told her to go away. She refused to leave and jumped in the car. As I drove, she was in the passenger seat, screaming at me. When I ignored her, she said, "You're not listening to me." After this, she grabbed the steering wheel. My car did a crazy turn into the gas station at full speed and almost hit a pump. That's when I jumped into survival mode. I grabbed her by the head and pushed her against the window until she let go of the steering wheel.

She ran into the gas station and told the attendant I had assaulted her. The police arrived immediately, and without asking what happened, they put me in cuffs. After my girl said to them that she was okay, they released me. On the way home, she apologized. And guess what? I apologized too. Things eventually blew over, but there were a couple of more incidents before I decided to leave.

The last straw was when I came home after an unknown curfew she enforced. When I walked in, all of my clothes and personal items were in garbage bags. I pulled out my cell phone to record her yelling and cussing at me. After having an incredible amount of footage, I pressed save. When I looked up, all I could see was her fist coming toward my face. She punched me in my right eye and continued to swing. I held her down until she was calm. When I let her up, she said, "I'm going to call the police. You're a Black man in America." She is Black, too, might I add. "They are going to get you before they get me." While holding her down, I didn't notice she had bitten me and took a chunk out of my shoulder. I had scratches on my shoulder, and my t-shirt was ripped.

I had become accustomed to the police coming, so I sat and waited until they arrived. Two White officers came, and again, they put me in handcuffs with no questions asked. As they escorted me out, the sergeant walked in. He looked at me and then at my girlfriend with a confused look on his face. He said, "Take those cuffs off of him and put them on her." That's when she lost it. She didn't think there would be a day when a White officer would take some time to observe what was going on. Instead, she relied on the history of police brutality against Black men and felt they would adhere to her false allegations. This time, I was asked if I wanted to press charges. I thought about the times I was cuffed, and she didn't press charges and told them no.

The sergeant pulled me to the side and asked if he could give me some advice off the record. "Leave that crazy bitch alone and never look back." I went to my mom's and paid my portion of the bills and rent until the lease was up. I still don't know what made me stay so long. I guess women aren't the only ones that can have Battered Woman Syndrome.

REFLECTION

This was a very tough story to hear, but it's something to address. When we think of abusive relationships, we usually think it applies to women being abused by men. But there are lots of men who have been mentally and physically abused by women. What makes this so sad is that a Black woman used the fact that her man was a Black man in America against him. Out of all the things Black men go through from just being Black, it's sad that he had to encounter such madness. Reading this story would make you wonder why our friend didn't leave at the first sign of abuse, but that's easier said than done.

CHAPTER 16
F*@# BOY MOMENTS

F*@# Boy

A guy with the body of a man and the mind of a perverted teenager. He has no heart, just a penis that he uses to paint the town.

—URBAN DICTIONARY

The unanswered texts with the read receipt. Mixed messages. Resurfacing after disappearing for days without any explanation. He could be as simple as the "Hey Babe" guy to as shady as "Claude the Fraud" that we read about in Part I. He will ask you out on a date and won't follow up to make plans, and when it comes to pursuing a woman, he has no ambition. He would rather let her do all the chasing because it feeds the ego. He thinks he's the prize and is everything but that. In our day, we called him a scrub. He has also been defined as a playboy. Generations later, he's a certified f*@# boy.

We recommend being careful when using this term and not throwing it around because you think all men fit in this category. Instead of being quick to label a guy a f*@# boy, it's essential to understand what this means and the key signs of one. Some women have misclassified a man as a f*@# boy simply because he wasn't interested in her. We have guy friends that had a f*@# boy moment or two while others went through an entire phase. A few of them were brave enough to admit they have had one of these moments. Here are some stories from our friends who used their loins to determine their behavior.

WANTING WHAT I CAN'T HAVE

When I first got to college, I had only one sexual experience. It was with my first love. Our relationship ended because she cheated on me with another girl. I showed up to campus fresh on some f*@# boy sh*t. I wanted to see if I had what it took to be "the man." I began messing with a bunch of girls and thought that was cool.

I ended up dating a girl named Brandy. When we returned sophomore year, she wanted to talk to me heavily. I didn't and told her I wasn't looking for anything serious. I told her the truth about where I was in my dating life while still sparing her a few details. However, I expressed that I was single and could do whatever I wanted, so it was her choice to mess with me. With Brandy wanting me so bad, I felt like I had the upper hand. She was a good girl, and I felt in control of our situation. I was doing my thing. I didn't want to be with her, but we still had sex. It worked for me because, as time went on, I realized we didn't have a connection outside of anything physical. Because one of my homies was a snitch, Brandy also knew everything I was doing.

There was one girl in particular that I liked. I didn't care if Brandy knew. She would come back and say, "I heard you were walking Aundrea to class." I wanted Aundrea so badly. She was a beautiful girl from St. Louis. Even though I wanted her, she had a guy back home. Since I couldn't be her guy, I tried to woo her as a friend. I would have sex with Brandy to curb my appetite before going to visit Aundrea. I just really enjoyed Aundrea's company and wanted her bad.

At the same time, I was doing Brandy real dirty. I would see her like every few days and call only for sex. It's such a crazy story because Brandy wanted me, but I didn't want her because I was interested in Aundrea. I only had sex with Brandy because Aundrea didn't want me. Anytime Aundrea hit me, I pulled up. I didn't care what time it was; I would leave. Wherever she wanted to go, I went. I smoked weed with her, and I didn't even smoke. I couldn't help it; I just wanted her so bad. I was willing to do whatever it took.

Brandy must have felt the same way because she was doing whatever it took to keep me around. Not only was she sexing me, but she was also spending money on me because she really wanted me to be with her. But if Aundrea called when I was with Brandy, I would leave at the drop of a dime. Aundrea ended up transferring to another school, but I will never forget her. Brandy and I messed around on and off for the next seven years. She was always available.

REFLECTION

This story is not just an example of a man treating a woman based on how she values herself. It's also an example of a narcissist. Brandy gave this guy everything. All she got in return was an emotionally unavailable man. We wonder how he would have treated Aundrea if she would have given this guy everything he wanted. He probably would have got tired of her too. We all know that guys will do whatever it takes to get the girl of their dreams.

Sometimes, women give a guy all the fuel they need to tap into their inner f*@# boy. It comes from a good place because you are so into this guy. Unfortunately, being nice isn't what will make a guy realize what's in front of his face. It's okay for girls like Brandy to let a guy put in some work, as we see in the case with Aundrea. Because she wasn't available in the way our friend wanted her, he did everything within his power to get with her, but she wasn't going.

OUT WITH THE OLD, IN WITH THE NEW

I was in a five-year relationship with DD, and we were beginning to talk about marriage and children. We lived together. One day, she told me she felt I was immature and irresponsible. I was, but as a man, that hurt to hear something like that coming out of my woman's mouth. I was careless with money. She was financially stable. During one of our arguments, she said she would never have a child with me.

I wanted to be married and have a family, but the relationship was now turning sour. It felt more like a mother and son relationship than a girlfriend and boyfriend relationship. Also, she was a daddy's girl, and I felt some way about it. If something needed fixing in the house, she would call him instead of me. I would come home, only to see her dad repairing something in the house. I'm like, *What's going on? This is our house together.* I got fed up, so I ended up moving on with another girl named Jada.

DD called one day and said she needed someone to look at her car. I told her to come to my house. I had moved in with my brother. She brought the car by, and I fixed what was wrong with it. She asked to see the new apartment. While showing her my bedroom, we talked. One thing led to the other, and while having sex, I kept looking at the time because Jada would be coming through in a little bit.

When we finished, I rushed DD out the door and told her I needed to head out. I got her out just in the nick of time. As she pulled off, I waved goodbye. DD left one way, and Jada came from the opposite direction. She saw me at the door and thought I was waiting for her. As I waved bye to DD, it looked like I was waving hi to Jada. She walked in, and I led her to my bedroom to finish what DD and I started.

REFLECTION

The only reason we put this story in this chapter is because he had sex with one girl and was gearing up to have sex with another. This is an example of a guy who can have f*@# boy moments and still be a decent guy. Based on his story, he wanted to be a good man to DD. He was just immature. He was in a relationship and was contemplating marriage, but shortly after, he was willing to engage in a new situation. It's important to note the admittance of his immaturity; perhaps that's why she continued to call her daddy when she needed things done.

As much as we want to place fault somewhere, we can see the flaw in both sides. Immaturity is a major factor in why relationships struggle to move ahead. Telling a man that you don't want to have a child with him is a real blow to his manhood. However, being a man admitting to immaturity, we can only imagine her side of the story. Overall it is best to mature and grow from the relationship before you engage in another situation.

BUT I MET YOUR MOM

I went on a date with my college buddy's sister. She seemed cool, and I was slightly interested in seeing what she was about. She invited me to go to a Maxwell concert with her at the Mercedes Superdome in New Orleans. I picked her up, and before we made it to the venue, I already knew this would be our last date. Just by our conversation, I could tell she was the clingy type. I found out, later on, she was like that with everybody. My mom and her girlfriends were at the same concert that night. I didn't think anything of it because everyone loves Maxwell. I also didn't expect to run into her because of the size of the venue.

My mom was a helicopter mom well into my 20s. Any girl that interacted with me would meet my mom. It didn't matter if they were girlfriends, friends, or anybody. My mother met anybody who came into my life, so it was never a big deal. She wanted to make sure if something went down, she knew who to question. I spotted my mom in a line waiting to grab drinks with her friends. Not thinking about this, I let the girl know I spotted my mom and had to say hello to her. I could not be rude. I mean, she did bring me into this world. My date grabbed my hand as we walked over. I wasn't thinking anything of it because I wasn't trying to pursue her in that manner. She wanted to pursue me. I held her hand as we walked toward my mom. After saying hello, I introduced them. We then grabbed some food before the concert began.

For about two weeks after our date, I dodged her text messages and told her I was busy. Since I knew her brother, I didn't want to ghost her completely. But she kept reaching out. I guess she felt a little more deeply about it than I did. One day, she called me. I figured I would just pick up the phone and let her know I wasn't as interested as she was. She asked if we could meet at this spot that had some delicious bread pudding. I agreed. While sitting outside eating, I had a conversation with her. I felt like I was ending a relationship that never happened. She went ape shit and started yelling, "But I met your mom!"

I told her, "Everybody meets my mom. It's no big deal." I also reminded her that she met my mom because we ran into her at the same concert we were attending. You would have thought I was getting down on one knee, proposing to her because she met my mama.

Then she said, "But we were holding hands."

At this point, I tried to get this crazy heifer away from me and prayed she wouldn't do some Louisiana voodoo. "You grabbed my hand!" I yelled back. In retrospect, I could see how other people may have acted in that matter, and that could be signs that things were going in a way that I didn't see them going. Still, you have to have conversations with people. Don't try to jump into a relationship because you met my mama when everybody meets her. It's not a big deal.

REFLECTION

Ladies, just because you met his mama doesn't mean that he's ready for a serious relationship. That's unless he's the guy from the *I Don't Want to Meet Your Mama* story in Part I. However, this is some classic f*@# boy behavior. This guy blurred the lines by even going on a date. He knew she was clingy but accepted the invitation to see Maxwell. I mean, we understand why you would want to go, but his concerts should be attended with someone special, and you were not into her. If you didn't want to hold her hand, you could have pulled it away.

Instead of dodging her calls and texts, you should have responded, letting her know that you weren't interested. To meet up with her again and get her hopes up is like firing someone on Monday morning when you could have told them at the end of the day on Friday. What's the point? You tried to be Mr. Nice Guy, but sorry sir, this was a f*@# boy moment.

REAGAN AIRPORT

While transitioning out of a relationship, I connected with someone from my college days. My live-in girlfriend and I had broken up, and we were living as roommates until the lease was up. I didn't know if my ex was going on dates or entertaining other people. I didn't care if she was. I wasn't dating until someone I had a real connection with started contacting me. She lived on the East Coast, and I was residing in the Midwest. I shared with her the details of my current situation, and she was okay with it. I didn't want my ex to know I was interested in someone else, so my new friend knew what times to call me before I got home.

One day, she told me she wanted to see me and asked if I would come out to the DMV (DC, Maryland, and Virginia area) to see her. I decided to grant her request and told my ex/roommate that I would be out of town for the weekend. When she inquired about where I was headed, I lied and told her I was heading to the DMV to check out some graduate schools. I wasn't ready for her to know I was going to see a new girl.

My new friend picked me up at Reagan National Airport. We were thrilled and greeted each other with a hug and kiss. As soon as we kissed, I knew this wasn't it. I didn't have that feeling. There was no spark. I instantly decided this wasn't going to work for me. Since we had an entire weekend to get through, I figured I would make the best of it. We made plans to go out for the night. We had a really good time catching up. When we went back to her place, we got into bed together. As we lay, I was on the other side of the bed. She noticed I wasn't trying to touch her and asked what was going on with me. I lied and said even though I wasn't with my ex/roommate, being in the space with her made me realize I still have feelings.

She said, "Okay." After getting out of bed, she put on her clothes. She then snatched the covers off me and said, "Grab your bags. I'm dropping you off at the airport." It's about 1:00 am, and I have no idea when the next flight would leave. This was during a time when you didn't have the luxury to just look up flights on your phone. She didn't care that it was the middle of the night. Instead, she dropped me off at the airport and sped off like a thief in the night.

Reagan is one of the smaller airports in the United States, and flights weren't coming in every hour on the hour. I approached the counter to switch my ticket. The lady working told me the next flight was at 10:00 am. It was almost 2:00 am, and I had nowhere to go. The nice lady told me, "You can spend the night in the airport." I didn't think it was such a bad idea. That's until I learned that the airport was about to close. I mean, completely shut down. The lights and heat went off, and I was sitting in a chair, unable to lay down. I was cold as hell and sitting in a dark airport. I went into my suitcase and put on a layer of clothes and eventually fell asleep while sitting up in the chair.

When I woke up, it was 9:00 am. People were walking around while I looked like the bum who slept in the airport. By the time I returned home, my ex/roommate and the girl from the DMV had already had a conversation. Thanks to social media, Facebook, to be exact, she messaged my ex and told her everything. They became comrades and exchanged information about me. Both of them had fun dragging my name through the mud. I learned never to take a trip where someone else is in control of where I'm staying and what I'm doing. I also learned the importance of ending a relationship before starting a new one.

REFLECTION

Okay, our friend definitely tapped into his inner f*@# boy, which is why he ended up sleeping in the airport. You weren't honest with your ex/roommate, and opened up someone's feelings and got her excited about a potential relationship. Only to leave her feeling crushed. He also didn't share with her the real reason he wasn't feeling her like that. As soon as he wasn't into her, he dipped without telling her the truth. Fellas, this is something a lot of you have a habit of doing. You would rather dip than have that hard conversation. When this happens, you have to be ready for the consequences that come along with it.

NOKIA 5300

I was dating a woman I will refer to as *Main.* She was delightful, caring, loving, and supportive. I met her at a friend's house party. It was a random night, and I wasn't expecting to meet any potential love interest. I had just ended a toxic relationship and felt broken.

While enjoying my time, Main approached me and asked what type of phone I had. Not thinking about it, I gladly showed her my newly purchased NOKIA 5300 slider phone. I probably dated myself with that information, but that shows you how long ago this happened. As I explained all of the features, she seemed intrigued. Main's interest in my phone left me wondering if she was interested in my phone or if this was a subtle way to shoot her shot. I no longer questioned her motives after she asked for my number, and things took off expeditiously from there.

Within weeks, Main and I were exclusive, and before we knew it, we were officially together. Problems began to arise as fast as the relationship started, and this was primarily my fault. I had just left a relationship, and BOOM immediately jumped into another without being fully ready to commit. While with Main, I was still entertaining other women.

I had one woman I sporadically entertained for years. She had mistress qualities, so we'll call her *Mistress.* This woman knew I was in a relationship and was comfortable with sex on the side. Mistress and I would discreetly meet for random sexual encounters. Together, we would come up with lies to tell Main when she questioned my whereabouts.

There were a few times when Main almost caught me cheating. One time, I was leaving Mistress's place on the other side of town. While driving, I stopped at a traffic light, and who pulled up on my right? It was Main, and she had just left an event at the same time I had finished hanging out with Mistress. From her vehicle, she called me on my handy-dandy Nokia and asked where I had been. I gave her the lie Mistress, and I came up with and told her I was leaving an event with my frat brothers.

I think it was at that moment that she figured out I wasn't shit. Main never caught me cheating, but something in her just knew that I wasn't right. I guess that's what you call women's intuition. Fast forward two to three months, I had planned a huge birthday party downtown. It had taken some time to plan, and Main helped with the planning and set up. She informed me of a family function happening on the same night and told me she would be late for my party.

As the night went on, I hadn't heard from her. She hadn't been answering my calls or texts. The event ended, and she never showed up. I called her several times the next morning but didn't hear from her. I went to her place, but she wasn't there. At this point, I was beyond worried. But then she contacted me later the next night. I was upset as hell on the phone that she missed my event.

Meanwhile, she was calm and in a chill state. She told me that she didn't make the event because she spent the night at her male friend's place. I became even more upset and loud on the phone while she continued in her chill state. I repeatedly asked what happened during this little sleepover. She initially tried to convince me that nothing happened, but I knew. Just like she knew I wasn't really with my frat brothers when she saw me at the traffic light.

After much interrogation, Main eventually told me that she slept with her male friend and wanted to pursue a relationship with him. She told me that I didn't appreciate her love and support, and I had taken her for granted. And I did. I can admit that now. One of the best women I had the opportunity to date helped me plan the party (that she had no intention of attending) so that I would have a great time while she slept with her best friend on my birthday. Now that's gangsta. Some gift, right? I was upset and hurt for years after. I knew that I had lost someone so special simply because I couldn't commit to keeping it in my pants.

Fortunately, ten years later, Main and I are great friends. All has been forgiven. She and her male friend never did quite work out, but it was something she had to experience. Just as I had to suffer the consequences of my careless actions, that experience changed my life forever. It's funny that it all started with a conversation about a Nokia 5300. That same phone that she called at the traffic light. That same phone I used to call and text her the night of my birthday. That same phone I used to hear her tell me that she slept with her friend and that we were over. Moral of this story: I'm glad I will never see a Nokia again. It always makes me think about the time I got played.

REFLECTION

To our friend who was brave enough to say he messed up with Main, thank you. Sometimes women need to know men's actions had nothing to do with them. We are glad that you two were able to become friends and laugh about this situation. We would like to point out three things that fueled these f*@# boy moments.

1. *This guy jumped into a new relationship before getting over the former one.* Instead of going through the emotions that come with ending a relationship, he tried to suppress them with something new. He tried to heal with Main and Mistress. Many men participate in f*@# boy behavior because they are broken men seeking validation by playing women.
2. *He was dealing with a woman who encouraged this behavior.* Because Mistress was okay with a physical relationship, she helped him come up with a lie to tell Main. Where is the girl code or sisterhood that we have abandoned to tend to our selfishness? At some point, we have to understand that as women, if we all said no to these ridiculous relationships, it raises the bar for all men. Mistress is one of the reasons, so many men think it's okay to have f*@# boy behavior.
3. *He had a Nokia.* No, that's just a small joke to keep you laughing. Kudos to Main, who was on to our friend and held her head in the

dating game.

STORY FROM AN OG

As it relates to my dating experiences, all I can say is, "it was hell when I was well, and I was seldom sick." I've had so many encounters that I could write an entire book, but I will spare you all the details. I was something else back in my day. I had a lot of women who wanted me, and I used my penis to paint the town. Keep that in mind, as you read this story.

It was a Friday night, and I was supposed to go to my lady's house. She was pregnant with my child. We had plans to hang out, and after I arrived at her house, I remembered I had a lady coming in from out of town to see me. I told my lady I was going to hang out with the fellas and would return a little later. I took a shower and headed to the Westside of Chicago to meet this fine young lady.

While my out-of-town guest was in the club waiting, guys were standing around her, wanting to talk. She dissed them by saying, "I'm waiting on my guy." One of the guys happened to be my friend. He asked her what man was keeping her waiting. After telling him it was me, she said, "When he gets here, I'm going to f*@# his brains out." I arrived at the club. We sat at the bar and had a few drinks. Soon after, I took her to the hotel where she was staying. After she did precisely what she told my boys she was planning to do, I told her I had to leave. I was supposed to head back to my baby mama's house, but I ended up at another spot where I met a new young lady. When we were leaving, she asked for a ride to her hotel downtown. At this point, it was early in the morning. About 6:00 am. While on our way, I thought to myself, *Okay, this is enough. I told my lady I was hanging out with my boys, and she's not going to believe me.*

I pulled over on the expressway and told the new lady, "Look, I was supposed to be somewhere else. I'm going to pull over, let you out, and give you cab money." But she refused to get out of the car. Like I said, I was wild during this time in my life. I carried a gun with me everywhere I went and always had liquor with me. I usually kept the gun in the trunk, but I put it under my armrest that night. I was going to another side of town and wanted to keep it close to me in case I had any trouble. Since she didn't want to get out, I told her, "I have something to get you out of the car." I got out of the car to get the gun out of the trunk. When I couldn't find it, I realized it was in my armrest.

When I got back in the car, she looked me dead in my eyes and said, "Are you looking for this?" She had my gun pointed at me. I sat there for a minute, frozen and wondering what I was going to do. Finally, I just swung at her. She hit the door and fell out of the car. We were on the highway where it was four lanes headed south, and four lanes headed north. She jumped up with the gun in hand, and I chased after her. She would stop, freeze, and keep running. We went across the four lanes headed south then crossed off the four lanes headed north. That's when she spotted a truck full of guys who were at work. She jumped in with them.

The next thing I saw were police cars surrounding me, and I wound up going to jail. I had no idea how I was going to explain this situation. I had white pants on with grass stains all over. I called one of my boys to bail me out. When he came, he looked at me and shook his head. He said, "I don't even want to know." He always reminds me of that story.

REFLECTION

This story read like an old Blaxploitation film. Which is why we decided not to go too hard on this OG. However, it makes us think about the young men who think they are playas in this game. They are nothing compared to this OG and the auntie who knew a fast one was coming. Jokes on you, OG. Can't outwit a woman. We don't have much more to say because, honestly, this story left us speechless. Don't be surprised if it's turned into a film or scene in a movie. All we can say is, every dog has his day. Just like the OG in the next story.

I'VE FALLEN AND I CAN'T GET UP

As I laid on the floor and looked up at the ceiling, I thought of a moment in time, 36 years ago, that led to this moment. I realize that the bump on my head and pain in my back does not compare to the pain that comes from my memory. It was a warm spring day in Chicago in 1984, and I was driving down Lake Shore Drive in my silver Corvette. I was living life as a 27-year old Black man, and it couldn't get any better than this. I raced down the Drive blasting *Jungle Love* by Morris Day in my speakers. I thought about how I had no worries, a thriving business, a plethora of women, and as the youngsters say, "a strong pull out game." I take that back. I had a few worries because though my game was superb, I tended to treat women too well.

They all wanted to be with me, and this was the extent of my headaches. Looking back, this was a nightmare, and I could have advanced much further in life had I not been so engrossed with my distractions. But hindsight is 20-20, and I have always worn glasses and am nearsighted. I guess in my wisdom at 63-years old, I see that this is where my vision is still blurry. Anyway, I stopped at several different women's houses on this day in time, and two were friends with each other. One knew I was dealing with the other but didn't trip much because the loving was so good. The other skeez was from Columbia and always had the best blow for the parties I threw at a nightclub I owned. They were both fine as hell and never felt three was a crowd. I had a main squeeze, though, and out of respect, I always came home to her at night. Her name was Allison, and after leaving my side pieces, I scooped her from our house to go pick out clothes for my brand-new baby niece.

Allison was polished, beautiful, and bright. The depth of our relationship was very promising. She had been around for my brother's death, assisted me with my businesses, knew all my family, and kept my secrets. Yet, I secretly was still searching for perfection in other women. I will never forget this day because things didn't get better how my uncles told me it would when you play the field. After finding cute little pink shoes for my little niece, we made our way to the hospital. My younger brother had his first child, and I never wanted to be bound by any children. I held this little girl, and somehow, I could feel she was the precursor to my life going in another direction.

Later while at home, Allison and I were watching a movie. Cable was fairly new, and we were excited not to see the lady who had fallen and couldn't get up. I never understood how you could fall and not get up and always laughed at this commercial. In the '80s, cable cords would hang from the house. As I was spooning on the couch with Allison, the cable goes out, and I hear someone yelling my name outside. "Calvin, Calvin!" As I listened to the woman screaming, I sat there thinking about how I could diffuse the situation.

The voice got louder as she moved closer to the door. Just then, I heard another woman yelling, "Calvin!" I thought, *damn, it's two of them, and one cut the cable cord.*

Allison sits up, turns to me, and says, "I know you didn't let your dirt come to our house!" She jumps up and goes to the door while I sat frozen. I couldn't come up with anything to say quick enough to stop her. She opens the door, and the two "buddies" were both standing there. I quickly learned that they called Allison at work the day prior and came to prove the two of them had been in our bed.

Somehow before cell phones and GPS devices, these detectives were well equipped to track down a suspect, and I was the criminal. I was guilty of stealing the hearts of these women, and this is when being a Gigolo lost all of its perks. Allison didn't entirely leave me that day, but I knew her heart was gone by looking in her eyes. She had been dealing with my BS for years, and I saw that this was the last straw. She slowly distanced herself from me and ultimately moved out, and I never tried to stop her.

Years later, I now am close to my niece as if she were my own. I listen to her dating experiences and find myself telling her to stay away from all the men who are just like me. After hearing her cries and relationship failures, I could see how much damage I had done in my youth. After failed businesses, fruitless relationships, two children I barely know by my 3:00 am's, whose mama's I knew much less, life never gained much luster from then. I looked for Allison in many women, and I never seemed to find her after that. It's funny how I played her thinking I could do better in my quest to catch perfection because I caught everything but that. Thirty-six years later, I got a Facebook page and searched my "one that got away."

I sent her a message, but she didn't reply. Instead, she tagged me to her wedding picture on her page for me, and all of my friends and family to see that she was happy. I was humiliated because, at that point, she was gone and was giving a huge signal she was not glad to hear from me. My niece told me I should have apologized to her because I never did, I guess my pride still had the best of me. Instead of apologizing, I mentioned Allison's faults to my niece as justification to not have faced her.

A few days later, I was standing on a ladder to water plants I had hanging from a high ceiling. My foot slipped, and I fell and could not move for an entire day. All the things you can imagine you can't do while immobile for 24 hours happened, and somehow that old 80's commercial was no longer funny. There was no one to call. Nor was my cell phone close, and unfortunately, neither was the bathroom—no Allison to save me.

In my bachelor pad, there was never a wife, never the pitter-patter of little feet, and in fact, I was a grandfather who didn't get to raise my children. Though once filled with top-notch women and the pick of the litter, my life left me understanding that the game had indeed played me. I laid in agony but not just from the pain in my head and back, but the pain in my heart that was proof I had been deceived. Like the women who had fallen for me and I abandoned, I had fallen and could not get up. I thought life as a player made me the man, but looking back, it only made a fool of me.

REFLECTION

Talk about pride coming before the fall. One thing about this story is that it is full of lessons. At his best, this man acted his worst and never thought to choose quality while he was at the height of his prime. He was too engaged in juggling women. He didn't know he would look as silly as a cat distracted with a ball of yarn. He sought an advantage over women, but time would reveal he was wasting his own time. It is easy not to see life passing you by when you commit to fruitless endeavors.

Because old unc' thought he was a professional player, he didn't expect that at 27, he would be forced into retirement. How many men are dealing with someone special who they know they don't want to get away but are treating her as if she is a permanent fixture? The biggest mistake is when people think good things last forever. We ask that while you are able-bodied, take the one you love off the shelf and make it forever. We would hate that it wouldn't be safe for you to water your plants all because you took your soulmate for granted.

CHAPTER 17
LET'S TALK ABOUT IT

"Can we just talk? Can we just talk?
Talk about where we're going? Before we get lost."

—KHALID, *TALK*

It's time for a little transparency. The topics in this chapter are kind of touchy, but significant in evolving our relationships with each other. There are some things that women only discuss with other women, and men only discuss with other men. To support our mission of changing the narrative, let's try something new and talk to each other. We want to bring to your attention issues that have been avoided. Some of them are a little taboo, but they play a massive role in failed relationships and generational curses in our community. Get ready for some honest conversations that can help us move forward during our relationship journeys. Grab a group of your best guy and girlfriends, read these stories together, and share your perspective with each other.

OUT OF MY LEAGUE

I was bored in the house on a Friday night when my best female friend Angela hit me up to see if I wanted to accompany her to her sorority sister Mia's 30th birthday party. I didn't have any other plans and figured I'd put on some decent clothes and hang out for a bit. I was also secretly crushing on Mia and didn't want to miss a chance to see her. Either way, it would be a fun time because her sorors were the TLC'S crazy, sexy, cool type. So, it didn't take much for Angela to convince me to go outside.

On my way to the party, I picked up a rosé champagne bottle for the birthday girl. The party was in a private hall located about an hour outside of the city. I arrived before Angela and waited for her so that we could make an entrance together. When she pulled up about five minutes later, we went into one of the liveliest birthday parties I had attended. The DJ was playing all of the hits from college. In real women fashion, Mia didn't make her arrival until about an hour later. It was only right that she made an entrance. The DJ started to play the latest Beyoncé song that everyone's mother, sister, and auntie loved. I looked up, and Mia was strutting in the room in some red heels and a short black dress that hugged her curves but didn't show too much. Birthday or not, her presence lit up the room. Not only was she beautiful, but she also exuded the type of confidence that I didn't feel in myself. I mean, I had my share of girls that I was messing with, but none of them exuded the type of energy Mia had with everyone she encountered. There was something different about this one. I had never experienced someone like her before.

Her presence had me barely able to speak. When Mia approached me, I froze. I hadn't frozen like that in a long time, if ever. It was as if she was some kind of superhuman. She greeted me and thanked me for attending her party. A few days later, I asked Angela to put me on. She told me just to shoot my shot. She let me know that a group of them would be attending a happy hour later on in the week and invited me to come. I went, but for some reason, I was too nervous to say anything. I never worked up the courage to approach Mia. To this day, I still don't know what made me freeze like Arnold Schwarzenegger in Batman when he played Mr. Freeze. It drives me crazy just thinking about it. She was just out of my league.

REFLECTION—ERIKA

Being a proud GIRL BOSS, I can attest that many women like me have got the short end of the stick when it comes to relationships. I have had men tell me I remind them of so many powerful women they admire yet, they have never made any type of move. They may flirt a little, but when it comes to pursuing me, they tend to go for the woman who seems less confident. A lot of men say they want a confident woman, and when one crosses their path, they don't know what to do with her.

Fellas, you may think that because a woman appears to be independent and got her own, that there's no use for you. But this couldn't be further from the truth. Yes, she's confident, but she's also a human being just like you. She makes mistakes and might be overcoming insecurities; you'd find it hard to believe that she even possesses. When they get rejected because they appear to be out of someone's league, it can cause some hurt and new insecurities. I am thankful that my friend admitted that he thought this woman was out of his league but sad because I know both parties involved, and they could have potentially made a great pair.

So, to the men who have met someone they feel is out of their league, I challenge you to give this type of woman a try. She is fearless and knows how to bring out the king in her man. Contrary to what you may believe, she's a leader but knows how to let her man lead. A woman who is walking in her purpose wants and needs a man who can cover her and provide the type of support she needs. The greatest thing about this woman is that she is ready to take care of a home, and in addition to her goals, your goals are meaningful to her as well. Whether you are in the beginning stages of starting your career, creating a new business, or bossed up with millions of dollars in your bank, this type of woman will take what you have and multiply it.

Now, there are a lot of guys who love this type of woman, but they too seem to be rare. In my experience, we have more guys saying, "somebody else will do you better." It makes me wonder how many amazing, single, self-assured women would be in a relationship if more guys sought this type of woman instead of going for the one who seems more convenient.

NIESHA

I used to think it was cute when I was younger, and a guy was too shy to admit he was crushing on me. As I grew up and became more mature in my dating life, I saw a pattern in my relationships. The men that I found myself dating in my mid-20s and early 30s felt that I was too ambitious, and our relationship eventually fizzled out. In the beginning, all the hype was about having a strong queen on their team. However, as I did things that drove my spirit and fed my passions, I was often told I was "doing too much." At times, it just appeared that it was easier to be "extra" in their eyes while I continued to pursue my dreams. It was almost as if it would've worked out if they only had to deal with a timid, dainty, and ditsy lady who always "went with the flow."

I've always enjoyed being confident in my truth of who I am and, more importantly, what I want in this lifetime. While I've always heard that confidence is a great attribute to have, in the atmosphere of dating, sometimes being confident can cause folks to feel teeny tiny. In being a strong woman who is sure of what she has to offer, why would I ever dim my light to make someone else comfortable? The answer to this question is why it's vital to be equally yoked with your person. When this is the scenario, experiencing bliss becomes more of a reality rather than a Cinderella-induced fantasy.

F.C.U.K.

In my industry, I go to a lot of events, conferences, balls, and galas. Most of them are the same: sociopaths, sycophants, rich White folks, intellectuals, industry leaders, and bleeding hearts. I don't even know why I go to them. Maybe I just want something to do, or perhaps I'm a sociopath. At the very least, there is always great food and booze. Cipriani, I love you. The Met, yessir. All-Star Weekend come through. Regardless, I am there. Live and in full effect. I am an active observer and participant in the social circus.

One night, I was at a charity event. It was fall, and nothing beats a perfect October night in NYC. I was walking the floor, hobnobbing, and making casual conversation. Out of the corner of my eye, I saw a beautiful woman who was dressed avant-garde. She had her hair pulled into two giant cornrows and was wearing large silver hoop earrings, a navy blazer, bell bottoms, and a deep V-neck blouse. She was ethnically ambiguous, her skin was olive, and she had hazel-ish eyes and full lips. I was mesmerized.

She was the unofficial star of the show that night. It seemed like everyone wanted to make their way over to speak with her. I could tell by her look, body language, and the expressions on her face that she wasn't American. Her accent had to be messing people up because they gave that curious squint and head nod that people do when they are confused yet still interested in a conversation.

The program for the night had begun, so I made my way over to her. I introduced myself and told her that I liked her outfit. I asked if she worked in fashion (everyone with an ounce of style will receive that as a compliment), and she replied, "No." She was a director of a non-profit.

"Celine" had a great voice and accent. It was French with a hint of British English. I asked where she was from. She told me her father was from London and her mother was from Africa. I asked her where in Africa, and she smiled, "Guess."

I said, "Senegal."

She replied, "Wrong Coast."

Then I said, "Madagascar."

Her eyes got bright, and she said, "Wow, you know your geography, huh? Sorry, that's close, but no cigar. One more guess, then I gotta go!"

I told her that I didn't want her to leave and that I was going to guess correctly. I stared at her and racked my brain. I thought of all the French African colonies in my head then cross-referenced them by being on the East Coast of the continent.

Celine sipped her drink and said, "You'll never get it."

I blurted out, "The Comoros!"

She laughed in astonishment and spat her drink out a little bit. I helped her with her mouth. She said, "Who told you that? There is no way you could have guessed that."

I told her that I have a photographic memory and that I won the geography bee every year from 6th to 8th grade. She laughed some more, and I asked her if she wanted to grab another drink outside of this bougie establishment. She said yes, and we went to another intimate bougie spot down the street and around the corner.

We spent about three hours laughing and drinking. Celine had one of the most interesting life stories I had ever heard. Her father was in the military and a professor. Her mother also held a Ph.D. Celine was born in the Comoros but lived in Paris, London, Nice, Rome, and Johannesburg. I was utterly lost in her eyes and enamored by every word she spoke.

We went our separate ways then spent about a week texting one another. I invited Celine to my place for dinner and a movie. We ate, drank, laughed, and made out. Then we took it to my bedroom and did what grown folks do at night. The sex was good. Celine was super passionate, and I loved how she said my name. We went for two rounds before I passed out. When I woke up in the morning, she was up and putting her stuff on. I took a good look at her body. Celine was tall and modelesque. She was different from my typical taste of the opposite gender. Typically, I like a bigger woman. She was about 5'10" and 130lbs. Small up top, skinny legs, and a bad case of nasatol (NO ASS AT ALL).

Celine and I hung out for about two months. Her conversations were engaging. I appreciated her point of view. Even when we disagreed, there was still some learning and exploration to be had. Her face was magnificent. It was almost like a work of art. I told her that too. I said she needed to be locked up in the Louvre, and people needed to pay a fee to be in her presence.

Despite it all, I had to let her go. I am incredibly superficial at times. I'm also one of those dudes who will take a body over a face. In the two months we were dating, I always thought about other women when we slept together. After a while, it made me feel bad. I felt like I was lying to myself and her. So, one day over dinner, I told her that I couldn't do it. I gave some BS reason. She was disappointed and a little hurt. But ultimately, whenever I saw her naked, my mind would make me think of other women, which was just a deal-breaker for me. C'est la vie!

REFLECTION

This story is relatable from both genders' perspectives because, as humans, we like what we like. It happens that you'll meet someone who is visually attractive with an exceptional conversation to match. You also greatly enjoy their company, but in your eyes, their overall physical appeal is not a solid 10.

However, does this matter 10 or 20 years down the line? Being superficial in our dating process can prevent us from giving and receiving the love we deserve. We aren't saying that you shouldn't be attracted to your partner. Yes, that's important. But at what point will we focus on the qualities that matter? Many of us get caught up in height and size while overlooking characteristics that are most important in a relationship.

This guy's preference for a woman's voluptuous body took higher priority than who this woman was as a person. We aren't knocking him, because it was his decision to make. But, it is also an example of why so many women have issues with body image. It sounds like this was an incredible woman who was dissed for something she had no control over. To think about all of the women who have been snatched up mostly for superficial reasons is quite sad. On the bright side, what may not work for some, works for others. Hopefully, this woman has met a man who can appreciate every part of her.

SMASHED THE HOMIES

There was a girl I knew in high school. We were cool but not close. We ended up at the same college living in the same dorm. I didn't make any moves during high school because I didn't see her in that way. Also, I was locked down and faithful. But college changed all of that. We ended up becoming friends, and a connection grew from there. It turned into some kind of weird sexual tension. We never made a move on each other. It turned out she was a virgin, and I didn't want any parts of that. She ended up getting a boyfriend, and I waited for ole boy to crack it. I was going to make my move afterward.

We flirted back and forth throughout the year. Since she still had a boyfriend, I left it alone and tried hollering at one of her friends. One night, a group of us were hanging out on my floor. I was planning to smash the friend. I'm putting my moves down, setting it up for later. When my homegirl from high school got a little jealous, I didn't think too much of it. Soon, she started texting me from across the room, trying to ruin the plans. I'm thinking to myself, you *have a man. I'm trying to smash your friend.* The night went on, I went to the dorm room with the new friend, and I ended up getting too drunk to poke.

My homegirl from high school hit me up the next day. We ended up in a little encounter, and things started to go in a sexual nature. Before we went all the way, she informed me that she smashed two of the homies from high school. I was surprised and ended up not even doing anything with her. I couldn't even finish. It was weird. I didn't know if it was because I liked her or the guy code. My guys and I made a code that we don't wax anything behind each other. We don't dip where another guy dipped in, and she smashed two of my homeboys. But apparently, they broke the code. I guess she was trying to knock down the crew.

REFLECTION

Before we dive into this story, we want to stop and point out that a lot of the stories from our guy friends have consisted of smashing and bagging chicks. Instead of them seeing a young woman as someone they wanted to pursue, they treated them more like objects they want to divide and conquer. For example, this guy didn't want a virgin because he had bad intentions. But he was okay with going behind another man. We are just as confused as he is. He didn't want a virgin but didn't want a hoe. Perhaps he wanted a virginal hoe.

Anyway, we all know that it makes a guy cringe when he hears that someone he likes has smashed the homies. It's funny how this guy was ready to have sex with girls who were friends but turned off when he found out this young lady did the same thing. The homie smasher is upset with another homie smasher. It's a delusional double standard that doesn't make any sense.

It's common for men and women to explore themselves sexually and sometimes excessively. We aren't surprised to hear the "smashed the homies" stories. From a health perspective, stories like this are like drinking your friend's backwash from their water bottle. Gross, right? So is running behind the vaginal and penile secretions of someone in the same circle. This is the same culture we want to annihilate.

DADDY ISSUES

I went away to school freshman year. I had no idea what I was going to do because I didn't like traditional American education. I set up a meeting to talk to my Academic Advisor, who wanted to know my interests. I told him, "Basketball and girls." By the time I had gotten to college, I had dealt with so many girls but never knew what they saw in me. So, it made me want to study them.

A lot of girls liked me for superficial reasons. They thought I was handsome. They liked my fashion sense and the fact that I was the star on the basketball team. But at the same time, I felt like a lot of things girls and other people were rocking with me for had nothing to do with me. The film *What Women Want* came out, and I became even more curious about what they wanted. I started down a journey of studying women and their behaviors. One weekend, I went home to kick it with my boys. We were a nice-looking group. One guy was 6'3, mixed, and had light brown eyes. You know, the pretty boy type. The other guy was dark-skinned and had a Morris Chestnut look that all the girls loved. When we were together, every kind of girl would approach us, and we had a plethora of options.

While at the bar, we noticed this girl walk in. It was hard not to because she was beautiful. She was the type of girl that made every guy want to shoot their shot. My tall, light-skinned friend went to talk to her and got shot down. Every guy that went over to her got shot down. Later in the night, we saw her staring at our group and tried to figure out who she was giving the eye. Everyone felt like they were turned down, so it had to be me. It turns out it was me that she was eyeing. She ended up approaching me and asked why I didn't want to talk to her. I told her, "I figured you turned down all of my friends, so you didn't want to talk to anyone."

She said, "What if it was because I wanted to talk to you?"

I said, "You would have come over here."

She replied, "I did." While we're going back and forth, I realized that she wasn't really checking for me. She was checking for the guy who wasn't paying her any attention. I wasn't any different from the other guys who approached her. I was just the one guy not giving her any attention. It only led me to think she had daddy issues.

She gave me her number, and we planned to go to lunch the next day. When I went back to the bar to talk to my friends, I told them, "Something about this chick tells me she doesn't stay with her father or parents, period." They were wondering how I came to this conclusion. "During our conversation, I felt like she was trying to prove that she's worthy of the man's attention that she wasn't getting. I believe that goes back to the relationship with her father." I explained to them.

I picked her up and realized she stayed with her grandma. It was starting to add up. She walked in the club, knowing she'd be able to demand attention. The person whose attention she couldn't get was her goal for the night. I enjoyed lunch with her, but it didn't go past that. I went back to school and continued to study girls.

REFLECTION

For someone at a young age to make such an observation is pretty incredible. Unfortunately, this is a common theme in the Black community. A lot of men and women have experienced absent fathers and even absent mothers. Most people who have been abandoned by their parents have not dealt with the hurt and pain they have caused. Women may enter relationships for the wrong reasons or look for men to love them like they wish their father had. They will even stay in a relationship well past its expiration date or accuse their partners of being just like their father. Men may not know how to be emotionally available to women or have a hard time giving and receiving love because it wasn't displayed in their childhood.

Broken families are a generational curse we need to deal with, and it starts with us addressing the hurt that it has caused and allowing ourselves to heal. Even if you grew up in a two-parent home, you might have a parent that was abandoned by one of their parents, and that can still impact how they learn how to love. These people deserve love too, and if they want to heal, as a community, we should take on the responsibility of helping to heal each other.

CHURCH GIRL

There was one girl that I re-met in college. I knew her in high school but didn't pay her too much attention. In high school, she was very homely looking and didn't put any effort into her looks. Her hair would be pulled back, skirts down to her knees. She had no style. When I met her in college, the curves had filled out nicely. She had changed her hair, and the skirts were a little shorter. So, I attempted to bag her.

She worked in the library. One day, while checking out my books, I figured I would see what she was on. I got shot down immediately. She told me she had a boyfriend. I got up and went on about my business. The next day, I was in the library writing a research paper when she came up to me and said I left so abruptly the day before. She didn't get a chance to get my phone number and wanted to hang out and get to know me. I told her I didn't think it was a good idea because she had a guy. If I were her guy, I wouldn't want my girl hanging out with the likes of me.

But she was very persistent. She thought it would be cool if we became friends because we were from the same hometown. We exchanged numbers. A few days later, she asked me to hang out with her and a group of friends. The fact that we were hanging out in a big group made me think that I had been officially friend-zoned. She let me know that everyone was meeting at her house and gave me a time and address. I didn't realize that she had told me to come over an hour before everyone else.

When I walked in, she had the Bible sitting on her coffee table, and a rerun of *Golden Girls* was on television. I sat on the couch, and she offered me a drink. I took her up on her offer, and she made me a vodka cranberry. While sipping my beverage, she told me she needed to finish a section in her Bible study. *I was like, Aight, cool. I guess I can watch the Golden Girls.* She was reading the Bible, so I did not expect anything to happen other than just hanging out.

When she finished, she closed the Bible and threw it onto the table. She said, "I can't take you teasing me like this." I was caught off guard. I didn't know what was going on. Imagine my surprise when she walked over to me, pulled my pants down, and straddled my lap. She continued to say, "You can't keep teasing me like this. You can't keep teasing me like this." Usually, I'm pretty good at talking, but I was in shock that this "church girl" was on me like this. We started attempting to do our business. She was going down and doing her thing.

I was like, *Okay, this is finna go down.* Then, as we were about to do the damn thing, her friends knocked on the door.

I heard a female voice say, "Hey, we hear you in there. Open up."

Church girl immediately jumped up, and I pull my pants up. She repeatedly said, "You can't tell anybody about this."

I told her, "Okay, cool."

She said, "We're going to finish this later."

I said, "Bet."

We went bowling, hung out, and got drinks. We called it a night with her friends. She invited me back to her place. We went to her room and finished what we had started after her Bible study. When we were done, she told me, "Please don't tell anyone." And I didn't. Until now.

REFLECTION

It sounds like this church girl has not matured in her walk or is struggling between her flesh and spirit. Her walk is between her and God, but we are trying to figure out why she felt the need to let our friend know she was reading her Bible and hop on him immediately afterward.

Not only was this distasteful, but it also sets up people on the receiving end of this scenario for confusion. It gives Godly women a bad rep because there is no reflection of great character in these kinds of moments. If she were mature in her walk with God, she would not be engaging in premarital sex.

NASTY NATASHA

In my early thirties, I met this very nasty girl, and I'm not talking about Vanity 6. For the youngins, Vanity 6 was a female group founded by Prince. Now that I have provided you with a brief music history lesson, I want to tell you about the time I became fed up by a girl who was not nasty in a sexual sense, well maybe that too, but she had the worst attitude I had ever experienced from a woman.

"It's not my fault that I'm a strong woman," Natasha told me as she stared at me from across the dinner table. "That's what's wrong with most men. They don't know what to do when they meet a strong independent woman."

"I can handle a strong woman. I'm not going to deal with someone with a nasty ass attitude such as yours." At this point, I was irritated. Natasha and I had been seeing each other for a few months, and her attitude seemed to get worst by the day. She was one of the most attractive women I had dated, very successful, but she was rude. Not to just me, but the people around us. I had invited her out to dinner to celebrate my new position at work. Across the table from me was one of the most beautiful women I had ever met. Aesthetically that is. Natasha had hair down her shoulders, beautiful brown skin, piercing eyes, and style to match. That's what initially caught my eye and made me approach her the night I spotted her while I was out with my friends. At first, I thought her attitude was cute, and the sex was superb. But she was down-right rude. If I were even one minute late for one of our dates, she would tell me I didn't respect her and her time, even when I gave her a heads up. She still found a way to go completely in.

Tonight's argument started because she was rude to our server. It was apparent that she was new to her job, and she messed up a couple of times. When she didn't refill Natasha's water in time, she let her have it. "Are you dumb?" Natasha asked the nervous young lady.

"I'm sorry ma'am, it's been jam-packed tonight, and this is the first day on the floor by myself." The waitress said.

"Yea, you're sorry, alright, a sorry excuse for a server. See if you get a tip!" Natasha yelled at her.

I looked at the waiter and mouthed, "I'm sorry." As soon as she left the table, I let Natasha know that her behavior was unnecessary. "Why are you so rude?"

"Because she doesn't know how to do her job."

"No, you are rude to people all the time. You snap at the drop of a dime and always find something to complain about." Last week, when I brought Natasha to my friend's cookout, she got in a heated debate with one of my homeboys about the state of our political system. Although her points were valid and much needed, my friend did not agree with everything Natasha said.

When he made a comment that didn't sit well with her, Natasha spat out, "what's wrong with you n*ggas! Like who raised you?" Because my homeboy was not as cool, calm, and collected as I am, I quickly interjected.

"What she's trying to ask is, what made you come up with that point of view," I told my friend, trying to lighten the mood. My friend just shook his head and walked away. I used that as my cue to take Natasha home. Because the sex was so good that night, I failed to mention how rude she was to my homeboy. But as we were sitting inside the restaurant, I figured this was the perfect time to bring it up. As fine as she was, I was ready to cut all ties with her.

"You were rude to my homeboy last week, now this."

"Whatever man, dude, was a weak ass n*gga," Natasha said as she sipped her cocktail.

I shook my head. Yes, this would be our last encounter. But, not before I took her home one last time. Like I said, the attitude sucked, but the sex was the bomb.

REFLECTION—ERIKA

This story reminds me of this woman I worked on a project with. She had one of the nastiest attitudes I'd ever encountered. She was rude, crass, and overall had an evil spirit. Everyone on our team wanted to flee from her. One day while working, a group of us began talking about relationships. This Nasty Natasha, in particular, started talking about the kind of man she wanted in her life. I couldn't believe the type of man she described. I mean, he was almost perfect from his height down to his bone structure. As she went on to share her non-negotiables, I thought, *how would she attract such a man?* I mean, she was a beautiful woman, but she was downright ugly on the inside. She didn't possess one quality on that list.

One of the worst things a woman can believe is that someone has to deal with their nasty attitude. It is also a mistake to think that an ugly disposition is equivalent to being a strong woman. Like Nasty Natasha, a man may enjoy you on a physical level, but it might only be so long before he excuses himself from the entire situation. To all of the Nasty Natasha's, it may be time for an attitude adjustment.

THE POWER OF FIGHTING THE P

This story is titled the power of fighting the P. I will use the initial because I want to use this word carefully and respectfully, and I know Erika and Niesha are trying to reach the world. In the late 90s, I had a successful career as a filmmaker. I worked with some of the largest television networks and produced a few films. Then my career suddenly came to a halt. It emotionally drained me, but it is what brought me to Jesus. This was new for me because I had never walked with Christ. As an African American man, I didn't grow up in the church. This was rare for someone in my culture. My family and I marched to a different tune.

Fast forward to the early 2000s, and I found a great church that had a men's ministry that focused on what was going on in the world. This church was innovative and brought up topics of abstinence, resisting masturbation and pornography, and renewing oneself to commit to the laws of Jesus Christ. With me being new to the Christian life, I was slowly changing my ways. I wasn't smoking and drank much less than I did before attending the church. However, I was having sex—lots of it. I mean, I was getting it in. My challenge was women who were attracted to me. If they weren't attracted to me, I didn't have a problem. But if they were, it was more tempting for me.

My temptations kept me in church trying to be a better man. One Friday night, while at home, I opened up a nice bottle of wine and created an online dating account. I matched with this young lady who lived in the Midwest of the West Coast. She was between California and Nevada. I matched with her not just because of her beauty but because her profile stated that she was a Christian. In her pics, you could tell she was short and very curvaceous. She gave me Erykah Badu, Jill Scott, and India Arie vibes. I was excited to meet her in person.

During our first conversation, I learned that she loved God, but she loves sex too and not just regular sex. She was into threesomes with men and women. She told me about two of her friends and sent their pics. One was tall, with an athletic build and dreadlocks. The other friend looked and dressed like a pop star. We talked for hours, and she told me about the different situations she had encountered. I was surprised (but not really) to find out that some of her encounters were with well-known pastors in LA. She also had been with a few R&B singers while on video sets with her Rockstar friend. She identified as a Christian but took priority in feeding her sexual desires.

We ended up meeting in person at a farmer's market in LA. While walking around, I told her I had just entered a doctoral program with a business component. We began talking about small business plans. We grabbed a seat at one of the booths, and she shared with me a business she wanted to start. As I sat across from this woman who appeared to be drawn to me, I was inspired to design her small business plan. Instead of trying to get physical with her, I helped her formulate her idea and develop it. We talked about how to target people and execute during the week of the Academy Awards. She planned the program with the two friends I mentioned earlier and made $20,000 that night using the plan I designed for her and my coaching.

I was attracted to her, but I didn't let the power of the p to take control. I felt like it was a test from God. This experience made me realize that I am called to support women in leadership. It was a struggle being around attractive women, but I had to overcome this power to answer my new calling. Overcoming my sexual desires was the precursor to the next three women I would help. I helped one draft a plan that led to a $4M grant for her to open a school.

To men out there, you will encounter plenty of beautiful women drawn to you during your purpose and calling. Not being able to overcome the power of the p has gotten a lot of us in serious trouble. When temptations arise, it can be hard to ignore your sexual urges, and this was once my downfall as a man. If you can deny the power of the p, you will have a newfound strength. Do I struggle? Absolutely. God brings those types of women into my universe, and I have to ward off the temptation.

The temptation for the woman I met online was so strong I had to block and delete her after her successful event. Of course, she and her friends wanted to "thank" me for my support. I knew I would fail that test, so I didn't want to play into it. Since I had discovered my new calling, and I didn't want to be that guy who sleeps with every woman he works with. Without God, it's not easy, but it's possible.

REFLECTION

The Power of the P is something that men have been fighting for years. There have even been number one songs written all about it. It has caused men to go crazy, make the wrong decisions, and hurt many women along the way. Truthfully, the power of the p is what has added to the generational curses that we experience today. It has been used as a weapon of destruction for many, many years. A lot of the stories in this book transpired because this power has been mishandled.

For this guy to recognize and address, it is more than commendable. The power of the p is something that many men deal with, and this story is the perfect example that there is only one way to conquer it—through the power of the Holy Spirit. This story outlines the spiritual battle that many of us deal with when it comes to sex. If not handled properly, these sexual strongholds will continue to divide men and women instead of bringing us closer.

We would also like to point out that this guy recognized that he would encounter many beautiful women, but that did not mean they should have a sexual relationship. If his loins would have moved him, he may not have recognized his gift of helping women in education.

CONTAGIOUS

This is a story about my experience with a married woman. I was fresh out of graduate school and new to the professional world. Some of my male colleagues and I would hang out during happy hour. One of my colleague's cousins would meet us out with her friends. She was a bad chick, and we would engage in great conversations. When I saw the rock on her finger, I accepted the fact that she was cute but married. Therefore, making her unavailable.

I was single but had a girl I messed around with consistently. We would have sex when we wanted to but agreed that we wouldn't have any attachments. However, this arrangement was built on trust because we had known each other since high school. We began an intimate relationship in college. Again, this was an on and off sexual relationship.

A few months into my new job, we hosted a conference at a hotel downtown. On our last day, we threw a party in our suite. My colleague invited the married hottie and her friends. At the end of the night, I asked to be in charge of cleaning, in exchange for having the suite to myself. I agreed. The married woman was flirting with me and giving me a lot of energy. I was like, *Okay, she's trying to "KICK it, kick it.*

I told her I had the room for the night if she wanted to stay. She acted resistant at first, but I could tell she was with it. When everyone left, we went into the bedroom, and that's when we got it crackin'. She stayed the night, and we got reckless. We weren't that drunk but didn't have any protection. I was smashing this chick raw. I didn't see it as a problem. After all, she was married. I guess I just assumed she was taking the proper precaution not to get pregnant. The sex was great, and we linked up a few times. At the same time, I was still messing with the chick I had been getting down with for years. One morning while getting ready for work, I felt a sting after urinating. I was in a rush to get to work, so I planned to call the doctor when I got there. The whole time, I couldn't focus on work because I was trying to get to the clinic quickly. At this point, I know how this goes. I'd been to college, and this is the package you don't want. I headed to the clinic, and it was confirmed that I had chlamydia. I was trying to figure out if it was from the married woman or the sex buddy.

My sex buddy and I weren't exclusive, so she didn't know what I was doing outside of her and vice versa. She and I were having unprotected sex as well, so this was quite the dilemma. I didn't know who burned me or who I burned. I left the clinic thinking; I've *been smashing both. One is married, and she wouldn't do that to me. The other doesn't give me information, so I don't know who she's dealing with.* I tried to think if there was anyone else I smashed or had some drunken nights I shouldn't have had. I was a little reckless during that time in my life but couldn't think of anyone.

I had more trust in my long-term sex buddy because I knew her longer. I'm not saying this was a reason to trust her more. I just assumed since I had been messing with her for so many years without catching anything. All signs were pointing to the married woman. I sent her a text, letting her know about my condition, she texted me back, saying she didn't believe me. My gut told me it was her. But then again, she and her husband had been together for 13 years.

I called my consistent sex buddy, who trusted me for so many years. I wanted to tell her in person, so I went to her house. She was hurt but appreciated the fact that I told her. Thankfully, her test results were negative. It turns out, it was the married chick after all. Her husband was in the military and would go on mission a couple of weekends out of the month. Some of those missions involved smashing random chicks. After our encounter with chlamydia, the married chick never called me again.

REFLECTION

This story is the reason so many people are turned off by marriage. What was created to be a beautiful union ordained by God has been strongly perverted. This is another story with so many layers. Let's start with the married, cheating woman. Men are not the only ones who step out in their marriage. Women might cheat for different reasons, but a cheater is still a cheater. Even though she had unprotected sex with someone who was not her husband, it is funny that the married one was deemed to be more honorable between the two women.

This is the perfect example of people getting into relationships, and recklessly doing things their way. To make matters worse, they are out here doing things their way and raw dogging during the process. We need to talk about the saints that are out here having unprotected sex with multiple sexual partners. We shouldn't have to tell you that unprotected sex with someone you barely know is dangerous, especially if married. But unfortunately, some grown folks are missing the memo.

While we strongly encourage the wait, a good rule of thumb is not having sex with anyone you don't see in your future, especially unprotected sex. But even with "safe" sex, things can happen. Raw sex may feel better, but it's just not something you should do with someone you don't know or trust. As we write this, it's crazy to think we are having this conversation with grown people about a topic we learned as a teenager.

We know that acts such as this can lead to STDs and unplanned pregnancies, yet we still engage in such activities. It doesn't make any sense. Actions like this lead to the continuation of generational curses because folks are out here having children with people they don't even like anymore. This is the reason God designed sex for married couples. Lastly, this story highlights that many people want to have sex without the responsibility of a relationship. It may be convenient, but it can also be dangerous. This guy made the girl from college his sex buddy, and as a result, put her health in jeopardy. Because there was no commitment, he engaged in any sexual escapade that was pleasing to him. These are just some of the things you risk when you want to have a "sex buddy."

CHAPTER 18
SHE'S THE ONE

Every time I think of her, I'm thanking You. And when I give my love to her, I'm thanking you. Loving her like Christ loves the church cuz you told me to.

—ISAAC CARREE, *HER*

You've heard the stories from guys who made moves according to their loins. If they weren't trying to smash, they were having some true f*@# boy moments. A few of them had encounters with women who tested their patience—making it hard to believe that there are men who want to settle down and start a family with the special woman they deem as the one. We heard from the ladies. Now it's time to hear from their soulmates. The guys in this chapter want to share their story of how they knew their wife was the one for them. Some of the stories are short and sweet, but it is an excellent example of when a man knows, he knows.

NIESHA, THE ONE

What stood out to me as far as knowing that Niesha was the one was that I knew she was different early on. Mainly after our first date, we engaged in really provocative conversations that covered everything from finances, sex, fears, wants, and desires. It was just a robust conversation from the get-go. I'm not saying that I knew from that point, but I knew that Niesha was significant early on. Based on my writing down what I was looking for in a woman, it was almost like lights going off. It was the first date, and obviously, you can't put that much ownership in something so early on because she or I could've turned into Dr. Jekyll and Mr. Hyde for all I knew. But what I can take ownership of is after we left that restaurant; I talked to one of my brethren, a close confidant of mine, and in my conversation with him based upon what I told him about Niesha he said, "she sounds fascinating."

What's crazy is that we just heard this sermon where my Pastor spoke about courting someone. Pastor Opal had a section just for the men, and his wife had a part just for the ladies, and I remember a day later, I shared it with Niesha. When I shared it with her I think she took about two or three days for us to debrief and we ended up having a real in-depth discussion based upon the principles of a woman and the principles of a man and how long does it take for you to know that someone is the one. How long is courting supposed to be, and if sex should be involved? It was one of the first times where I delved into an in-depth conversation that was not about sex but was more so my soul speaking. I knew those were building blocks I was building with a woman that I would want as my wife.

In conjunction with that, on our fifth date, we were at a Jamaican restaurant called Pearl's, and she brought out 285 questions. I found it intriguing because, based upon those questions, I think she was solidifying her life. The questions covered finances, sexual preferences, raising a family, I mean we covered just about everything. We didn't go through all 285 items in one day, obviously, but we would do about three a day. I looked forward to those conversations and learning more about her. I also looked forward to Niesha learning more about me. On that particular date, she said something real prolific regarding knowing that I was still kind of "in the land."

She told me in a nutshell, "Just don't play me like a sucka." She went on to say, "If you are out there it is against my control, but don't play me for a sucka and act as if you're not." She was on a journey of celibacy, and in two weeks, we went on about five dates so clearly everything was moving fast, and at no point did I act as though I wasn't out there. Niesha told me, "I know you didn't join me on this journey in particular, and I know this is probably odd to you, but if you're gonna be out here the land, and think you're gonna be messing with me, don't have unprotected sex, don't bring no baby home."

It was weird, but it was one of those moments when I was like, *damn, now I don't want to do anything to mess this up, because what's the point?* This made me look at a lot of women differently, and from that point on, I couldn't be with anyone else but her. I wanted to spend all of my time with her. I wanted to continue answering all of those questions and learn what ignites her spirit. I wanted to see if what ignites both of our souls could complete this union, and it did. From the first time we went over scripture together to that date at Pearl's with the 285 questions, and that particular conversation, it was a mash-up. I was like, *damn, I am really into this woman, and I want this to work.*

I cut everyone off and told Niesha everything that was happening. She heard some of the phone calls, saw the texts, and the emails. I always kept Niesha in the know of everything, and because we had built something so open with the communication, the scriptures, and the questions, it was easy for me to share things with her. I would say, from the date at Pearl's, I knew that Niesha would be my wife.

$14 UNTIL PAYDAY

I started seeing Naledi as the one early when we started dating. One particular moment was when we went on a date to the Dodgers' game. I was working as an assistant and living check to check at the time. I had $14 to my name a week from payday, and Naledi had tickets to the game. The old me wouldn't have gone because I was broke, but I had read an article that money shouldn't stop someone from living life, so I decided to take this advice. I went to the game with Naledi and hoped to have a good time since I didn't have to pay. We had passes for free parking, so I didn't have to worry about that. I purposely didn't plan on ordering food. It was 85 degrees, though, so I bought us a $6 bottle of water that was big, and we shared it.

The game was fun, and when it was over, Naledi asked if I wanted to get something to eat. I didn't have any plans for the rest of the night, but I told her I didn't want to hang out. She wanted to know why. I did want to hang out but couldn't tell her that I didn't have any money. She wanted to grab something to eat before heading home, so I agreed to go with her. When we got to the restaurant, Naledi looked at the menu. She asked what I was going to get, and I told her nothing. Naledi looked upset and asked why I would go to dinner if I weren't going to eat. Our date was headed in another direction, and my not telling the truth was making it worse. I had to tell Naledi that I didn't want to order because I couldn't afford it. It was excruciating and embarrassing to tell her my truth. My pride was hurt, but it was liberating.

Naledi was supportive of me after telling her the truth. I'll never forget her next question. She looked me in my eyes and said, "Are you hungry?" I just nodded my head. Naledi paid for my meal, and we had one of the most real conversations that night. We have been keeping it 100 ever since. And here we are five years later, married.

RIDE OR DIE CHICK

A month after we started dating, Tiffany invited me to hang out with her and her family on the 4th of July. They would be celebrating her mother's birthday, and she wanted me to meet some of her family members. The venue of the gathering was about an hour away, so we drove separately. I had to be at work the next day, but we had so much fun. I didn't pay attention to the time. We kicked it all day well into the night. When it was time to leave, we trailed each other. Since it was late and I had to be up early, we were both speeding. About five miles before our exit, I got pulled over by a police officer. Tiffany pulled over to wait for me. I told her to keep going, and I would catch up, but she said, "No, I'm going to wait."

Then the officer said, "If you don't go, I will call another officer over, so you get a ticket too."

I told Tiffany, "Get the heck out of here. It doesn't make sense for both of us to get a ticket."

Tiffany looked at both of us and said, "We're both gonna get a ticket, then."

In my mind, I was like, *Okay, she's a rider.* At that moment, I felt she was the one. You never know if it's going to work out, but I knew I could rock with her.

MY WIFE, MY BEST FRIEND

We started as friends in 1980 while we were both in college. I would go to her house to kick it with her, and soon after, we began dating. I knew she was special because we would have the type of conversations I didn't have with other women. We talked about things we wanted in life, like family, houses, jobs, and cars. You know, the things people in their early 20s aspire to have. The more we dated, the more we liked each other and ultimately fell in love. One of the fondest moments we had together was when we discovered we were going to have our first child. About three months after our daughter was born, we got married.

I am always reminded that she is the one for me. In the early stages of our marriage, we didn't have much. We were very poor, and she still stood by my side. Seeing all of this, I said to myself. *This is the one.* My mom always said if you don't have anything and a woman stays by your side, you know she wants to be with you. Several other things let me know she was the one. One of these is the first meal she made me. I remember it like yesterday. I went to her house, and she had made smothered chicken, rice, greens, and cornbread. If she was throwing down like that, I knew she liked me. She still makes the best meals for me. Thirty-eight years and two beautiful daughters later, I am truly blessed to have married my best friend.

ONE MONTH

To simplify it, I knew after a month of dating that Izoha was the one for me. From the time we'd met, we had an unspoken connection that felt amazingly organic, fresh, familiar, and grounded. Everything I'd longed for in a mate, I knew I'd finally found. For me, I saw a woman who strived for many of the same ideals in relationships, family, and financial goals. To this day, these things remain true. Though we have many differences, as all people are different, I found the person I pray to grow old with. With this person, my life has infinitely changed for the better, and I thank God daily for this blessing.

SHE MAKES ME FEEL LIKE A MAN

How did I know my wife was the one? So, it wasn't a particular moment. I think it was just progression over time. I met my wife Ebonie when I was almost 16. We met April 29, 1998, and started dating May 8, 1998. We met at a convention, and I asked for her number. She took mine instead. We went for a few days and didn't talk because I accidentally wrote down the wrong number. She thought I did this intentionally until she ran into my buddy at the mall, who told her that wasn't the case, and he gave her the correct number.

I realized she was special the very first time we talked. We talked for five hours on the phone about profound and intimate topics. I asked questions about her family, and she asked questions about mine. We talked about our likes and dislikes, and she even got emotional and began to cry and open up about some things in her life. The first conversation struck me like *wow, she could be the one.* Thinking back, it wasn't a conversation you had in your teens. We were ahead of our time with the intellectual discussion we had. Not only did I find her extremely attractive, but we connected on a mental level.

From May of 1998 to September of 1999, we spent countless hours together and had never even got into an argument. We were both accommodating to each other. We knew how to compromise. From every aspect. We got into a disagreement because I wanted to hang out and party with one of my buddies, and she didn't want me to. Her mom intervened and said, "let him go hang out with his friends." That was the only actual argument in over a year of us being together. We got along and enjoyed each other's company

Fast forward to the year 2000. We had our first son. We became teenage parents. The way she took care of our son further confirmed that she was my wife. Less than a year later, she was pregnant with my daughter. By 2001, we had two kids. She moved into an apartment, and I came later. I could tell that as far as progression, Ebonie had ambition. We were both in school. She made up her mind that she would have her place with or without me. We never broke up, but I was living with my mom and stayed with Ebonie part-time. It didn't matter to her because she was going to make a way for her and the kids. We never separated, but I could tell from her mindset and how she was moving that she would be okay if that were the case.

As we continued to move forward in our relationship, we lived together in a low-income apartment at the time. While we were still in college,

Ebonie told me, "I don't want to live here. I want to live in a nicer place." So, we moved into a townhouse. Again, she's taking care of all the household situations, and even managing the bills. I'm helping with everything, but she had the vision. Fast forward, I get a job after graduating from college. At that point, I told her not to worry about work, and we moved into another house. The same type of vision moving forward.

In the meantime, family was important to both of us. We hosted Thanksgiving with our families. We shared a common interest in family and love. At this point, people are putting pressure asking when we are getting married. I didn't want anyone to pressure me because I knew she would be my wife. She was faithful, loyal, took care of my kids, and I loved her more and more every day.

Most importantly, she made me feel like a man. We walk side by side, but at the end of the day, she gives me the utmost respect. She doesn't make me feel less of a man. She makes me feel like THE man. To know that I'm the head of the household is a feeling I can't even begin to explain. She lets me know I can lead and trusts me enough to follow the direction we are going. We make decisions together, but for a man to have a woman that will allow you to be a man without trying to pull you down and make you feel like you're not worth anything is priceless. I feel like I'm spoiled. She makes my plate not because she's old school but because she wants to. It makes a man feel like a man. It might seem minimal, but she never disregards what I say, and she trusts me.

In 22 years of being together, I can't recall a time we went a full day pissed at each other and not talked. That shows both of our dedication to compromise and bend for each other. She allows me to be a man. We both have successful careers. I feel like the protector and provider in my home. That goes so far for a Black man; it's hard to explain. Every man needs an Ebonie! In 2005, I proposed on Christmas and the rest is history. I love her, and I'm so glad that we chose each other to be the one.

PART III

CHAPTER 19
THE ANTIDOTE—KINGDOM RELATIONSHIPS

Two are better than one because they have a good return for their labor. If either of them falls down, one can help the other up.

—EPHESIANS 4:9-12

We've laughed, we've reflected, and we've reviewed the red flags, and since we have retained your attention thus far, stay with us as we introduce and welcome you to a new school of thought. In full disclaimer, we understand that this section may not be for everyone, and some of you may have just come for the laughs, and that's cool too. But for those of you who would like to continue further, there are some things we want to discuss before we bid you adieu. As women of faith, we want to inspire you to view this topic from a perspective of faith while we simultaneously highlight cultural habits that have been damaging and restrictive in our relationships.

We have witnessed so many ladies within our network of friends preparing for their future spouses, and we noticed a spiritual element to this preparation. What does this entail? There is a large group of women who are aware of what they desire in a relationship and are positioning themselves accordingly. For such women, positioning for a future spouse may look like clearing away baggage from the past, correcting negative behavioral habits, and tackling health and body goals. One of the major consistencies in this trend is that they are all actively seeking purpose. These women are committed to their path of improvement with their future husbands in mind. What we have also observed is, they're being intentional about developing a relationship with God first.

For every ten women in full preparation, perhaps we may know two men qualified to date them. This is not to say unqualified men are on the rise. Still, currently, women are seemingly the spearheads compared to men who are engaged in transforming themselves and prioritizing marriage right now. As women, we are naturally receivers, and what we believe to be the cause of our trending transformations is simple. The Most-High God is pouring out his spirit, and the receivers by nature are most receptive.

The major shift happening in this world is available to everyone, and we are encouraging you to get in tune. The old habits that yielded no return for our generation need to be put to rest, and we invite you to join us in doing the work to redefine the culture. In the current era we live in, we cannot afford to continue with business as usual, especially regarding personal relationships. The trending dating culture signifies death to the potential legacies we can build together as men and women and leaves almost nothing left to desire for the children of our futures. Right before our eyes predominate quality pairings are dying off, and our pairings may be one of the most important and influential areas of our lives. With that being said, stories like "*Goodnight Daddy*" and "*Bye Felicia*" must cease to exist. The time has come for us to take social accountability of each other and dismantle the popular beliefs that embrace dysfunctional situationships, the side piece, and the serial dater. Let's begin to change the narrative.

So, what do we think is the antidote to rid us of bad dating experiences? God. In case you missed it, God is looking to develop his Kingdom, which is the season we are in. We are here to be fruitful, and this starts with being in relationships that lead to kingdom marriages. But before we are ready for this kind of marriage, we must be willing to do the work on ourselves before pursuing one another. Unlike a typical relationship, the kingdom relationship is God-ordained and assists you with your God-given purpose. Meeting the love of your life, having someone to share your space with, or being relationship goals is fine. Still, the kingdom relationship, most importantly, has the ultimate purpose of glorifying God, which we won't do dating the "Felicia." When God ordains your relationship, its fruit extends beyond you, and many will be blessed through this union. Kingdom marriages defy generational curses and groom you both to be your best self. When God joins two people together, you get the privilege to witness his multifaceted plans, and his design includes your marriage. Let's all start by being open to giving God a try, and for those of you who are currently in a relationship, it is never too late to rebuild the foundation based on his principles, and this is what we would like to explore.

Let's break it down biblically. In Genesis 2:18, God says, *it is not good that man should be alone; I will make him a helper comparable to him.* To be comparable means to be similar in quality. The woman God created for Adam was perfectly crafted just for him. God put Adam in a deep slumber, while he prepared Eve, and as he slept, God removed one of his ribs and created her. Y'all know the story, so we don't have to go into detail, and if you don't, visit Genesis 2:18-22.

We've taken note of the high occurrence of people pursuing or who pursued relationships with their motives and did not consider God in their choices. Imagine if we went into potential relationships with our purpose for our lives at the forefront of our minds? If we had truly understood our purpose and worth, we would not have accepted the excess red flags that we previously ignored. Now we realize that everyone has to grow. But there are people well in their 30's, 40's, and even 50's who still possess toxic habits that are not allowing their relationships to thrive, and we want to explore some ideas as to why.

THE SLEEPING ADAM & IMPATIENT EVE

The first idea we want to bring to the congregation is that of the sleeping Adam and impatient Eve. As we mentioned, God put Adam in a deep slumber while he took one of his ribs to create Eve. We found an abundance of oblivious sleeping Adams (men) and too many impatient Eves (women). As we discussed earlier, it is the women right now receptive and being prepared by God while a lot of men are still sleeping. But the sleeping Adam and the Eves in preparation only signify that there will soon be an awakening of the Adam, who was most likely unaware he was sleeping. Just as God produced Eve while Adam was deep in slumber, he is now doing the same thing for a lot of men. There are often devastating results of waking a sleeping Adam too prematurely in a woman's impatience, just as it would have been had Adam awakened during the removal process of his rib.

While God is doing his surgeries, he allows men to sleep while they are not even comprehending that they are in season to receive their wives. Some men are being led by God to prepare their garden for Eve's arrival, and do not realize their steps are being supernaturally guided. Then there are others gazing eyes on their "Eves" every day and do not recognize her and are wasting time taking her for granted. Let us not forget about those happy sleepers. They are the ones who have chosen their slumber over the action of choice required of them. Whom enjoy the ways of the world and because they feel time is on their side, become entangled with multiple women; manipulating, and stringing them along in attempts to avoid a commitment. Although the male-to-female ratio may appear to be in his favor, it is only a trick of the enemy to distract him with so many options that he's too overwhelmed to choose. He will be so engulfed with loving his distractions that he can never fully serve God. Though he may not be in love, he's in love with his opportunities, and meanwhile, there is only one Eve perfectly fashioned for him. As he actively continues to close his eyes, he does everyone a disservice, especially himself, and delays writing his signature and legacy in the earth.

With the same respect, impatient Eves, who are engaging in waking a sleeping Adam before his time, even if the two of you are compatible, you could be trying to entice your Adam out of season. While Eve waits, she should develop the fruits of the spirit, and one of which she lacks is the patience and longsuffering that are must-have character traits for a kingdom marriage. The mere fact that you are impatient shows there is a little more time required to spring forth. It would be more in her best interest to cultivate those character traits, and sometimes the sleeping Adam is still left in his slumber, surprisingly because you are not entirely shaped yet. As much as you are looking at your biological clock ticking or your 15th time being a bridesmaid and not a bride, God could be using your season of singleness to perfect you for no ordinary marriage but a kingdom one.

Just because she thinks she is ready and it's time for a man to take notice, we still are on God's perfect timing for our lives, that is, if we are fully submitted. God will hold no good thing from his children, so trust your time is approaching. We suggest that while you wait, get in position for the blessing you would like to receive. By seeking the Kingdom of God first, you allow Him to prune and chastise you. Become committed to the journey of walking with God to heal and shape you to His purpose.

The goal of marriage is to glorify Him, and our jealous God does not want marriage to become an idol. Look to become intimate with God so He can instill his principles of a covenant. Though you may feel that you are marriage material are you ready? If you ask God to show you whether or not you are prepared, he may say you need to learn to be obedient. He may be saying you need to establish boundaries in your friendships or detach from unhealthy relationships. He may tell you, you talk too much, are a little too snappy, have soul ties to your exes, or keep a messy home. You can do all things through Christ that strengthens you (Philippians 4:13), and he can renew and transform your mind (Romans 12:2). We are here to walk this path with you, and we want to invite you to ride this wave. If you are single, appreciate the pruning so that when your Adam or Eve arrives, you are prepared and walking confidently in your calling.

These are just ideas, but we wanted to bring them to your attention because being in the wrong relationships doesn't only produce heartbreak. They can also add to generational curses and lost destinies for you and your children. We want to get to the bottom line, so you can be in a relationship that bears good fruit. Just like kingdom relationships glorify God's Kingdom, the enemy's relationships glorify Satan, and we are turning our backs from walking in ways that signify a lack of understanding that. Hopefully, we didn't go too deep for you guys. We just want to engage in a conversation that will help us explore why so many people are unable to give and receive the love they have been longing for.

CALLING ALL WOMEN

ERIKA

A significant component in kingdom relationships involves understanding our roles as men and women. In the current era in which we live, a lot of people reject the idea of having gender roles. Men have to be men, and we have to allow them to be that. We are not here to serve as their mothers because that is not our role. We cannot force them to wake up, and as leaders, they must be led by the Holy Spirit before they lead us.

However, as women, we can use our influence with the way we live our lives, and it can impact the man as he submits himself to the will of God. Again, the female-to-male ratio may look like it's in a man's favor, but because there is still a lack of quality women with Godly understanding, the dating pool is not as suitable as the man believes it to be. Even if a woman is a good woman, she serves as a counterfeit if she is wrongly paired with the wrong man. We are here to empower both the women and men to start their conversations with God first on the steps they need for Him to deliver their spouses. The women of the present must seek our Heavenly Father on what to accept and reassess their "list" to avoid becoming improperly paired.

There are so many people, both men, and women looking for quality partnerships. Yet, they lack everything on the laundry list they are looking for. Many times, it's because they are uninterested in allowing God to do something new in them before they pursue a partner. Yes, there are some very loyal men and good women out there, but unfortunately, some rotten apples are making it hard to be receptive to even the most genuine people connecting. Many of the men are blinded to their true wives and prefer the counterfeits because she is a good time or doesn't hold him accountable for genuinely being the man God is calling him to be. While that is the case, there are those women who celebrate the "Futures" and couldn't spot a "Russell" if their life depended on it. Likewise, the "Futures" of our day cannot recognize the potential present in a "Ciara" that he was incapable of awakening. Many women wondered what the key to Ciara's prayer that manifested Russell was, but oftentimes, it's the painful experience of a "Future" that has us crying out for God's intervention. Similar to Niesha's experience that led to the wait.

WHY CIARA'S PRAYER WON'T WORK FOR YOU

NIESHA

Speaking of Ciara, I want to take a quick commercial break to let the ladies know why Ciara's prayer will not work. We see a lot of women are praying for their mate, and that's great. But some of us are praying out of context. When singer-songwriter Ciara's pictures of her beachside proposal to the Seahawks Quarterback and Super Bowl champion Russell Wilson hit the waves, people lost their minds. The saints were full of joy and excitement given her past dating experiences with previous lovers, especially her ex-fiancé rapper Future. Due to the nature of their careers, the ending of this relationship made public headlines. This left Ciara's fans feeling like they went through the break-up with her.

Russell and Ciara's display of love and joy caused many single ladies to question their dating journeys and how they could achieve this type of blessing and life. The hashtag #Ciaraprayer popped up all over social media and prompted the question of how she could go from dating a Future to having an actual future with a Russell. The couple's love was indeed one of a kind. Not only did Russell love Ciara, but he also loved her child. He was intentional about the plans he had for her, and they made it known that they were practicing "The Wait." This inspired single women to crack the code to this prayer that unlocks the blessing. This relationship was the encouragement that good and Godly men do exist but require intervention from our divine intervener and faith that He will deliver!

It was the joy that Ciara exuded in every photo she took that made the desire for what she had become an obsession for some women. Many wanted to know the prayer that guided Russell to seek her and desire her to be his wife. I am here to share with you that I have cracked the code for everyone who wants to know what Ciara prayed. What Ciara prayed was HER

PRAYER. It was for HERSELF. It was for her needs and desires. And more importantly, it was customized to her heart. Meaning, her prayer was based on what she needed in her life. She has also shared that it was a multitude of prayers, not just one. In addition to Ciara praying, Russell was praying for her. It's a two-fold activity that is done individually to gain collectively.

God has prepared your person just for you. When the time is right, you will have your moment of bliss. Stop with Ciara's prayer and anyone else's prayer. Get to cracking on your prayer to get lit in love the way you want and deserve.

***

Okay, back to our regularly scheduled program. It's only right that we address women not receiving their desires because some ladies deal with men who are fresh out of a relationship with women who lack quality. The woman that the man will entertain will say a lot about how he will treat you because his resumé of women is his standard. If those women did not inspire or command respect, it minimizes the man's potential as iron sharpens iron. When the quality woman arrives, he may not know what to do with her. Whether he does or not, we want to take a stab at what it takes to attract what you need.

Our advice is that if you are looking to meet a quality man, it will start with being a quality woman. A quality woman is a woman of virtue, rooted in purpose, and with a clear vision of the direction, she wants to go in her life. This woman has values and brings out the very best in a man and does not use manipulation to bend his will for her needs. In the words of Uncle Stevie Wonder, *she doesn't use her love to make him weak, she uses love to keep him strong.* Yes, she's *That Girl.* So here are a few ways to know if you are dealing with a woman of virtue.

1. *She is God-fearing.* The fear of the Lord is the beginning of wisdom (Proverbs 9:10), and this woman possesses a lot of it. She is morally guided and walks with a confidence that God is her ultimate

provider. This woman is slow to speak, and when she says something, it's usually profound. She thinks before she decides and is more patient than other women. Though far from perfect, she "prays about it" and will also cover you in prayer. She stands in her faith that either way, God will produce to her, his very best.

2. *She adds value.* This type of woman will accept a man's help, but at the core, she is the ultimate multiplier. As we mentioned in the reflection from the *Out of my League* story, we shared, if you give her a little, she expands in excess. By nature, she's ultimate "flipper." She is fully aware of what she brings to the table, and upon commitment, your life will expand. When a man is with her, people notice his positive change. As a result, her presence is felt in her absence.
3. *She has standards.* Setting a standard serves as a sense of protection, and without one, you are susceptible to whatever. The standard doesn't just weed out quality, but it also encourages the pursuer to be held accountable. When there is a standard, someone who is interested will walk away because they do not want to level up or meet you at your level and do so consistently.
4. *She is NOT superficial.* The things that she likes in you says more about her than it does about you and she has no interest in the surface level character. She is attracted to you, but in love with the way you think and how you treat her is what she values the most. She respects the actions you take and is attentive to your words because she knows that out of *the abundance of the heart his mouth speaks* (Luke 6:45).
5. *Her heart is pure.* She is not preying on you; she's praying for you. And as some women have a way of being manipulative, this woman is the epitome of selflessness. She wants you to do well in life and is neutral in advice and doesn't speak out of selfish motives. She's with you for who you are and will stand by you through thick and thin.

The woman who is pure at heart just naturally takes the position of a best friend.

6. *She is responsible.* She tends to the things that are in her care and does not need anyone to oversee her. She is capable of handling her tasks sufficiently and works as a good team player. She prioritizes her work and will complete all of her goals before she engages in the fun. She can work independently and may even be a boss but works better paired and knows that two are better than one.
7. *She is willing to learn.* She is smart but teachable and always striving to be the best she can be. Because she is ready to learn, she is always listening and open to her self-discovery. She understands she doesn't know everything and is attracted to a man who supports her, one who will push her success to the max. If he points out areas where she needs to grow, she accepts his input. She will come as she is but won't stay that way because she is always evolving.
8. *She will adjust her attitude.* She is the exact opposite of a Nasty Natasha. She does not expect a man to tolerate a bad attitude. Instead, she is accepting of pruning. She may have to jap every now and again but only occasionally, as she will adjust her attitude accordingly.
9. *She allows her man to grow.* When you are with this woman, you will not feel stagnant in your growth. With her, you can be everything you're called to be without feeling like she's lagging, and you're carrying her along the way. She will add to your growth in a healthy way.
10. *She possesses life skills.* As much as society pushes that cooking and cleaning are roles of women, they are just life skills, but we do ask that women possess them. The woman is the first nurturer and is the trainer of her children, so she sets the standard. The woman is the keeper and heart of her home. Why leave the responsibility of

its care in the hands of someone else?

11. *She's not trying to fill a void with you.* We know Mary J. Blige said she's searching for real love, and we all sang along. However, the woman who is not looking to fill a void is not looking for love. She's looking to love. Prior to you, she took accountability for her healing and got rid of the specific issues we talked about in this book. You will enjoy this woman, and she will treat you like an addition and not her savior.
12. *She's a Proverbs 31 woman. God validates her.* Lately, we have been asking our guy friends if they are familiar with the Proverbs 31 woman. Most of them have heard of her but are not familiar. We realized that there's a large group of quality women who are preparing to be Proverbs 31 women, and men don't even know how to identify them. We know good men who are choosing women for all of the wrong reasons. We want to encourage every man who has a strong understanding of their God-given purpose to become familiar with the Proverbs 31 woman, so they can know what to look for. We believe it will save you a lot of stress and heartache.

CALLING ALL MEN

Fellas, now more than ever, is the time we need you to step into your role as the man you are being called to be. That is if you aren't already. And if you are, please give a copy of this book to a friend who needs to hear this. In simpler terms, there are too many "Futures" and not enough "Russells." Our intention is not to offend or bash anyone. But since we believe it is time for men and women to rise, we are okay with doing whatever it takes to address what's happening in the world of relationships. Most of our toxic dating behaviors come from the culture we live in, where music plays a huge role.

Since we let the ladies know why the Ciara prayer wouldn't work for them, we want to continue with Future and Russell to explain what we mean.

There is a lack of men tapping into their full potential. When men operate with a Future mindset, it adds to the generational curses that have been placed upon us. It doesn't just affect us, but it also affects the ones coming after us by encouraging an anti-marriage mentality. When a man with a Future mindset hurts a good woman, it can take a long time for her to recover. Please, please, if you meet a good woman, step up to the plate or step out of the way for another man who will. While we may appear to be superwomen, we're not, and as the headship, we ask that you lead in handling us with care.

Now, if you are an Eve and are ready to meet your Adam, a man with the mindset that rapper Future portrays to be in his songs is not the way you want to go. He said it himself in his song with Drake, *Jumpman. Chicken wings, and fries; we don't go on dates.* Which tells you, he's limited in being chivalrous. In one song or another, he's continuing to say to us, *chase a check, never chase a b*tch.* But he's not the only one. Too many men have adopted this mentality and have reenacted the songs that destroyed us in the relationship category. Women flock to these men because they perceive them as charming, attractive, and have all the things we think we should want. This toxic ideology is so mainstream we have settled and accepted it, and, in the end, both men and women are not getting what they want. In redefining the narrative, we have to spot out the "Future" quickly, so we won't waste time in the wrong place and for too long. Some of us have no way of knowing, but as a heads up, here are some ways to spot one:

1. *He is emotionally unavailable.* Like the guy in the *I Want What I Can't Have* story, he's emotionally unavailable. Most men with this mindset are not looking for anything too deep and engage in shifty behavior. The foundation you build if it's rooted in sex can gauge the way he will receive you. Don't get us wrong how

you start is not always how you finish, but typically the emotionally unavailable man is not too committed. He can have sex with you on multiple occasions, but the depth of your connection is minimal.

2. *He is abusive.* The man who shows any tinge of anger or jokes about fighting or having to put his hands on a woman for any reason should be avoided totally. If you find he throws things, gets aggressive in a disagreement, it's a huge red flag that you should never take lightly. It is no guarantee that these things mean he will put his hands on you, but those things are more of an indicator that he might. Better safe than sorry, and we ask that as soon as you notice this to simply just move on.
3. *He's not intentional.* A guy with no intentions will dodge deep conversations. If you ask what his intentions are, he gets offensive. You will find yourself in a situationship as quick as Usain Bolt coming down the track field. You should never press the issue of being in a titled relationship with someone who "just wants to see where it can go" because most likely, it is going nowhere.
4. *He's selfish.* A man with this mindset is only focused on himself. He will do bare minimum things if he likes you enough with the intent only to pick you up and put you down as he sees fit. Rarely will he ever do anything for you that calls for him to sacrifice himself, he's the worst kind of man because you have to question his motives behind what he does for you. You may find yourself practically begging for bare minimum treatment, and when he spends time with you, he will act as though he has done you a favor.
5. *He's superficial.* Like a woman, he's a man with a list, and whether the list is about you or him, he's going to let you know

he has one most likely on the first date. All the reasons he's a good man have all roads leading back to his earnings. He wants to impress you, but we ask that you pass because this man is ill-equipped to recognize your worth. His interest in you is simple and short, and he most likely sees you as his bracelet. As he treats you as a trinket, don't feel bad. He doesn't have much he wants to say. As long as you look good on the passenger side, he's happy about the date.

6. *You can't call him in an emergency.* There's nothing worse than giving your body to someone you can't call during a 911 situation. If you catch a flat and he cannot help, delete him right away.
7. *He's irresponsible.* A guy with this mindset doesn't take care of his responsibilities. If he has a job, he job hops a lot with no plans or vision of what he wants to do with his life. If he has children, he does not take care of them or decides how he treats his children based on their mothers' feelings and their relationship or lack of. He is not a provider, careless with his money, and cannot be relied on. He looks to a woman to assist him as he seeks to drive her car and won't even put gas in it, change the oil, and will let it throw a rod. He will live in her house without paying bills and has plans for her income tax check well before tax season. As far as we're concerned, this man is tainted and should be avoided like the plague.
8. *He's unfaithful.* Someone unfaithful is by default a liar, so how can you build on a faulty foundation? It's impossible to stay sane with this man because when he's gone, you won't know to be sad or hurt because you will go back and forth, asking if he's cheating or dead. He's just that unreliable. You can't trust him at the drop of a dime, and something about his aura says health

risk. Because he has not mastered controlling his flesh, don't be surprised if you end in a clinic.

9. *He preys on weak women.* This is the guy who will prey on women with low self-esteem. You would never know he is insecure because he portrays himself to be nothing short of a king. Strong women repel him, and upon meeting, he presents himself as every woman's end all be all to maintain his options. However, truly confident men understand that they are not for everyone and will not waste time seeking just anyone's validation. The man that preys on the weak is looking for your yes and the yeses of the neighborhood. No matter how much you grant your approval, he will always seek the attention of someone else. He is not seeking a woman. He is seeking an advantage to use and abuse you, and no matter what you do, it is never good enough. Stay away from this man. You have nothing in common because as you want a partner, this man looks for a pawn.
10. *He treats every woman the same.* He has no discernment of the woman for life or the chick of the night. He is incapable of adjusting his approach for either of these women, and you will find that his inadequacy is offensive. No one is perfect; however, this man is not interested in changing, he doesn't understand he's been rolling around in a cesspool and at best only worthy of that pool's prized pig.
11. *He's not spiritually grounded in God.* He will say he believes in God but never engages in reading a Bible, listening to a sermon, or even downloading a Bible app. He only talks about God when it's convenient for him, and he is lukewarm at best. He says he is spiritual, but from the looks of his actions, you don't know what spirit he is operating in. Some days, you aren't going to

feel like praying for yourself and will need him to cover you, but this man will only cover you in confusion.

NOT ENOUGH "RUSSELLS"

As women writing this book, we can't tell men how to be men, but from a woman's perspective, we can tell you what we need to create a kingdom relationship. We aren't saying a guy with the "Russell" mindset is perfect; in fact, there is a thin line between a Future and a Russell. A Russell can tap into his "Future" qualities if he's just not that into a woman or is not ready. In the event the woman is exceptional, the man who is not prepared will pick apart any reason he can find as an excuse to continue his various pursuits, and it is not as personal as it may feel. The core of a "Russell" is an honorable man, and he possesses a variety of qualities, including the following:

1. *A man who is God-fearing.* The definition of a God-fearing man is contingent on who is doing the surveying, but we have found that a truly God-fearing man looks very different from other men, and his circle of friends and hobbies do as well. We have to say more about this man because he is a collection of all the men listed. He is the caterpillar in the maturation process to becoming the butterfly we call the "Ephesians 5" man. Good men may have a few good qualities, but the God-fearing man at least the one we believe to be the prototype is past his pruning season and is gifted with all traits. This type of man has already established his relationship with God and fears a life without Him. A kingdom man seeks counsel from the Most-High first and is already submitted to His will for his life. You will not question his ability to lead because he would have already been walking in his calling before he met you, and you will know this by his fruit. Like the God-fearing woman, he will pray for his spouse and lead his children properly. His circle of friends is

those of his same caliber. They encourage restoration, growth, and prayer long before they ever advise their homeboy to leave their girlfriend or family.

2. *A man who knows what it means to be a covering.* This man will prioritize your safety. The man who knows how to be your covering will protect you spiritually, physically, mentally, and emotionally and will not abuse you in any way. He gives valuable advice, is a gentle leader, and can discern the things you can't express. This man is of extreme support because he understands that even the most responsible woman needs a supportive partner. His ability to do so makes her feel at ease, and men lead well when the woman has been made to feel at ease first.
3. *A man with integrity.* We are in dire need of men who mean what they say and say what they mean. Some men consider themselves to be upright if they tell a woman the truth regardless of how it will make her feel even if it may hurt her. But the way we see it, a man with integrity will simply avoid intentionally putting himself in any position that would compromise hurting her at all. We are not expecting perfection. We all understand that there will be times when we are confronted with uncomfortable things, but what we are expressing is that this man is willing to own up to his mistakes and do the work necessary to correct certain behaviors. The road to improvement always begins with being honest about things first.
4. *A man who is aware of his purpose.* A man not connected to his God-given purpose may be too busy spending his time on personal interests instead of focusing on what God is leading him to. This man almost always lacks a clear direction for his life, and if he has no direction for his life, as the leader, where can he lead you? Usually, a man without a vision for his future always returns to his past. Don't be surprised if a few exes are lurking around. The

purposeless man will always be the distracted, all over the place, and the "let's just hang out, guy." The man rooted in his purpose will recognize the virtuous woman when she enters his life. He is an awakened Adam and can sense that his rib is missing. He has already been made aware that his helpmeet is tailor-made to fit and assist him with his calling he has already committed himself to, and the "Bye Felicia" just won't do.

5. *A man who is responsible.* He is a provider and is secretly happy in that position. We have heard many men tell independent women that sometimes they did not pursue them because they did not feel needed by her. Some men pride themselves on being needed, while others don't want the pressure of being needed. Women have to be discerning on which they are dealing with. The man who feels the pressure in being needed may only use the fact that you need him as an ego booster. Sometimes he'll come through, and sometimes he won't. The man who wants to be needed is a builder and takes his responsibility to support himself and his family seriously. Even if he has children from a failed relationship, he sees his children as a badge of honor and inheritance from the Lord and treats them as such. The responsible man is strategic about his plans and understands that senseless relationships will drain his finances and waste his time. Therefore, he is selective of who and what he entertains.
6. *He's a true gentleman.* He doesn't play Mr. Nice Guy; he is Mr. Nice guy. This man is a true gentleman and reveres all women, whether worthy of respect or not. He is careful to consider your circumstances and factors them in before he decides to pursue you. The gentleman will not lead you on or waste either of your time if, at any point, he finds that he cannot go the long haul with you. He is not reckless in his pursuit and will not rush physical intimacy. Of

course, he has sexual desires but is unmotivated by them. He wants to get to know you and will gently handle you in speech even when he does not agree with you, and you make him upset. In the end, you will appreciate this man and his ability to handle you delicately as it takes real strength to remain the gentleman with or without appreciation.

7. *A man who is intentional.* When men go to fill out an application for a job, they are not only aware they need a job, but well before applying, it is clear to them if what they are looking for is a part-time job, a full-time gig or a career. Likewise, men are also aware of their intentions in pursuing a woman. He knows if he is just passing the time, looking for a fly by night, rebounding, or ready for something more profound. Even if this man does not know for sure who you will be to him in the future, early on, he does know where he is in life and what he is open to receive. If he doesn't know his intentions and does not make them known to you, he might be the "oh she's beautiful how can I waste three months of her life" guy.
8. *He's faithful and loyal.* Regardless of what is presented to him, the man is fiercely disciplined and devoted and considers his family first. He's loyal to his partner to her face and behind her back, and through the way he lives his life, you will never doubt that. He is happy to be committed and understands he is representing his family.
9. *He's an Ephesians 5 man.* It does a disservice to tell you to read Ephesians 5 without telling you how we feel about this man. The "Ephesians 5" man is the God-fearing man on steroids practically. He is the epitome of what we want to receive. He's the butterfly fresh out of the cocoon, really more like a unicorn. This man is what women are fasting, praying, blocking exes, breaking soul ties, working out, growing their hair, whitening their teeth, getting

deliverance, and taking cooking classes for. The Ephesians 5 man is not for anyone but the Proverbs 31 woman.

He makes himself a living sacrifice and denies his flesh of temptations for her daily. In his strivings, his face is against sexual impurity as he has decided to present himself to his wife without blame. Ephesians 5:5 tells us, *no whoremonger will have any inheritance in the Kingdom of Christ.* The fear of the Lord has renewed this man's mind, making him turn his back on fleshly ways.

Somewhere he's fasting and praying and has sought out deliverance from things that make him imperfect for his Eve, whether he knows his rib or does not. It's funny to note that before a caterpillar turns into a butterfly, it has to fast first before its emergence. We see that the Ephesians 5 man is spiritually developed similarly. His wisdom is seasoned and comes from the experience of selling out to the Lord. He reads the word of God and is in tune with the guidance of the Holy Spirit. In his dealings with his wife, he is an imitator of Christ, and she is made clean through his ministering. Though he may attend church, he does not rely on a pastor because he has studied to show himself approved to God and will be pastoring his own family. This man is not only the one, but he is a part of the remnant of chosen men that God says is fit for His Kingdom, and subsequently; as a result, this is the man we endorse.

BRINGING OUT THE KINGDOM IN EACH OTHER

Now that we've shared a few qualities of a kingdom man and kingdom woman, it's time to bring them out of each other. Truth be told, there is a man and boy in every male, and in every female, there is a woman and a little girl. The perfect example is Gucci Mane. Yes, Gucci Mane. Remember, you are talking to two ladies who love the Lord but know our music. Anyhow, let's take it back to 2011 when Gucci made the song, *I Don't Love Her.* In this song, he lists all of the things he loves about a woman, including how she sexes him, but "he doesn't love her," and there's that Future mentality at best. However, fast forward to a 2017 song, and he's saying, *spend a week with Gucci, and I'll boost your self-esteem.* This reflects that of a changed man. The saints witnessed this man transform from an overweight convict to Debonair La'Flare. Gucci's glow-up was so out-of-sight that some people actually believed this man had been cloned. As out of this world as that may sound, he is a perfect example of what can occur when you surrender to your inner royalty title and position in the Kingdom. Don't get us wrong. It's is not to say that this is or is not a kingdom marriage only a mere illustration of the transforming qualities of a real woman.

It is possible that Gucci wanted to make some changes on his own, but a better bet was that he was influenced by the woman who spoke to the man in him. His wife, Keyshia Ka'oir, recognized the king he was capable of being and helped bring it out of him. She overlooked that ice cream cone he tattooed on his cheek and believed that underneath the layers, there was a diamond. This is a man who had plenty of women chasing after him because of his money and fame, but it was Keyshia who ultimately took reign. With this in mind, we have to understand that to reach the light in someone, sometimes you have to be willing to help pull them out of the darkness. Be okay with some imperfections and be inspirational. It boils down to how much you are willing to invest in the Kingdom that you are called to have together. Why not go for yours? God promised it to you, and it's yours to have if you want it.

Taking all of these ideas into consideration, we want you to continue beyond this book to explore the ideas shared, including kingdom relationships. Toxic relationships aren't something that can be changed overnight, and it will take more than a book filled with funny stories to solve all of the problems happening in the world of dating and relationships. We hope that you have been encouraged, inspired, and ready to be intentional while seeking purpose and keeping your head in the game.

CHAPTER 20
KEEP YOUR HEAD IN THE GAME

"No matter what you endure in life,
don't let anyone steer you from keeping your head in the game."

—ERIKA & NIESHA

ERIKA

I pray this book made you laugh while simultaneously exploring habits that have held you back from giving and receiving the love you truly deserve. In all transparency, writing this book has helped me heal from wounds that I didn't realize still existed, and recognize patterns that have hindered me from experiencing a successful relationship leading to marriage. Sharing my story with you helped me explore situations that made me feel like I couldn't keep my head in the game. Most importantly, this book has held me accountable for the decisions I've made in the past. I will no longer entertain situations that make me feel like love is not possible.

Being single is not always easy for me. There have been times when I felt love was not in the cards for me, and I wanted to throw it in the towel altogether. I have lost count of how many times I have been the third wheel on a date, have encountered family members trying to diagnose my singleness or had to heal from a counterfeit. My dating experiences led to almost believing that maybe my life was just different. I mean, after all, I am living my dream in other areas of my life. So maybe I can't have it all. Now I am wise enough to know that this is a LIE. Each experience has better prepared me for what's to come.

So, what does it mean to ***keep your head in the game?*** It means that no matter what you endure, you won't use it as an excuse to throw in the towel. This doesn't just apply to your relationships. When you are faced with obstacles and can't see yourself on the other side, keep pushing. A scripture that helps me in times of despair is Deuteronomy 30:19, and it reads, *Today I have given you a choice between life and death, between blessings and curses. Now I call on heaven and earth to witness the choice you make. Oh, that you would choose life, so that your descendants may live.* Choosing to keep your head in the game has less to do with you than it does for the people who will be impacted just because you chose life.

Your decisions play a role in your family and those coming after you. In times of trouble, don't choose to live a content or mediocre life. Choose to live your best life, one that is fruitful in every area. When you feel less than worthy, look in the mirror, and pay attention to the dope person God created you to be. And if you are still in the dating game, embrace your current season and enjoy every moment.

NIESHA

When E and I decided, in the final quarter of 2019, to write a book about our spicy, sometimes sad, enlightened, and hilarious dating experiences, who knew we would get to this place during a global pandemic? There's something to be said about being determined and convicted because it will drive you to accomplish the goal before you no matter what. It was important for me to reflect on what drove my acute transition of breaking my poor dating habits. So often, I would hear the definition of what crazy entailed. But it wasn't until I was turning 35 that I understood that I was crazy all this time. I was crazy to believe that my love and support of my exes automatically meant I would receive it back. I was crazy to think that I could make someone's potential work for my benefit while never seeing any effort extended from my exes. I was crazy to believe that I would ever have a king when I dismissed myself as the queen I knew I was but failed miserably at keeping my crown on straight.

Now don't get me wrong because I'm never saying I wasn't a great partner in my previous relationships. I was dynamic, and I say this humbly. I'm funny. I'm respectful. I refused to call a man out of his name no matter what transpired between us. Most importantly, I am loyal. Despite all of these amazing traits, I still found myself getting cheated on, lied to, and sorely let down in reciprocity. See, I knew that because of the exceptional values that Queen Marilyn Diane and King Joe Earl instilled in me, the settling for BS had to end at some point in my life. As their daughter, I always felt that I owed it to them to do my absolute best in life, including bouncing back from some epic fails.

When it finally clicked for me, it was almost as though I was a new creature. I began to attract individuals whom I believed were within my league. Insanity is doing the same thing over again and expecting different results. While we have all been there, there is no reason why we should stay there. This brings me to the reason why writing this book was necessary and, at some moments, therapeutic in unwrapping the sweet and sticky moments of my journey. A scripture that was a focal point for me in my new way of dating (practicing celibacy) was the promise God shared with me in Psalm 37:3-4: *Trust in the Lord and do what is good; dwell in the land and live securely. Take delight in the Lord, and He will give you your heart's desires.*

And let me tell y'all that HE CAME THROOOOOOOOOOOOUGH! He blew my mind, heart, and, more importantly, my faith in Him led to Ephesians 3:20 being my entire life. I gave it all up to Him to orchestrate as I was willing to be obedient. I was down to do whatever I had to do not to get another spiritual whooping and secure my king. I am not an average or basic woman, and I knew that God's man created just for me would reflect the new creature he made me be. My phenomenal king Bryan Forbes is every bit of what was on the long wish list I created in 2014 and beyond. He is my heart's delight and my mind's safe house. He is my answered prayer, tenfold.

My hope for you is that on your journey to keep your head in the game, you never sell yourself short. Believe in what you deserve. Identify your passions. Execute the steps to walk in your purpose so you can watch God manifest what's yours to have.

ACKNOWLEDGMENTS

ERIKA

To my Heavenly Father, thank you for thinking of me enough to CREATE me. To know that God loves me is the most beautiful feeling. It's because of your love that I can love others. Thank you to my parents Leonard and Beverly McCall, who have shown me the importance of using friendship as your foundation. Thank you to my amazing sister Tiffany who always reminds me that I am ERIKA RESHANDA MCCALL and my brother-in-law, William. The two of you show me that love is possible and that it can show up in the craziest ways. Thank you to my Grandma Candias, who is on her knees praying for me every night. To Niesha, I am so grateful for our sisterhood. Thank you for joining in on this journey. I don't care what you say. You ARE a writer. Thank you to my cousin Marcus McCall for believing in my vision and dream of starting a publishing company. My aunts, uncles, cousins, and friends who continue to support me and love me unconditionally. There are way too many to name, but I love each one of you. To my future King, I can't wait to share our story and continue to build God's Kingdom together!

NIESHA

First, I give my Heavenly Father total praise for loving on me in such a way that it defies natural thinking on the subject. I praise GOD for working supernaturally in my life repeatedly and having testimonies to share his grace and fresh mercies. I want to thank my HusBae, my King, my bestest friend after Jesus, Bryan. Babe, thank you for being beyond my greatest prayer answered and for being consistent in the way you show me, supreme love. Your covering over me is the peace GOD provides to me through you, and I'm so very thankful for these facts. I love you looooong time.

To my extremely phenomenal Parents, Marilyn & Joe. There was never a question in my heart that GOD blessed me with the absolute greatest parents for me to have. Thank you for drenching me in your unwavering love, unending support of my dreams, and the countless sacrifices you've displayed all of my life. Y'all are seriously, the absolute greatest of all time, and this is not up for debate ever.

To my dearest, feisty and beyond beautiful Grandmothers, Aretha Lucas, and Eula B. Jefferson. Thank you for always allowing me to be my sassy, opinionated, one of a kind and respectful self around ya'll at all times. Most importantly, thank you for cementing in my heart how vital having a relationship with Christ is and forever will be. To my Grandfathers, Israel Jefferson and Baba Griot Leonard Lucas for instilling in me the importance of being a leader and not a follower.

My NaNa Sweets, Heide, Leonardo, Troy, Randy, Keno, thank you for being a spotlight of joy in my life and always gathering me up when necessary. To my very incredible In-Loves (not In-Laws) and my extended Forbes/Ayre family, may GOD continue to bless you always in all ways. To all of my loved ones, my Tribe & friends who are my family that have continued to pour into me and be a light in my world, thank you always.

To my Ace, Erika, I can't express in words really how incredible you are, but what I can say is that your presence adds such value to my life that is priceless. Writing a book with my sister-friend has been a dream turned reality, turned bright future. Thank you for always being a true testament of the goodness GOD intended for me to witness in my lifetime.

Lastly, to my future little giants, thank you from the top of my heart for being the greatest catalyst for me and your Dad to create a living legacy and generational wealth for you to take advantage of in full abundance. I'm so looking forward to nurturing your anointed lives to be everything GOD created you to be for his Kingdom. My love for you has no end.

Erika & Niesha

A special thank you to each and every person who shared their story. You all helped make this book a HIT! Thank you to Marcus McCall for believing in us and supporting this project. Shout out to our beta reader Sian Ferguson. You helped get us in the right direction. A very special thank you to Jillian McLeod. You played a significant role in helping us deliver the message that was in our hearts. We couldn't have made it to the finish line without you.

ENJOY A PREVIEW OF DON'T WAIT, CREATE
BY ERIKA R. MCCALL

Do you have an idea that you've been waiting to put into action? Don't be stingy. The world is waiting for your gift. The purpose of *Don't Wait, Create* is to make sure you don't waste another minute sitting on your talents. It's time to unwrap your unique gift and share it with those who will be significantly impacted by your calling.

In *Don't Wait, Create,* Erika shares her story of going from a volunteer to executive and, eventually, business owner. By sharing her story, she will help you identify and execute goals that are intentional and produce quality work. This book teaches you how to navigate obstacles instead of running away from them—in the end, using failure to strengthen your knowledge and expertise. Enjoy a sneak peek into this book!

***

It's 2010, and I'm standing in the kitchen reading the unedited manuscript of my debut book Go for Yours, to my mother and grandmother. *"So, what does it mean to Go for Yours? Some call it grinding; others call it hustling. No matter what the case is, to Go for Yours means you don't wait on an opportunity—you create it."*

I began to envision myself at the local bookstore, reading to a supportive audience. As I finish my sentence, both start to clap and telling me how much they enjoyed the words typed on about twenty pages. My grandmother grabs the short manuscript and begins to pray, "Lord take it higher, and higher, and higher." At that moment, none of us were aware of the journey ahead. We had no idea that the words I had just shared would one day turn into a business, brand, and nonprofit foundation, among other things. We were just enjoying a moment together—three generations of women. Who at the time, hadn't realized the infinite possibilities that had been manifested through prayer. Ten years later, and I am still trying to fathom where my journey has brought me.

It's hard to believe when just a decade ago, I was living in my grandmother's basement in Chicago with a limited vision of what was in store for my future. At that time, I wanted to publish a book but was oblivious to the process. Not to mention, I had a full-time job. When would I have time to complete this book? Maybe it's just a pipe dream. These are thoughts that crept through my mind from time to time. My mind began to shift when I witnessed what was supposed to be a book of quotes turning into a compilation of stories about young people who are brave enough to step out on faith and reach for the stars. The people I met and interviewed during this process were extraordinary. Instead of focusing on my lack of knowledge, I tapped into my faith and believed if God did something miraculous for them, He could do the same thing for me.

Today, I'm sitting in my one-bedroom apartment in North Hollywood, California, as a published author and business owner. Once again, I envision myself in front of an audience reading *Don't Wait, Create.* This time, on a 10-city book tour to a crowd filled with new and familiar faces. As I continue to imagine all the places and experiences my journey will bring, I look forward to all of the creators this book will help birth.

While anticipating all the lives that will be touched, I can't help but think about whose life my journey has impacted the most. That person is me. After deciding to begin creating the opportunities I had been waiting for, I met a brand-new person in me that had been waiting to make its debut. In my first book, I hid my story behind all the people I was writing about. It wasn't until after publishing *Go for Yours* that I realized how impactful my story is. I am most excited to provide you with an authentic story that will help you give birth to whatever vision has been placed in your soul. I believe that you possess everything you need to bring all your dreams into fruition.

Truth be told, I have been sitting on this book for over three years. Can you believe that someone who encourages people to create instead of wait did the same thing? Thankfully, God's timing is perfect. If I had published this book prematurely, it wouldn't have done you or me any justice. Within the last three years, I learned more strategies to help you during your process of creating. As you move forward in this book, you will be provided with practical tools to help you create opportunities to live out your God-given purpose. Pay close attention as I use my experiences to elaborate on key concepts and messages that will help you jumpstart whatever you are being called to create.

During our time together, I want you to grab your Don't Wait, Create journal and start thinking about what dream you are ready to bring to life. Whatever it is, I pray the same prayer my grandmother prayed. Like my dream, I pray yours goes higher, higher, and higher. Let's get to creating!

***

CALLED TO CREATE

"For we are God's handiwork, created in Christ Jesus to do good works, which God prepared in advance for us to do.

—EPHESIANS 2:10

You were created with intention. You were created with a purpose. You were created to CREATE. Your arrival on earth was not by mistake. When I think about all of the relationships developed that led to us being here, it blows my mind. Hence the reason I solicited my parents to write the foreword of this book. Think about it, not only did our parents have to meet, but their parents, your great-grandparents, and so on. You, my friend, were intentionally designed for a time such as this. With that said, it's time to stop waiting for a miracle to happen before you start creating. You are the MIRACLE that has already happened.

Imagine you have an incoming phone call, and it's God on the other end. You pick up, and He gives you a specific assignment only you can accomplish. You aren't provided with all of the instructions, but special abilities to complete the mission. It may not be in the form of a call or text, but the ideas tugging at your heart, keeping you up at night, is God calling you to create. Your gifts, skills, and talents are the superpowers He has given you to carry out your vision. It wasn't until I began to fully embrace that I was created for a particular purpose, that I lived my dream confidently. Once you decide to fully embrace what you are being called to do, you won't feel like you are following a dream. It will be the exact opposite. The world around you will begin to change, and your dream will follow you. You were called to create something that could change the world, shift the culture, save lives, and the time to do it now.

There was a time when I felt I was on the outside looking into the lives of people that have unleashed their power to create the types of opportunities that most people, sit, and wait for. As I observed, I watched people fulfill dreams with confidence, allowing nothing to stand in the way. Curiosity made me put my observations to test and join a unique group of individuals who have created a lifestyle filled with purpose. When I put away my old way of thinking and moved in the direction I was being called to, the world around me began to change. I discovered a rare group of innovative leaders who merge their ideas with technology, education, or any resource to help them leave a lasting impact on the earth. They worked hard, yet smart, and were willing to go the extra mile most aren't willing to. Some wake up at the crack of dawn to work on a new project while others wait until the sun goes down to bring forth their ideas. One thing that stood out was the fact that they defined success on their terms.

Some of the people I encountered were climbing up the ranks in Silicon Valley, while others were developing a blueprint in their parent's garage. A few of them spent numerous hours in the studio, creating music that will eventually shift the culture. I even met some in middle school, high school, and college preparing to become the next powerful attorney, physician, teacher, or whatever they have set their mind to do. There were several whose future depended on their next slam dunk, home run, touchdown, or tennis match. Different desires, but similar qualities, that make them stand out in a world where most people are afraid to do something extraordinary.

I have met so many amazing souls from various cultures and backgrounds, but all have one thing in common: the desire to create something well beyond their imagination. The greatest discovery was to find out that I possessed similar qualities. The dream that felt so far away was waiting on me to realize the supernatural powers that have been intentionally downloaded in my DNA. That miraculous power took me from being a shy girl who was raised in the midst of cornfields and told she was a horrible writer, to a confident woman who has embraced everything she is being called to be and has broken word curses that have been spoken against her in every area of her life.

There is no doubt in my mind that you are one of the unique individuals I just described. You have a special gift ready to make room for you as soon as you decide to create rather than wait. If you are having a hard time believing me, it's okay. I have done the dirty work. Only to come back and tell you that you have everything you need to begin your journey of creating.

DON'T WAIT

"Good things come to those who wait, not to those who wait too late."

—BILL WITHERS, JUST THE TWO OF US

WAIT

verb (used with object)

1. to continue as one is in expectation of; <u>await</u>: *to wait one's turn at a telephone booth.*

verb (used without object)

1. stay where one is or delaying action until a particular time or until something else happens.

Most of us who were called to create, are sitting on talents that God intended for us to use. It's not because we don't recognize them; it's just easier to think that we will fulfill our calling "one day" when the time is right—leaving us waiting instead of creating. The definitions above describe two forms of waiting. I want to explore both because there will be times when you have no other choice but to wait. In our daily lives, we wait for our turn in the check-out line, our rideshare to arrive, or a movie to start. In more serious instances, we wait until we have completed the required courses to graduate, meet the right person to get married or have enough money to take a trip out of the country. This type of waiting is active and intentional.

I am speaking to the people who stay where they are and delay action until something other than themselves comes to help them achieve their goals. Much time and talent have been wasted because people are waiting on an outside factor to pursue what is already meant for them to achieve. The most popular form of delay comes from waiting for people to give us permission or provide us with an opportunity. This is the quickest way to rob yourself of what you were created to achieve. This type of waiting is toxic and can steal your joy, leaving you to feel defeated, depressed, and hopeless. How do I know? Well, it almost happened to me.

A few months before reading my manuscript in the kitchen, I was on a flight, 30,000 feet in the air traveling from Atlanta to Chicago. I had just finished bringing in the New Year with my line sister, Tiara. Together, we declared that our year would be like none other we have ever experienced. Typically, flights coming back from a festive weekend consisted of on and off naps until I land. This flight was different. As I sat on the plane, I began to write quotes in my journal. One of them being *Go for Yours.* I have loved this phrase since the very first time I heard it from my good friend Anthony "Ant P" Peterson while in college. He was trying to convince me to make a move on my crush by telling me, *Go for Yours.* I didn't take his advice at that particular moment, but the words always stuck with me. By the end of the flight, I had made up my mind. That year, I would write a book, and it would be titled *Go for Yours.*

Initially, my idea was a coffee table book filled with quotes and examples of young people who modeled them. As I continued to write, my vision grew. The small paragraphs typed in my Google drive turned into pages highlighting the accomplishments of people who served as an example of everything I was documenting. The thought of publishing became a huge passion of mine, but something held me back from fully committing myself to my newly found dream. The obstacle that stood in between me and my vision was my full-time employment.

Fresh out of graduate school, I had landed a job at a private university in Chicago as the Assistant Director of Diversity & Leadership. I loved everything about my position because it allowed me to work with talented young people excited about their future. Before receiving my master's degree in Higher Education, I worked in the field of Social Work. As a case manager, my job was to reunite families who fell victim to the foster care system. This career didn't last long because it was challenging for me to work with people who didn't seem to want my help.

Finally, I had a job that would jumpstart my career while providing me with my own office, salary, and benefits. In my mid-twenties, with very few responsibilities, this position contributed to my plan of living the adult lifestyle I had envisioned for myself. In the next couple of years, I would be able to do things people in their late twenties did, like purchase a home, start a family, and work my way up to an executive position. To facilitate my plan of action and save money, I moved into a small room in my grandmother's basement.

As excited as I was about my new passion, it was not enough to leave a job that provided me with financial security. Therefore, I decided to wait a little longer, write in my spare time, and save money to publish my book while continuing to implement my initial plan. Writing became my "dream on the side." After work, and sometimes on the weekend, I would sit at home for hours writing and creating story concepts. Eventually, my dedication to creating *Go for Yours* became so strong that it became a huge part of my life. When students came to my office in need of encouragement, I would refer to some of the stories I was writing.

When summer approached, my job became so demanding that I didn't have time to write. On top of that, my supervisors began to micromanage me and put me on a six-month Performance Improvement Plan (PIP) because they felt I wasn't performing up to their expectations. This shifted my focus to dedicating my time to keeping my job and improving my performance to prove that I was an exceptional employee. That same summer, I took a trip to New Orleans to attend my sorority's national convention.

When packing my bags, I noticed a year-old copy of *Black Enterprise* sitting on the coffee table that I had only used for decoration. I grabbed it so I could have something to read on the plane. Again, 30,000 feet in the air, I became inspired while reading the articles in the magazine about young entrepreneurs who created their very own opportunity for success. I read in amazement about Jerome Boykin, who at the age of 23 started a parking lot cleaning business after losing all his belongings in Hurricane Katrina and made $850,000 in revenues his first year in business, eventually becoming a millionaire. I also read about siblings Lorielle and Brandon Broussard. They started Barackawear, a t-shirt company, and created Barack the Vote t-shirts in support of the 2008 election campaign for President-Elect Barack Obama.

When I returned to Chicago, I sent Jerome Boykin an email informing him I was inspired by his story and wanted to interview him for my book. A few days later, Jerome contacted me, letting me know he received my message. He said he usually didn't get a chance to call people because of his busy schedule, but my email stood out to him. Jerome was the first person I interviewed and encouraged me to complete *Go for Yours.* Interviewing Jerome inspired me to seek more personal stories. I discovered so many influential trailblazers who had great stories of success.

Another of my favorite stories was about Kari Miller, who I became familiar with after researching people with triumphant stories. Kari became a Gold Medalist after losing her limbs in a horrific car accident. It wasn't until she experienced this accident that she learned how to play volleyball. I remember reflecting on all the compelling stories that would motivate my readers and admiring them for being confident enough to pursue something they were passionate about.

Closer to the finish line, it was time to provide a brief synopsis of my book. I leaned into some friends to help me come up with the perfect description. *"Go for Yours, a guide for ambitious, faithful, and progressive individuals who yearn to break the conventional models of living."* I was about to publish a book encouraging people to do something brave while doing the exact opposite. This made me question the real reason I was waiting so long to do what was tugging at my heart. Deep down in my spirit, I knew this book would take me beyond having my own office and climb the ranks in Higher Education. Where I was headed, there were no limits to how far I could go. Still, there was something subconsciously preventing me from moving forward in the direction I was yearning to go. I wanted to leave my job to see where my vision would take me, but the thought of being broke and never making it out of my grandmother's basement made me wait a little longer.

By the end of the year, *Go for Yours* came to a standstill. Publishing was still in my plans, but I didn't have a real deadline. On one of the coldest days of the year, I was in the house watching Kimora Lee Simmons' *Life in the Fab Lane.* She was somewhere in Los Angeles, at a restaurant, sitting outside under the sun, at a business meeting with her shades on. I recalled the meeting I had earlier that was facilitated in a small and stuffy conference room. I began to envision myself creating my schedule, taking meetings outside in the warm weather, and actively living my dream, making real boss moves. In the back of my mind, I knew *Go for Yours* was the key to making my dream a reality. I don't know if it was the stillness of the winter or the lack of sunshine, but at that moment, my dream couldn't have seemed further away. My present condition made it hard for me to see what was right in front of me.

A few weeks later, I headed to work amid the first big snowstorm of the year. I couldn't help but think about what life would be like if I decided to follow what had been continuously tugging at my heart. I dug my car out of the snow, warmed it up, and headed to work. When I arrived, there was an email from my supervisor requesting a meeting to review my PIP. Before heading to her office, I opened my desk drawer and grabbed the letter of resignation that was sitting there for months. I didn't know what it would lead to, but it was time for me to practice everything I was writing about and finish my project. In my meeting, I provided my supervisor with two weeks' notice. I was asked to leave that day.

I will never forget the disrespect I experienced while packing up my office. I called two of my friends and asked them to help me clean out my office. While packing, we could hear my supervisor and the Dean of Students laughing and talking about what was taking place. As we closed the last box and went to grab the flash drive from my computer, the Dean entered my office, snatched the flash drive out of my hand, and accused me of trying to steal the university's files. I still have no idea why she would think I wanted any of their files, but the adrenaline in my body caused me to snatch my flash drive back from her. She could have everything else, but on that flash drive was my manuscript and the key that would open the door for what was lying ahead.

As I reflect on the events that led to the decision to follow my dream, I can't help but think about why it took me so long to leave a job that didn't value me instead of beginning the path of creating an opportunity that was already waiting for me. Honestly, I was too scared to break a tradition that encourages you to obtain a degree, get a job, start a family, and retire—in that order. For years, hundreds of thousands of people have been pursuing dreams based on society's standard of living. Instead of defining it on their terms, they have measured their success based on others' opinions.

My experience has taught me, there is nothing wrong with achieving the goals mentioned above, but it shouldn't be based on the world's terms. It's okay to start a family first, before tackling your professional goals. Or put your personal goals on hold to achieve professionally. You can also pursue everything you want at the same time. This is your life, and you only get one. Now more than ever, people are breaking conventional models of living and refusing to be boxed in. They don't even believe there is a box. But for every person shattering boxes and creating their path, there is someone stuck on a more comfortable and safer route waiting for the perfect time or circumstance to pursue what is truly in their hearts. Too many people are living an unhappy mediocre life because they are afraid. Instead, they water down their vision to fit in with the traditional idea of how they think life should be lived. I can say without hesitation that deciding to create *Go for Yours* saved my life. It helped me discover my purpose and provided me with many experiences filled with lesson after lesson. Despite the accomplishments, I would be further along in my journey if I hadn't waited.

STAY TUNED FOR DON'T WAIT, CREATE!